FLYING SAILORS AT WAR

FLEET AIR ARM OPERATIONS DURING THE SECOND WORLD WAR

Seafox K8575. The seventh production Seafox built, this aircraft was delivered to the FAA in July 1937 and was later allocated to HMS *Neptune*, a sister ship of HMS *Ajax* and *Achilles* of River Plate fame, although K8575 seems not to have survived after September 1939.
Fleet Air Arm (FAA) Museum

FLYING SAILORS AT WAR

FLEET AIR ARM OPERATIONS DURING THE SECOND WORLD WAR

Volume 1: September 1939 – June 1940

Northern Europe, Norway, North Sea,
North and South Atlantic

Brian Cull

with Bruce Lander and Mark Horan

DALRYMPLE & VERDUN PUBLISHING

Above: Fairey Swordfish L7652 '2', L2728 '8' and one other unidentified Swordfish coded '6' from the Torpedo Training Unit, Gosport, circa mid-1939. L7652 was struck off charge on 10th April 1940 following an earlier accident, although L2728 went on to serve with several squadrons until at least May 1944. *via Newark Air Museum (NAM)*

Flying Sailors at War
Brian Cull with Bruce Lander and Mark Horan
Fleet Air Arm Operations during
the Second World War
Volume 1: September 1939 – June 1940
Northern Europe, Norway, North Sea,
North and South Atlantic

ISBN 978-1-905414-14-7

First published in 2011 by
Dalrymple & Verdun Publishing
33 Adelaide Street, Stamford PE9 2EN
United Kingdom
Tel: 0845 838 1940
mail@dvpublishing.co.uk
www.dvpublishing.co.uk

Editor Martin Derry

Printed in England by
Ian Allan Printing Limited
Riverdene Business Park
Molesey Road
Hersham KT12 4RG

Title page: A flock of Rocs, 13th August 1940. This image received the title *'Destroyers of The Fleet Air Arm'* by the British media of the day. The accompanying caption read 'The striking power of the Fleet is greatly increased by the Blackburn Roc. This fine machine embodies the multi-gun turret used in the Defiant with such devastating success against the Nazis'. If nothing else, five Rocs in a formation such as this did at least look intimidating. The image also illustrates a number of variations in roundel and camouflage applications, variations with the upper fuselage fairings either side of the turrets (allowing them to traverse) and, in one aircraft's case (second from rear), no pilot canopy. Doubtless it was the censor that removed any trace of the aircraft serial numbers and equally any reference to the unit employed. *via NAM*

CONTENTS

DEDICATION

To the memory of Fleet Air Arm historian and author Ray Sturtivant – 'Mr Fleet Air Arm' – who died in August 2008: to 'Gentleman' Jack Lee, who also passed away in 2008: to aircrew of all nations who lost their lives defending their beliefs and principles during the period covered by this study and, to those veterans who have since followed them to a better place.

ACKNOWLEDGEMENTS

First and foremost Brian wishes to record his thanks to his wife Val for her encouragement and continued support during the period of researching and writing this volume, and for her practical assistance from time to time. With possibly a further four or five volumes to follow, one can only hope that her patience and understanding will continue.

Margaret, Viscountess Thurso (widow of Lt-Cdr Guy Brokensha DSC) is to be thanked for providing material, letters and photographs, as is Professor David Brokensha (Guy's brother), and also Professor Alan Macfarlane, an acquaintance of David Brokensha. Other veterans who have been contacted, albeit several years ago by Bruce Lander, include Lt-Cdr Eric Monk DSM, Lt-Cdr Bob Kearsley and Lt-Cdr Freddy Charlton DSC. The diaries of Lt(A) Graham Hogg DSC (killed 1942) and Sub-Lt(A) Stephen Griffith, (killed 1941) have proved invaluable, as have memoirs of the period written by Major Dicky Partridge DSO (*Operation Skua*), Vice-Admiral Sir Donald Gibson DSC (*Haul, Taut and Belay*, plus correspondence), Lt-Cdr Dick Bartlett (*One Man's War*), Capt Desmond Vincent-Jones DSC, who provided a wonderfully written account of his time with Number 806 Squadron and Cdr Geoffrey Hare DSC, who also provided an account of his experiences. Flt Lt Jim Pickering AFC kindly provided information concerning RAFVR pilots who flew with the FAA. Sadly, most of these gallant gentlemen are no longer with us.

Others who have contributed directly or indirectly to this volume are authors Peter C. Smith, whom we thank for permission to use quotes from his excellent book *Skua;* the late Ray Sturtivant for permission to quote from his books including *British Naval Aviation* and *Fleet Air Arm at War;* Chris Shores (*Fledgling Eagles*); Wayne Ralph (*Aces, Wingmen and Warriors*); Chris Goss (*The Sea Eagles*); and Don Kindell *(Naval-History.Net)*. Thanks also to Peter Cornwell (eminent aviation author), and TOCH/RAF Command stalwarts including Paul McMillan, Dave Williams, Errol Martyn, Alex Crawford, Henk Welting, Adriano Baumgartner, Bjorn Hafsten, Horst Kube, Juha Vaittinen, Ronnie Olsthoorn; Eggert Norðdahl. Also Catherine Smith and Anna Clarke at the Research Centre, RNAS Yeolvilton: the staff at the National Archives and at Bury St Edmunds Public Library are also thanked for their assistance.

Brian and co-authors Bruce Lander and Mark Horan wish to thank Martin Derry and the late Steve Thompson for their expertise and support in helping to produce the first of this series on FAA Operations during WWII.

They say in the Royal Air Force a landing's okay
If the pilot gets out and can still walk away
But in the Fleet Air Arm the prospects are grim
If the landing's piss poor and the pilot can't swim

Fleet Air Arm Song Book

Left: Supermarine Walrus crew about to depart on a sortie. Note the RAF pilot.

PREAMBLE

IN THE BEGINNING

1911 Four Royal Navy officers (three RN, one RM) learnt to fly fixed wing aircraft.

1912 January. Acting Commander C R Samson successfully took off from a platform, approximately 100ft in length, erected above the fore-turret and bow of the battleship HMS *Africa* whilst moored.

1912 May. Samson took off from a 112ft platform erected above the fore-turret and bow of the battleship HMS *Hibernia* whilst the vessel was under way; this was the first successful launch of an aeroplane from any moving warship.

1913 In the presence of a group of RN officers, a Sopwith type 'C' seaplane with a 225 hp Sunbeam engine took off from the water at Calshot equipped with an 810lb 14-inch torpedo.

1914 The Royal Naval Air Service was formed out of the Naval Wing of the Royal Flying Corps, a month before war broke out. By 1918 it had 3,000 aircraft.

1915 The first aerial torpedo attack in history was made on a Turkish merchantman in the Dardanelles, Turkey. Flight-Commander Edmunds, operating from the seaplane-carrier HMS *Ben-my-Chree* took off from the Gulf of Xeros in a Short 184 seaplane carrying a torpedo and petrol for 45 minutes. Although the ceiling of his aircraft with this load was less than 1,000 feet, he crossed the Bulair Isthmus and made a successful attack. The merchantman was sunk. Five days later Edmunds repeated his success by sinking another Turkish vessel on 17th August 1915.

1915 HMS *Campania* was converted from a liner and equipped for launching seaplanes mounted on light trolleys along a ramp extending from bridge to bow. The aircraft landed on the water, and were sometimes collected unbroken. She could carry up to six reconnaissance aircraft and six fighters. In 1916 the vessel was refitted and, following earlier experiences, incorporated many modifications relating to the operation of aircraft and allowed for up to seven Short 184s and four fighters to be carried.

1917 The 'large light cruiser' HMS *Furious* was converted prior to completion to accommodate a hangar and a 228ft flying-off deck forward in lieu of its fore 18in gun and turret. From this deck, land planes (i.e. wheeled undercarriage as opposed to floats) were operated with some success. Only one flight per aeroplane was possible, as there was no landing-on deck aft and the aircraft had to be ditched and salved as opportunity offered. Squadron Commander E H Dunning DSC, flying a Sopwith Pup had, on 2nd August 1917 successfully, albeit precariously, landed on the flying-off deck. He succeeded again on 7th August, but later that day was killed whilst attempting the feat for a third time. He was the first pilot to succeed in landing on a moving vessel. Later, the aft 18in turret was removed and a 300ft landing-on deck was constructed aft of the vessel's funnel and superstructure, although the air disturbance created by the superstructure caused many pilots to comment that they preferred to land in the sea!

1918 1st April. The Royal Air Force was formed by the amalgamation of the RNAS with the RFC.

16th September. Converted from an incomplete liner ordered by Italy, HMS *Argus* was commissioned as the world's first aircraft carrier to be completed with a flush flight deck; i.e. one devoid of obstruction. Too late to perform operational duties in WW1, *Argus* proved successful and helped to develop carrier operations in the early post-war years.

1920 HMS *Eagle* emerged as the first British carrier fitted with an island superstructure, having been converted from a battleship ordered by Chile prior to WW1. Eagle was at this time partially incomplete but was sent to sea in order to conduct trials with the island structure and its effects, if any, on aircraft operations caused by wind eddies and air currents across the flight deck. The results were acceptable and *Eagle* was returned to the builders for completion and later commissioned into the Royal Navy on 20th February 1924.

1924 February. HMS *Hermes*, the world's first aircraft carrier to be specifically built as such was commissioned into the Royal Navy, having been laid down in 1918. The Japanese vessel IJN *Hosho* is credited as being the first aircraft carrier in the world to be designed as such. *Hermes* was laid down and launched before *Hosho*; however, the latter commissioned in December 1922.

1925 Following an elaborate reconstruction, *Furious* rejoined the fleet with her superstructure removed to leave an almost uninterrupted flight deck. In this form *Furious* proved very successful and consequently the two 'half-sisters' *Courageous* and *Glorious*, each originally armed with four 15in guns, were taken in hand for a similar conversion which incorporated larger hangars than *Furious* and thus enabled them to carry a larger complement of aircraft.

1938 16th November. HMS *Ark Royal* was commissioned. She was the first big British carrier to be designed and built as such from the keel up and incorporated many of the technological and operational lessons obtained during the 1920s and 1930s. *Ark Royal*'s design included a large complement of aircraft and a very heavy anti-aircraft battery consisting of eight twin 4.5in guns plus lighter anti-aircraft weapons.

1939 Since 1924 an unsatisfactory system of dual control had persisted between the Air Ministry and Admiralty concerning the governing, provision and control of naval aircraft. Following an official enquiry in 1937, the Admiralty regained full control of its aircraft on 24th May 1939.

On 18th July 1918, seven Sopwith Camels were launched from the aircraft carrier HMS *Furious*, their mission to attack the German Airship Sheds at Tondern. En route one Camel developed engine trouble and had to abort, returning to land safely back on *Furious*; the remaining six flew on to their target and, sweeping in low over the German base, dropped twelve 50lb bombs. Both airship sheds were set ablaze destroying Zeppelins *L54* and *L60* inside; thus the attack was a complete success with the Germans caught completely by surprise. On the way back however, one Camel ran out of fuel and the pilot was killed attempting to ditch his aircraft. Three of the other aircraft had to divert to land in neutral Denmark, their pilots being interned and the remaining two Camels reached the British flotilla where they safely ditched their aircraft and were picked up by the destroyer HMS *Violent*. This was the outstanding carrier-launched air strike of the Great War and demonstrated the potential of the aircraft carrier, a potential that was to be fully realised in the Second World War. In fact, had the Great War continued and not ended in 1918, plans were being made to launch a strike against the German High Seas Fleet at its anchorage in 1919, a strike which foreshadowed those against Taranto (1940) and Pearl Harbor (1941).

From its birth, naval aviation in the Royal Navy had struggled against both hostility from traditionalists and indifference from politicians; however, due to the courage of its pioneering pilots and the foresight of some higher-ranking officers, it had seen the development of the ship-borne aircraft as a potent weapon. The years between the wars however saw the Fleet Air Arm and naval aviation as a whole suffer from both inter-service rivalry and government policies which kept spending on Britain's armed forces to a minimum. For most of these years the Navy's air arm, whilst disembarked from their ships was under the control of the Royal Air Force and as such was very much a 'Cinderella'. The ships were provided by the Navy, the RAF provided aircrew whilst the Air Ministry provided the aeroplanes; an unwieldy, inefficient and unsatisfactory arrangement. Following the Inskip enquiry of 1937, the Navy, in 1939 at last regained sole control of its air arm, their Fleet Air Arm. However, the main reason it lacked modern aircraft stemmed from the total lack of foresight and imagination of the Board of Admiralty, who were responsible for the edict that:

> 'It is not necessary for the design and performance of shipboard aircraft to be comparable with shore based aircraft as we cannot foresee any occasion when one will be in conflict with the other.'

When war broke out in September 1939, the Royal Navy possessed seven aircraft carriers of which only one, the *Ark Royal* which commissioned eight months earlier, was of modern construction and design. She could accommodate six squadrons and was serving with the Home Fleet. Of the remaining six carriers, *Glorious, Courageous* and *Furious* had been converted from large light cruisers, while *Eagle* had begun life as a Chilean battleship but had been purchased prior to completion and converted from 1918. *Hermes*, however, enjoyed the distinction of being the first custom-designed carrier and embodied many of the features later recognised as standard; she was just completing a refit at Plymouth. Finally, the small training carrier *Argus* completed the complement, having been converted from an Italian liner, the *Conte Rosso*, in 1918. She was based at Arbroath and was equipped mainly with Fairey Swordfish. Until shortly before the outbreak of war *Argus* had been operating as a parent ship for Queen Bee (adapted Tiger Moth) radio-controlled target aircraft. The Navy also possessed the seaplane carrier *Albatross*. She had been built for the RAN but was handed to the RN in 1938 as part payment for two cruisers transferred to the RAN. Capable of carrying up to nine Supermarine Walruses and fitted with a catapult, she was only able to retrieve aircraft from the sea by hoisting them aboard by crane. There was a second, far more ancient seaplane carrier in the Reserve Fleet at Chatham – HMS *Pegasus*. Commissioned at the end of 1914 as HMS *Ark Royal*, she had operated up to eight seaplanes in the Mediterranean during the Great War. Taken out of active service in the early 1930s, she was renamed *Pegasus* in 1934 and commenced a period as a trials ship for catapults, aircraft recovery and training.

Ark Royal	Captain: A J Power CVO Commander Flying: Cdr F M R Stephenson
Glorious	Captain: G D'Oyly-Hughes Commander Flying: Cdr G Willoughby DSO DSC
Courageous	Captain: W T MaKeig-Jones Commander Flying: Cdr E M C Abel-Smith
Furious	Captain: M L Clark DSC Commander Flying: Cdr(A) R P Peyton
Eagle	Captain: A R M Bridge Commander Flying: Cdr A P Colthurst
Hermes	Captain: F E P Hutton Commander Flying: Cdr G G Poole
Argus	Captain: H C Bovell

PRINCIPAL TYPES OF FLEET AIR ARM AIRCRAFT IN SERVICE BY 1939

Blackburn Roc

A development of the Skua fitted with a rotating electrically-driven turret mounting four .303 Browning machine-guns and situated aft of the cockpit. Although briefly used operationally it was not a success.

Blackburn Skua

A single-engined, monoplane fighter-cum-dive-bomber. New aircrew were slightly disconcerted to be told that the dictionary definition of a Skua was 'a gull which folded its wings and dived into the sea.' Fortunately, despite its failings, it was surprisingly reliable.

Fairey Seafox

A single-engined two-seat spotter-reconnaissance seaplane distinguished by having an open cockpit for the pilot with an enclosed position for the observer. Generally they were carried at sea by catapult-equipped cruisers and Armed Merchant Cruisers. Approximately 64 production models were received into service from April 1937.

Fairey Swordfish
A single-engined, three-seat biplane torpedo-bomber capable of carrying bombs in lieu of a torpedo. Some were equipped as floatplanes. The Swordfish was affectionately known in service as the *Stringbag*.

Gloster Sea Gladiator
A biplane fighter, effectively the standard RAF Gladiator fitted with an arrester hook and dinghy stowage. Highly manoeuvrable but slow and obsolescent.

Supermarine Walrus
A single-engined amphibian reconnaissance 'pusher' biplane. These operated mainly from catapult-equipped battleships and cruisers and could carry a small quantity of bombs. Known affectionately within the RN as the *Shagbat,* 162 were in service with the RN and Commonwealth navies at the start of World War II. [1]

FLEET AIR ARM ORDER OF BATTLE, HOME FLEET, SEPTEMBER 1939

At the outbreak of war the FAA possessed just five land bases in the UK. Known as Royal Naval Air Stations, they were also given names with an HMS prefix. All were commanded by the RAF:

RNAS Lee-on-Solent (near Portsmouth)	HMS *Daedalus*	Wg Cdr W J Seward
RNAS Eastleigh (near Portsmouth)	HMS *Raven*	Grp Capt E O Grenfell
RNAS Ford (Hampshire)	HMS *Peregrine*	Grp Capt H W Penderel
RNAS Worthy Down (Hampshire)	HMS *Kestrel*	Wg Cdr W Underhill
RNAS Donibristle (Drem, Scotland)	HMS *Merlin*	Wg Cdr B A Mallet

RNAS Hatston (near Kirkwall, Orkney) HMS *Sparrowhawk* opened on 2nd October 1939 as a shore base for units embarked with the Home Fleet at Scapa Flow and was commanded by Captain C L Howe.

AIRCRAFT CARRIERS AND AIR SQUADRONS HOME FLEET

North and South Atlantic Trade Protection
Commander-in-Chief Admiral Sir Charles Forbes

HMS *Ark Royal*		
800 Sqn	9 Skuas, 3 Rocs	Lt-Cdr G N Torry
803 Sqn	9 Skuas, 3 Rocs (to end Sept)	Lt-Cdr D R F Cambell
810 Sqn	12 Swordfish	Capt N R M Skene RM
820 Sqn	12 Swordfish and 1 Walrus	Lt-Cdr G B Hodgkinson
821 Sqn	12 Swordfish	Lt-Cdr G M Duncan
HMS *Furious*		
816 Sqn	9 Swordfish (3/10/39)	Lt-Cdr J Dalyell-Stead
818 Sqn	3 Swordfish (23/10/39)	Lt-Cdr J E Fenton

HMS *Courageous*		
811 Sqn	12 Swordfish	Lt-Cdr S Borrett
822 Sqn	12 Swordfish	Lt-Cdr P W Humphreys
HMS *Hermes*		
814 Sqn	12 Swordfish	Lt-Cdr N S Luard
HMS *Argus* (training carrier) from 11/39		
767 DLT Sqn	Swordfish	Lt-Cdr J A L Drummond
770 DLT Sqn (formed 7/11/39)	Sea Gladiator/Skua/ Tiger Moth	Lt-Cdr C A Kingsley
HMS *Albatross* (seaplane carrier)		
710 Sqn	6-9 Walruses	Lt-Cdr H L Hayes

Note: For the sake of completeness HMS *Eagle* was in the Indian Ocean on 3rd September 1939 allocated to the China Station. 813 and 824 Squadrons were aboard, each with 9 Swordfish. At this time HMS *Glorious* was stationed in the Mediterranean with 802 Squadron (6 Sea Gladiators) and 812, 823 and 825 Squadrons each with 12 Swordfish.

WALRUS/SWORDFISH CATAPULT SHIPS HOME FLEET

Battleships			
HMS *Barham.*	1 Swordfish floatplane	701 Sqn	Lt-Cdr W L M Brown
HMS *Malaya.*	2 Swordfish floatplanes	701 Sqn	
HMS *Valiant* (refitting)	2 Swordfish floatplanes	701 Sqn	
HMS *Rodney.*	1 Swordfish floatplane	702 Sqn	Lt-Cdr R A Phillimore
HMS *Resolution.*	1 Swordfish floatplane	702 Sqn	
HMS *Nelson.*	1 Swordfish floatplane	702 Sqn	
HMS *Queen Elizabeth* (refitting)	2 Walruses		
Battlecruisers			
HMS *Repulse.*	2 Swordfish floatplanes	705 Sqn	Lt P E O'Brien
HMS *Renown* (refitting)	1 Walrus	705 Sqn	
HMS *Hood.*	1 Walrus		
Cruisers			
HMS *Belfast.*	1 Walrus	712 Sqn	Lt-Cdr G A Tilney
HMS *Edinburgh.*	1 Walrus	712 Sqn	
HMS *Suffolk* (refitting)	2 Walruses	712 Sqn	
HMS *Norfolk* (refitting)	1 Walrus	712 Sqn	
HMS *Cumberland.*	1 Walrus		
HMS *Glasgow.*	2 Walruses		
HMS *Newcastle.*	2 Walruses		
HMS *Sheffield.*	2 Walruses		
HMS *Southampton.*	2 Walruses		
HMS *Effingham.*	2 Walruses		
HMS *London* (refitting)	2 Walruses		

With war imminent, ships of the Royal Navy and the German *Kriegsmarine* began taking up their war stations. There was much activity in the South Atlantic, where merchant ships of all nations were engaged in providing Europe with the fruits of the Southern Hemisphere. At any one time, many hundreds of British, German and neutral freighters and tankers were criss-crossing the southern waters with their wares. Mainly unarmed, these soon became sitting targets for the belligerent warships, whose crews were awaiting orders to strike. In the northern waters, the main concern of the British were the convoys bringing food and materiel from Canada and North America, which similarly were to become helpless targets for Germany's as yet small but expanding U-boat force.

An hour after war was declared at 11:00 on **3rd September 1939**, Blenheim N6215 of 139 Squadron took off from RAF Wyton, Cambridgeshire with Flg Off Andrew McPherson at the controls. He was ordered to fly to the Wilhelmshaven area and airfields in northwest Germany, carrying Cdr Charles Thompson RN from HMS *Ark Royal* as observer and Cpl Arrowsmith as gunner. The flight was uneventful and some 75 photographs were taken of warships and other military objectives. The following day McPherson repeated the sortie, but this time had Lt-Cdr Philip Yorke aboard as observer; thus the FAA was represented in two of the first operational sorties of the war.

Lt Bill Lucy DSO. The Fleet Air Arm's first ace.

1. EARLY OPERATIONS IN THE ATLANTIC AND NORTH SEA

Northern waters September – December 1939

'Two torpedoes hit us almost simultaneously … there were two explosions, a split second apart … as if the core of the earth exploded, and the universe split from pole to pole, it could sound no worse … the hot blast which followed tore at the skin on my face and plucked at my clothes. There was something Satanic about it, and unreal. In the sudden deathly silence, which followed, I knew that the ship had died.'

Lt(A) Charles Lamb, HMS *Courageous*

On 9th September 1939, HMS *Courageous* with a three-destroyer escort left Plymouth for anti-submarine duties in the Western Approaches. At 10:30 next morning (**10th September**), one of her patrolling Swordfish attacked a submarine contact some 280 miles south-west of Ushant and, at 12:50, another made an attack 270 miles west of Ushant. During these operations Lt Bill Playfair flying P4090 of 822 Squadron was unable to locate the carrier at the end of his patrol and was lost with his crew, Sub-Lt(A) Harry Wheatman and N/Air Fred 'Ginger' Frizzell. Fellow 822 Squadron pilot Lt(A) Charles Lamb wrote:

'We lost our first aircraft and crew. The pilot was one of our flight leaders, a very experienced aviator named Bill Playfair. When they returned after a patrol the ship was obscured by cloud, low on the water, and although they flew right over the ship and we saw them; they failed to see us. Searchlights were shone up into the clouds, and star shells were fired, but there was no further sign of the aircraft.

'I had an interesting conversation with our squadron CO, Pat Humphreys [Lt-Cdr P W Humphreys]. "Has it occurred to you, sir, that they might have been shot down?" "Shot down! Don't be an ass! We're miles from anywhere out here." The tragedy had given me the opportunity of saying something that had been bothering me for a week. "I know it's a very remote possibility, but it isn't impossible; and I think it is time we armed the aircraft guns." The Swordfish had a Vickers gun in front, which was fired by the pilot by pressing a button on the control column; the gun then fired through the propeller. We also had a Lewis gun in the rear cockpit, which was fired either by the observer or the air gunner – if one was lucky enough to be carrying such a luxury as a third member of the crew. "You've been watching too many films about the last war!" said Pat Humphreys, scathingly. "What on earth do we want bullets in our guns for?" "Because they are more useful with them than without," I replied, equally scathingly, and was rebuked for being impertinent.'[2]

Courageous arrived at Milford Haven late on the 10th, and departed next day bound for Plymouth. She and her escort were delayed en route when they provided cover and assistance for two destroyers that had collided while escorting Convoy *OB.2*. Both HMS *Vanquisher* and *Walker* were badly damaged, with 14 ratings killed on the former.

Meanwhile, HMS *Ark Royal*, which had ventured into the North-Western Approaches, also on the 9th was soon in action, her aircraft attacking a submarine contact some 150 miles north-west of Cape Wrath on 12th September. Two of her escorting destroyers, HMS *Faulknor* and *Firedrake* were detached to carry out a search, but failed to make contact. Three more destroyers joined her screen on 14th September, shortly before the carrier was attacked by *U-39*. Two torpedoes passed astern and one actually detonated in her wake. The enormous column of water caused by the exploding warhead alerted the escorts and they immediately moved in for a counter attack. As *Ark Royal* steamed on and out of danger, the destroyers gained sonar contact and commenced a depth charge attack. The first pattern of depth charges dislodged the U-boat's engines; the second blew her to the surface in a sinking condition. The destroyers opened fire but ceased as men began to appear on deck. The whole of the submarine's company – 43 in all – abandoned ship and were taken on board *Faulknor*, *U-39*'s skipper was Korvettenkapitän Gerhard Glattes, who was only 23 years-old and several of his crew were teenagers.[3] A few minutes later the U-boat went down in a torrent of foam and bubbles becoming the first German submarine to be sunk in World War II.

A section of three Skuas from 803 Squadron led by Lt-Cdr Dennis Cambell were flown off in the afternoon to protect the ship from further such attacks, and one of these found an abandoned steamer, the grain-carrying SS *Fanad Head* – bound for Belfast from Montreal – about 100 miles away. She was lying stopped, with her eight passengers and crew in several lifeboats in the calm sea around her. *U-30* (Korvettenkapitän Fritz Lemp) was on the surface and was trying to sink her with gunfire. She was in the middle of a patch of oil some 50 feet in diameter and was obviously surprised by the arrival of Skua L2957/A7K flown by Lt Richard Thurston RM, who immediately carried out a dive-bombing attack. Unfortunately for the Skua crew, the bombs detonated almost directly under their machine, which caught fire and was promptly ditched. Both Thurston and his observer PO(A) Jock Simpson suffered severe burns but managed to evacuate their sinking aircraft, whereupon they endeavoured to swim towards the sinking freighter, which had been boarded by a small party from *U-30*. Simpson failed to reach the boat and was lost, while Thurston was recovered by one of the German sailors, Gfr Ohse, who bravely dived into the sea and pulled him to safety, despite himself having been slightly injured by shrapnel from the Skua's bombs. Lt-Cdr Cambell then arrived on the scene, releasing his bombs on what they believed was the submarine but was probably the burning wreck of the downed Skua! Turning towards the *Fanad Head*, they saw two men swimming, whom they believed to be two of the German submariners left behind when *U-30* crash-dived. In fact, the swimmers were Thurston and Ob.Btsmt Hinish, who had indeed been left on the surface. *U-30* then resurfaced and Cambell made a strafing attack before it hastily crash-dived once more. Having radioed for assistance, two sections of Swordfish were scrambled from the *Ark*, led by Lt-Cdr James Fenton, the Observer CO of 821 Squadron aboard Lt(A) Michael Clifford's aircraft, these being passed as Cambell headed back to the carrier.

At this stage the third Skua, L2873/A7M flown by Lt Guy Griffiths RM arrived, having spotted the freighter on the horizon. As they circled the ship, the crew were surprised to see *U-30* alongside. They decided to make a diving attack and, on releasing their bombs, suffered the same fate as Thurston's aircraft – the bombs detonated prematurely and brought down the Skua. The aircraft sank almost immediately, taking the observer PO(A) George McKay down with it. Griffiths swam over to the freighter and was able to climb aboard, whereupon, he too, was taken prisoner by the boarding party. With all this aerial activity, Korvettenkapitän Lemp ordered the boarding party to return with the two prisoners, all of whom were required to swim over to *U-30*, following which the *Fanad Head* was sunk by a single torpedo from the U-boats stern tube, after four fired from the bow tubes all malfunctioned. When *Ark Royal*'s Swordfish arrived, the *Fanad Head* was still afloat but listing to port. As they prepared to attack *U-30*, a torpedo was seen to strike the vessel amidships and, with her back broken, she settled with her bow and stern rising skywards, before sliding beneath the calm waters to leave only the lifeboats and an ever-widening circle of flotsam to mark her grave. One of the Swordfish observers remarked afterwards:

> 'It was a moving sight to see this small cargo vessel slowly covered by the calm sea. All six Swordfish attacked the vague shape of the submerged U-boat with bombs, which fell so close that the crews of the Swordfish were convinced that they had sunk her, but later evidence showed that she returned to Germany after landing one of her wounded men in Iceland. With her she took the crews of the two crashed Skuas, the first naval airmen to be made prisoners of war.'

U-30 was severely damaged in this attack and by a follow-up attack by three destroyers and sprang several leaks; two of her crew were injured, but she eventually reached Iceland, where the two injured men were put ashore for treatment. However, Griffiths and Thurston remained aboard and were taken to Germany, the submarine having been undertow for two weeks. From his eventual POW camp, Lt Guy Griffiths RM later wrote:

> 'I went out in my machine to look for a submarine, which was supposed to have sunk one of our merchant ships about 500 miles out from Ireland in the North Atlantic. Three machines went out, and I searched for the ship. My observer, a Chief Petty Officer, suddenly shouted to me: "There's a merchant ship on the horizon, let's look at it." Well it was about 20 miles away, but away we went. When we were almost on it my chap said: "Go low so that I can see its name". So down I went to sea level, and slowed down. Suddenly, just as I got alongside the ship, I spotted the sub alongside the far side of the ship! Up I went, but the sub had already got half submerged, leaving me no time to get to a safe height to bomb from. So I took a chance and bombed from a low height in order to hit. My first bomb missed by about 20 feet, and my next blew me up with the blast! I hit the sea at 200 mph at a steep dive and went straight down without stopping. I tried to get out of the cockpit but was jammed in with a stuck roof. When I was almost out of breath, I managed to break free and came to the surface. My observer was killed at once, for I never saw him again. I looked for him, but with no luck. I then found that I was nearly a mile away from the merchant ship, in very cold water, with flying clothes on, and not a little

knocked about. Somehow I got there, and clambered aboard the merchant ship. On board were some of the submarine's crew who were collecting the ship's papers when I arrived, also on board was one of my squadron [Lt Thurston], who had done almost the same thing as I had. A few minutes later up came the submarine and we were taken prisoner; the ship was torpedoed almost at once, and once more we were submerged.'

The *Fanad Head*'s crew and passengers were eventually picked up by the destroyer HMS *Tartar* and put ashore in the small Scottish port of Mallaig.

On 16th September, HMS *Courageous* departed Plymouth for anti-submarine hunting in the Western Approaches. She was joined outside the breakwater at 09:30 by destroyers *Inglefield*, *Ivanhoe* and *Impulsive*. A fourth, *Intrepid*, which had not completed embarking depth charges, departed Plymouth later in the day and joined them at 15:00. Next day (**17th September**), *Courageous* was 350 miles west of Land's End when she was spotted by *U-29* skippered by Korvettenkapitän Otto Schuhart who had observed a Swordfish and 'followed' it, assuming that its parent carrier would be nearby:

'At the time it looked like a hopeless operation. Because of the aircraft, I could not surface and my underwater speed was less than eight knots, while the carrier could do 26. But we were told during our training to always stay close and that is exactly what I did, following him submerged.'

Courageous' Swordfish had been in the air searching for signs of U-boat activity following a distress call from the 5,000-ton British freighter *Kafirstan*, which had been torpedoed by *U-53* (Korvettenkapitän Ernst-Günther Heinicke). One of the aircraft dropped a bomb on the submarine, causing her to dive but inflicting no damage. Meanwhile, Kapt Schuhart continued to trail the carrier for one-and-a-half hours, losing distance all the time, but eventually, at 19:40, he found himself in a favourable position to launch an attack, firing three torpedoes from less than 3,000 yards: 'The vast size of the target upset all normal calculations and in any case I was looking straight into the sun.' Lt(A) Charles Lamb of 822 Squadron, who had just entered the wardroom with his observer, Lt Robert Wall:

'Two torpedoes hit us almost simultaneously, just as Wall and I were stepping into the wardroom. I had said to him: "What are you going to have?" but he had no time to answer because at that moment there were two explosions, a split second apart, the like of which I had never imagined possible. If the core of the earth exploded, and the universe split from pole to pole, it could sound no worse. Every light went out immediately and the deck reared upwards, throwing me backwards, and the hot blast which followed tore at the skin on my face and plucked at my clothes. There was something Satanic about it, and unreal. In the sudden deathly silence which followed, I knew that the ship had died. In the wardroom passage the deafening silence was broken by the tinkling of glass, breaking somewhere; and the tiny sound of trickling water. There was also a persistent whisper of noise, which at first I failed to identify. Then it dawned on me that it was the sound of men breathing. The bulkhead behind me was now partly underfoot; and facing aft, I was standing with my left foot on the deck, which sloped upwards to starboard at an amazing angle. My other foot was on the wall. In this position it was obvious that the ship could not remain afloat for long. The silence was frightening. I supposed that the ship's engine had been blown to bits. All that remained was a great hulk, not a ship, lying on its side. The port side of the flight deck was only a few feet above sea level. The next few hours were unforgettable.'[4]

When the torpedoes ripped open the carrier's side at 19:40, she rolled over to port at such an incredible angle it was obvious to all on board that she had been struck a mortal blow. In the first few seconds the whole length of the port side of the flight deck hung suspended a few feet from the sea, crushing the ship's boats, which burst through the sea up to the surface, swept from their stowages on the decks below. In those opening seconds, the aircraft in the hangar slid to port, crashing against each other and against the port bulkhead, adding greatly to the uneven top weight and increasing the ship's list; furniture in the mess decks broke from deck fastenings and slid crazily to port; petrol tanks burst, flooding down into the decks below, and an evil slick of oil and petrol quickly spread over the calm sea, surrounding the ship with an inflammable mixture which might burst into flame – and a massive explosion – at any moment:

'When I had recovered my senses from the stunning blast, I remember thinking "I must get my Mae West at once." But before I had moved from the darkness of the room I heard a voice calling for help in a pleading tone, which couldn't be ignored. Inside, by groping about, I found that a big, glass-fronted bookcase had been wrenched from the bulkhead by the blast and had fallen on top of the Principal Medical Officer, a huge pot-bellied Surgeon-Commander. With the strength born of the desperation inspired by his cries it did not take long to lift it – just enough for him to crawl out and up – and we both stood in the half-light, panting. Then he peered at me by the light from the scuttles – which I was horrified to see were open - and thanked me. I felt that there was no time for courtesy and I propelled his colossal bulk into the passage, which led straight aft to the quarter deck. A long way away, the doorway out to the deck was flooded with sunlight, like a bright light at the end of a long tunnel, inviting everyone to safety, and I left him plodding through the dark passage towards its salvation.'[5]

Having retrieved his Mae West, Lamb made his was to the deck:

'The contrast between the pitiless blackout of the cavern I had just left and the wide beam of sparkling light stretching across the sea from the horizon was quite incredible. There was to be no let-up to admire the scenery. A little group of aviators were manning the starboard 4.7 gun, mounted on a pedestal by the guardrails on the quarter-deck, and I looked aft and saw a horrible sight: in the wide path of the shimmering light on the water, silhouetted against the sun as it sank below the horizon, were the twin periscopes of the U-boat which had just torpedoed us, pointing upwards. The thought that our hidden enemy was lying just under the surface, gloating at the sight of a great ship writhing in her death-throes, was obscene, and I hurried up the sloping deck to join the group. Lieutenant Ingram had taken charge. Assisted by the others he had wrenched a ready-use shell from its bulkhead-stowage and rammed it into the breech. He was trying to train the barrel downwards, by the hand mechanism, which at first none of us understood; but eventually we succeeded. "Do you know how to fire this bloody thing?" Ingram said fiercely. "I'd like to blast him to hell!" I had to admit that I didn't. The firing of ship's guns was not included in the Training Manual for Aircraft Pilots, and none of us knew what to do next. Pulling what we thought was the trigger had no effect. "Think they are operated by electricity," I said, dumbly. It was just as well, in some ways, that we were unable to explode the shell, because at that moment the head and shoulders of an astonished stoker appeared, clambering over the stern, gazing straight into the barrel of the gun. He had been blown into the sea on the port quarter and was seeking temporary refuge, back on board, before being swept astern, and the prospect of being blown to pieces by a bunch of young lieutenants was not at all to his liking. He was about to drop back into the less unfriendly sea, when Kiggell [Lt(A) Launce Kiggell] and I dashed aft and dragged him on board. I think he thought we had all gone mad and were about to blow his head off.

'Then the Commander's face appeared above the quarterdeck, looking down from the seaplane platform, which protruded over the quarterdeck below, and shouted "abandon ship" several times. His face was grey with anxiety. Men were diving into the water in all directions, some from the flight deck, which was fully 70 feet above sea level. I felt slightly sick at the sight and watched with my heart in my mouth as Sub-Lieutenant Oxley, one of our young pilots, made the same attempt. High above our heads he sprang out into the air, wearing his Mae West, his chest arched forward and his arms spread wide in a swallow dive, and I grimaced with relief when he missed the bilges and plummeted into the sea. Kiggell laughed. "Typical!" he said. "Only Jumbo Oxley would abandon ship with a swallow dive!" He was doing it to make sure that he missed the bilges.

'Back on the quarterdeck I saw that the stern had risen even higher and it was time to go. Only the three men from the Reserve Fleet remained at the rails, plus one Lieutenant (A) who looked as though he was going to be sick. He was one of Kiggell's squadron [811] and I listened with horrified curiosity to their short conversation. The lieutenant said that he felt too ill to swim and was going down to his cabin for a bottle of brandy he had secreted in a drawer. Kiggell told him not to be crazy. It was obvious that there was no time to go below quarterdeck level – or anywhere inside the ship – but the lieutenant refused to listen and disappeared through the doorway into the darkness. Perhaps he preferred to go this way. I have since wondered whether he was unable to swim and was too proud to say so, but have discounted that theory as too improbable. Perhaps he was just thirsty. Whatever his reason, he was never seen again.'[6]

Survivors were picked up by the escorts and the American steamer *Collingsworth* that happened upon the scene of carnage, as did the Dutch liner *Veendam* and British steamer *Dido*. They were transferred from the merchant ships to destroyers and arrived at Devonport on the evening of 18th September. Lamb had swum towards the destroyer *Impulsive* and was quickly hauled aboard. One of the first to greet him was his observer, Lt Wall:

'Those who were fit enough were kept very busy helping *Impulsive*'s men deal with the half-drowned men who were hauled on board. There was a lot to do. We applied artificial respiration to those who needed it, and then put them into a hot bath and gave them some fire-water to drink. By the time I arrived on board all the normal spirits had been drunk and all that was left was neat Pimms; but it was a wonderful reviver after the taste of that oily sea-water. I asked Neil Kemp if he had any news of Simon Borrett, the CO of the other Swordfish squadron [811], and it was a strange coincidence that when we had dressed in our makeshift clothing we walked out on deck and saw him going past, stretched out on a Carley float. His body was rigid and he was unconscious. Fortunately the ship was stationary at the time and it took only a few minutes to get him on board. I carried him down the deck and was shocked by his lack of weight: I might have been carrying a boy of ten. We put him into a hot bath but his eyes remained closed. I tried to persuade him to swallow a little neat Pimms but he was an abstemious chap and resisted, even though unconscious. "Try again," Neil said, "that little drop almost brought him round." I tilted the bottle against his teeth; his eyes opened for a fleeting moment, just long enough for him to say: "I – don't – think – I'll – have – any – more – thank – you," before he lapsed into a coma again. I said to Neil: "Even when out for the count, Simon still behaves like a gentleman! Anyone else being forced to drink against their wishes would have been far less polite!"

'Together we carried him to a settee, lying head to toe with the Commander [Cdr Claude Woodhouse],[7] who was looking awful. His face was a stricken grey, but when I asked him if he was all right he nodded. I could see something was wrong and put my hands under his blanket and found that he was soaking wet and shivering with cold. So I rubbed him down with a towel, ignoring his protests, and was greatly helped by a young Midshipman Andy Aitken, who was also from our squadron in *Courageous*. We wrapped him in a dry blanket and stretched him out on the settee again. Then Aitken and I found a number of empty bottles and filled them with hot water and stuffed them all round the outside of the blanket. During the night I looked at him occasionally and saw that his colour was returning. He seemed much better in the morning. There were others not so fortunate, and a number of men died during the night. Some of those deaths were unnecessary – one in particular. When a man is feeling low, and is cold and dispirited, and has been subjected to shock and perhaps injury, it is easy for him to drift into a torpor from which he may not wish to recover, unless something is done to jerk him out of his apathy. I learned this simple fact of life that night, but at the expense of a man's life. He was stretched out on deck by one of the hatches leading down to the wardroom flat. From one direction he had to be stepped over, and since men were carrying comatose bodies down the ladder, he provided a dangerous obstruction. I knelt down beside him and asked him if he would mind moving, thinking he was only asleep, like hundreds of others strewn about the ship's decks. He said: "Bugger off," without opening his eyes, so I left him in peace for a while. Later I tried again, but he said: "For Christ's sake leave me alone!" He was there all night and I spoke to him several times, and asked him if he was all right, or needed anything, but always received the same brusque reply. In the morning he was dead.'[8]

Lt Hank Rotherham, Senior Observer of 811 Squadron, was also a survivor:

'I could hear the roar of water flooding in and breaking down bulkheads. The ship listed to port and before long the order to abandon ship was given. I went down to the radio room, for I doubled as Signals Officer, made sure that everyone there was clear, and then went on down the starboard ladders. I met a warrant officer, rather elderly and a bit frightened. "I can't swim, Sir", he confessed. The destroyers were close now, and I thought to myself that the years of playing water polo were finally going to pay off. I gave him my life jacket. I never did see him again and often wonder what became of him.

'The ship kept on going over to port, and I made my way down to the starboard bulges where a few others had gathered. A young Sub-Lieutenant suddenly said, "I'm going down to my cabin to get my flask." He was in our squadron, and I had heard him joke about keeping something ready for just this sort of emergency. He began to clamber awkwardly back up the side of the ship. This was so stupid with help close at hand that I was suddenly angry and shouted, "Come back you bloody young fool! It'll be hell down there with everything falling about." Nothing I said had the slightest effect, however, and he disappeared from view. I never saw him again. Apart from this one piece of foolishness though there was no panic. Some brave men on the other side of the ship slipped into the water and unhooked a cutter as the ship heeled further. Their work saved many lives later.

'The ship lurched forward and seemed to shudder beneath us. She was obviously going under, so I dove in and did a fast fifty yards to get clear. I stopped, and looked back while treading water. The stern reared vertically in the air, with all four propellers stopped. I thought it strange that they were not turning. I could see two men clinging to the ensign staff at the very extremity of the stern ... they were waving. *Courageous* went with a rush, and rafts and baulks of wood came up to the surface with sudden violence. I could see the two destroyers quite close, and a merchantman lying stopped a little further off. There was a raft not far away. I was swimming towards the raft when I saw two men in the water and turned aside to help them. As I took hold of the first the other floundered around and got hold of me by the shoulders. I shook him off roughly. "Can't take you both", I told him. He agreed breathlessly and let go. I towed the first man over to the raft, but when I turned back for his companion he had gone. Once aboard the raft I realised just how cold it was, my teeth were chattering and I could not stop them. The raft began to get overcrowded, and as the merchantman was by now much closer I plunged into the sea once more and swam to her.'[9]

Another survivor, 822 Squadron Observer PO(A) 'Murgy' Brown recalled:

'On deck I helped a seaman hack a Carley float loose, and after a struggle we managed to drop it into the sea – and it was promptly seized by a group of swimmers and paddled away. I slid down the ship's side, hitting every ringbolt with my backside on the way, and into the water. Looking up as I drifted past the stern, a huge propeller ticking over a few feet from my head, I saw a Marine officer calmly smoking a fag as he ditched his confidential books over the side, before diving in. Suddenly a huge wall of water loomed up, higher than the ship's side, and I went under. When I eventually surfaced, lungs bursting, *Courageous* had gone – taking more than 500 of her company with her.

'The destroyers, including *Kelly* were bustling around by now, dropping depth charges all over the place; no joke for those of us in the drink – it was like being kicked by an elephant when they went off. I swam towards one of the destroyers, but never seemed to get any nearer. It was dusk by now, and I'd nearly had it, when I spotted a merchantman nearby, an old tramp bound for Liverpool from Sierra Leone. I made for her and managed to reach her as darkness fell. I was a good swimmer, and surprised that I was so exhausted – until I realized that I hadn't inflated my Mae West! Apart from being frozen stiff, I was all right, but others, who had seemed OK in the water, had first-degree burns and begged to be put back when they had been pulled out.

'At midnight the tramp steamer's passengers were transferred to the destroyer *Inglefield*, which had come alongside, looking for survivors. We then searched the area until morning, picking up a few bodies, and continued patrolling for another two days before we were put ashore at Plymouth. Some survivors had been picked up by an American liner, and been given the full VIP treatment by the passengers – fitted out with civvies, hob-knobbing with film stars, and all set for a run ashore in the USA. They got a shock when Mountbatten [*Kelly*'s commander] turned up and took them aboard!' [10]

In *Kelly*'s crowded sickbay, Sick Berth Attendant PO Bert Male made his patients as comfortable as possible:

'They were all exhausted, and had bad burns, lacerations, shock, and internal damage from gulping the oil. One man, a stoker, was carried below to the mess. He had slid down the ship's side when she had heeled over and the barnacles had torn his back and his buttocks and hands and he was in a very bad way. The gash bucket in the mess was full of tea leaves and scrapings off our supper plates. When the poor sod saw the bucket he fell on his knees and, stuck his hands all torn and bloody right into it. "Don't do that, old matey," I said, and tried to pull him back, "you'll get blood poisoning or something." "I don't give a shit," he said, "it's cool, cool, cool ..." When I looked closer I saw that he was pissed as a newt. The Yanks had poured a bottle of whisky into him, and had given them thick blankets and warm clothes.' [11]

Courageous' captain, Captain William MaKeig-Jones was among the 518 Royal Navy personnel, 26 members of the Fleet Air Arm and 36 RAF servicing crew who were lost. Among the FAA personnel lost were seven aircrew including three from 811 Squadron: Lt Hugh Walton-Wilson, Lt(A) Thomas MacDonald and PO(A) Bernard 'Taff' Owen, while 822 Squadron's Sub-Lt(A) David Williams and Sub-Lt(A) Gerald Pollard were lost. Also among the fatalities were two 811 Squadron TAGs, N/Air Reg Byrne and N/Air Alfred Marsh, of whom one remembered: 'Alfie had last been seen sitting on the bilge keel as she lay wallowing upside down. He couldn't be persuaded to let go because of his inability to swim.' Sadly and somewhat surprisingly, the inability to swim cost the lives of many sailors. All 25 of *Courageous*' Swordfish were lost. It was then rather belatedly realised that the use of aircraft carriers in anti U-boat hunting groups was far too dangerous for the carriers and they ceased forthwith.

At 05:10 on the morning of 25th September, HM submarine *Spearfish* put out a distress call reporting that she was unable to submerge following an attack by German anti-submarine forces while on patrol off Horn's Reef, and was currently off the coast of neutral Denmark. Four RN destroyers were already off the Norwegian coast in order to cover *Spearfish*'s return, and these were joined by two cruisers of the Humber Force and two more destroyers. Two other light cruisers, also at sea, proceeded well into the approaches of the Skagerrak and met the crippled submarine to provide cover. Meanwhile, further support was provided by the battlecruisers *Renown* and *Hood*, three more cruisers and six destroyers that departed Scapa Flow later in the day. Finally, the *Ark Royal* together with battleships *Nelson* and *Rodney* and four destroyers set out from Scapa Flow to provide overall cover for the return of this sizeable force, all of which returned safely despite German air attack. The crew of a He115 reconnaissance from I/KüFlGr.106 reported being fired on but not hit by one of the British warships.

With the bulk of the Home Fleet now at sea, the Oberkommando der Marine organised a search for the British warships, a total of 18 Do18s from 3/KüFlGr.306, 2/KüFlGr.506 and 2/KüFlGr.606 being sent out from Sylt on the morning of **26th September**, followed later by nine He59s from 3/KüFlGr.106 (attached to KüFlGr.406). One of the Dornier crews spotted the Fleet through cloud at 10:45 in the Great Fisher Bank area, and reported its location, which was about 250 miles north-east of Heligoland. Two more Dorniers soon arrived on the scene. No defending fighters were in the air, but soon three sections of Skuas were scrambled, as recounted by Lt-Cdr Cambell, CO of 803 Squadron:

> 'It was a perfectly clear day in the North Sea, and we had not been going long when we were picked up by three Do18 flying-boats, which circled around the Fleet on the horizon. Nine Skuas of 800 and 803 Squadrons were immediately launched in a free take-off, each sub-flight of three aircraft attacking a different shadower. We rushed to the attack with great delight thinking this was our big chance, blazing away with the only ammunition we had, which was .303 ball. This was unlikely to do much damage unless we hit something vital, but one of our sub-flights was successful, due to one bullet going through the radiator of their Dornier, which had to come down in the water due to the loss of its coolant.'[12]

The confirmed victory was credited to Lt Bruce McEwen and his observer PO(A) Brian Seymour, who had been busy right up to the last minute organizing the other TAGs:

> 'A TAG's work was never done, even at the best of times, let alone in this mad rush. I was responsible for getting all the information on the positions of ships in the vicinity, the call-signs and codes of the day, and for looking after the observers' gear. It was also my job to maintain my wireless set in first-class working condition – if it failed in the air, the TAG was on the bridge in front of the Captain when he got down. That was as well as manning the aft-mounted Lewis gun, of course. And there was no special hot meal laid on for us before a patrol, like the commissioned aircrew had. The Admiralty knew as much about flying as Nelson did – with slightly less excuse.'[13]

Having completed his many tasks, Seymour took off in L2873 with Lt McEwen, who was not his usual pilot. They were led by Lt Charles Evans[14] and accompanied by Lt Bill Robertson.[15]

> 'We strained our eyes through the mist and murk. Suddenly we sighted a dark, mottled shape low on the water, indistinct because of the clever camouflage in blue, green and grey – but definitely a Dornier. McEwen opened up with his four forward-firing Brownings, then I raked the German with my Lewis, with the Dornier firing back all the time. After a second attack the Dornier went down and flopped into the water like a shot-gunned duck. The Germans broke out their rubber dinghy, and the flying boat sank. It was the first enemy aircraft of the war to be shot down by any Allied force. It was also the *Ark*'s first aircraft victory, and for the officers there was a Black Velvet party.'[16]

Their victim was M7+YK of 2/KüFlGr.506. Both Evans and McEwen had fired at the Dornier, and eventually it was driven down by McEwen and forced to alight on the sea. The crew of four – pilot Ltn.z.See Wilhelm Freiherr von Reitzenstein, observer Ltn.z.See Emst Komer, Uffz Walter Hecht and Uffz Fritz Schmalfeld – were picked up by the destroyer *Somali*.

Later, a second seaplane approached the ships and another section of 800 Squadron Skuas was scrambled comprising Lt George (known as 'Ned') Finch-Noyes, Lt Ken Spurway and PO(A) Harold Monk, known as 'Eric'. The flying boat was intercepted, as the latter recalled:

> 'Unfortunately, the C-in-C allowed the Dorniers to fly around the Fleet, and for a long time only one was attacked. We were limited to only one attack each on our Dornier. I was last to attack and the Dornier's slipstream was visible on the sea so I ignored my reflector sight and watched my bullets from the four machine-guns making ducks and drakes all over the Hun. He must have been riddled like a colander but his "fans" kept turning and I often wondered if he reached home. That was my first action and very disappointing too.'[17]

It was reported that the 'Dornier' eventually alighted off the Dutch coast due to engine damage and that one crewmember had been wounded. However, records suggest that while a German seaplane did land on the sea off the Dutch coast, it was in fact a He59 float-plane of M2+JK of 3/KüFlGr.106 that had put down with an engine out of action. However, whether this was Monk's victim is not clear. Next day the crew was rescued and the Heinkel was later salvaged by a German minelayer.

The shadowers had meanwhile signalled the position of the Fleet, and at 12:50 nine HeinkelHe111s from II/KG26 were promptly despatched from Westerland/Sylt led by Hptm Martin Vetter, followed at 13:05 by the detachment of four Junkers Ju88s from II/KG30 under Ltn Walter Storp. Expecting just such an attack, the *Ark*'s captain (Captain A J Power) had ordered that all the petrol from the tanks of the Skuas should be emptied so that they would not bum easily, and had them stowed below decks. He had decided that any air attack would be met by the ships' anti-aircraft defences. The German bombers duly arrived overhead in heavy cloud, the Heinkels bombing from low altitude, but in level flight, and missing. Ju88s then appeared and dived on the ships. Ltn Storp scored a direct hit on HMS *Hood*, but the bomb bounced off the deck without exploding. Obgfr Carl Francke dropped two SC500 bombs aimed at *Ark Royal*, but only obtained a near miss. He returned claiming that he might have hit the carrier. Lt-Cdr Cambell had just returned from the Dornier-intercept sortie:

> 'After returning to the ship, the Fleet started to return to Scapa Flow. At about 14:00, I was having a late lunch when suddenly there was an almighty bang and the ship shook like a jelly. It appeared that one of the German bombers had dropped a bomb just ahead of the ship, but Captain Power managed to swing her clear and she had ridden through the explosion, shaken herself, but suffered no substantial damage.'

PO(A) Monk was also on his way to lunch when the attack started:

> 'After landing on, I went out on to the lower weather deck to walk down to the mess for a late lunch. That was the instant the bombs exploded alongside the port side. I was drenched and wondered why one bomb made black smoke and the other white.'

Lt-Cdr Richard Phillimore, OC 702 Walrus Squadron, aboard HMS *Rodney*, recalled:

> 'A signal was received that a Hudson aircraft would be closing the Fleet – and most of us had never seen one. It duly appeared, low down, and was passing some message by Aldis when we were aware that three aircraft were nearly vertical above us. One of them went into a near-vertical dive over the *Ark Royal*, dropped a bomb at about 1,000 feet and made its getaway below the level of the tops of the masts, while all the close-range weapons of our force were trying to train quickly enough to fire at it and avoid hitting the other ships. Then, when it was near the horizon, it would climb again and stand by for another run.
>
> 'My action station was in the armoured tower, providing a front seat at a most spectacular display. My recollection is that the three aircraft attacked singly, each carrying out three runs. It was dramatic in the extreme, with the *Ark Royal* taking violent evasive action as soon as a plane was committed to a dive and with the *Rodney* and *Repulse* doing their best to conform. No hits were scored on either side, although Captain Power reported that the last bomb had broken crockery and taken off some paint from the ship's side. This was one of the many times the Germans claimed to have sunk the *Ark Royal*, almost certainly because shortly afterwards she, with some of the destroyers, left for Rosyth, while the rest of us returned to Scapa. Not seeing her, they thought they had sunk her.'[18]

Later in the day further reconnaissance noted two battleships and covering forces heading west, but no carrier. At once the German propaganda machine leapt upon this, announcing that Obgfr Francke had sunk the *Ark Royal*. He was awarded the Iron Cross and promoted to Leuntant. As darkness fell a Do18 again saw the ships and reported the carrier present, but nothing was done to stop the story going out to the world's press.

Earlier in 1939, whilst still at peace, a notice had been sent to RAFVR centres, inviting part-time pilots to volunteer for a two-week attachment to the Fleet Air Arm, to be spent on an aircraft carrier. Subsequently this was changed to a three-week stint, and as a consequence most of the volunteers in civilian occupations had to drop out. Upon mobilisation in August of that year, some 40 RAFVR pilots, each of whom had a minimum of 100 hours flying training, and most of whom had previously volunteered for the two-week carrier trip, were posted to the Fleet Air Arm airfield at Donibristle on the Firth of Forth. At this stage, the FAA had only recently been returned solely to Royal Navy charge, and many of the pilots who had previously served in the Fleet squadrons had transferred back to the RAF. Sgt Jim Pickering, one of the chosen few, recalled:

> 'We were amongst the first RAFVR recruits and were politically aware of the German threat. We had responsible civilian occupations, or were being trained for them. We had no career expectations in the RAF. There was little realisation in 1939 that there would be a long war or any expectation that Germany would win. I think most of the mobilised reserves of all the forces expected to be back in their civilian occupations in a year or possibly two. Most RAFVR pilots hoped and expected to join operational squadrons on award of the RAF wings.'

The first batch of new arrivals – thirteen RAFVR Sergeant Pilots (Sgts D K Ashton, D H Ayres, H W Ayre, O R Bowerman, R J Hyde, E N Kelsey, J B Marsh, R O'Donnell, J Pickering, F N Robertson, L W Sturges, W J Timms and B Wigginton) and 12 FAA pilots – at Donibristle were allocated either to the Torpedo Spotter Reconnaissance Flight to fly Swordfish and Blackburn Sharks, or to 769(T) Fighter Squadron on Sea Gladiators and Skuas. Operational training was to include deck landings on HMS *Furious*. Indeed, the first RAFVR pilots to arrive were posted to the TSR Flight, this being considered the better posting by the Navy, since it involved attack, while fighters were only defensive. The later arrivals were admonished for being too late for posting to the TSR unit, but most were in fact pleased to have got on to fighters. Sgt Pickering and two others soon found themselves in the front line (on 16th October):

> 'Jack Marsh, Drac Bowerman and myself were taxiing out for some formation flying in Skuas when a matelot on a bike rode towards us waving his arms (we had no reliable radios). He persuaded Bowerman and myself to stop, but Jack, intent on other things, took off. Our instructions from the matelot were to disperse the Skuas, switch off, and stand by our aircraft, which we duly did. We were then able to hear the air raid sirens, followed shortly afterwards by the crump of bombs in the distance, ack-ack bursts above and the sight of a flight of Spitfires chasing a Ju88. We heard the rasping note of eight machine-guns firing in unison, then the all clear, and we were told to return the aircraft to the tarmac. With no aircraft to formate on him, Jack returned and found that a bullet, obviously fired from the ground, had passed between his left arm and chest. We had seen the first air raid of the war by German aircraft on British soil – and once again, with that genius for doing the wrong thing, the FAA had grounded the only three Naval fighters that could at least have given chase.'

After six weeks at Donibristle, eleven of the RAFVR pilots were posted to 770 Squadron at Lee-on-Solent in company with eight FAA pilots; the other two RAFVR pilots – Sgts Robertson and Hyde – had purposely failed the course and returned to the RAF, being posted to 66 Squadron on Spitfires. At Lee-on-Solent, the group boarded the old training carrier *Argus* to continue deck-landing training off Toulon, in the safety of the Mediterranean. The first fatality occurred on 26th November, when A/Sub Lt(A) Malcolm Pike, night training with 770 Squadron, was killed when his Skua L3022 crashed into the sea.

Elsewhere during this period the nation experienced further naval tragedy on **14th October**, when *U-47* sank the battleship *Royal Oak* in Scapa Flow. In total 833 officers and ratings were lost. Fortunately, most of the Fleet was at Loch Ewe although the old seaplane carrier *Pegasus* was in the berth next to *Royal Oak*. Mistakenly identified by *U-47* as the battlecruiser *Repulse*; she was not damaged. *Pegasus* was in the forefront again the following month when she formed part of the escort for Convoy *FS.38* from Methil, on the Firth of Forth to Southend.

803 Squadron, now shore based at Hatston lost a Roc on **23rd October**, L3063 failing to return from a patrol off Wick. PO(A) Len Tregillis and his TAG N/Air Bob Eason were the unfortunate crew. Early the following month saw the arrival on posting to 803 Squadron of Capt Richard 'Birdy' Partridge, one of the Navy's rare Royal Marine pilots, who had been instructing at Eastleigh. It proved to be a busy time for him, honing the pilots on the finer points of combat, though it was routine and mundane, until **25th November**:

> 'A signal came through to say that major units of the fleet were being shadowed by enemy aircraft north-east of the Shetland Isles and 803 Squadron's commander decided to take four Skuas up there to deal with the situation. I was one of the four and we took off at about 13:00 in very squally, poor weather. We eventually found the ships about three hours later, only to be told to return to base immediately as enemy aircraft had departed. The weather was deteriorating and darkness not far off so 803 leader decided to land and spend the night at Sumburgh in the Shetlands where there was a small (very small!) aerodrome and a Royal Air Force detachment. We all managed to land safely and refuelled, spent the night there and returned to Wick early the next morning. I think it may be interesting to realize that at the time of which I am writing there were only about 15 Royal Marine officers flying with the Fleet Air Arm and yet in 803 Squadron where I was Red sub-section leader my No.2 and No.3 were both Royal Marines, Of course without fail we were dubbed "The Thin Red Line." '[19]

Five days later, Capt Partridge was advised of an immediate move – to help form a new fighter squadron at Hatston, which was required to counter increasing Luftwaffe reconnaissance in the area. Four Sea Gladiators were despatched to Hatston from Donibristle to form the nucleus of the unit, which next day (1st December) officially became 804 Squadron under the temporary command of Partridge until the CO-designate, Lt-Cdr John Cockburn, arrived. Meanwhile, at Wick where the FAA had lodger facilities with No.13 Group RAF, six more Sea Gladiators were taken from storage and put into service, flying over to Hatston to bring the squadron up to strength.[20]

Meanwhile, at sea, *Furious* was involved in convoy protection and lost one of her Swordfish on **27th November**. On this occasion the crew were fortunate and Sub-Lt(A) Sid Appleby of 818 Squadron and his crew were rescued and returned to the ship. The carrier was part of the escort provided for the 20,000-ton liner *Duchess of Richmond*, which was carrying British civilians being evacuated to Canada. On her return journey to the UK, *Furious* was required to form part of the protection for Canadian troop convoy TC.1 comprising four liners, the *Monarch of Bermuda* (961 troops), *Empress of Britain* (1,303 troops), *Empress of Australia* (1,235 troops) and *Aquitania* (2,638 troops). The battlecruiser *Repulse*, light cruiser *Emerald* and two destroyers accompanied *Furious* and the convoy. Because of the severe cold, the carrier was unable to launch aircraft due to frozen hydraulic lines until several days out from Halifax. On 17th December, the convoy arrived at Liverpool. Unknown to the troops was the fact that they had narrowly escaped what could have been a major sea disaster. The outward-bound passenger liner *Samaria*, showing no lights, had passed right through the convoy unaware of the convoy's position. It struck the wireless masts of *Furious* on her port side, struck a glancing blow on the port side of the next ship astern, the *Aquitania*, then passed close down the starboard side of the third and fourth ships sailing in line ahead. It was a close call.

Lt(A) Charles Lamb, a survivor of the *Courageous*, found himself posted to newly formed 815 Squadron at RNAS Worthy Down under the command of Lt-Cdr Simon Borrett, formerly CO of now defunct 811 Squadron, who had recovered after a fashion from his ordeal:

> 'The Swordfish was a sturdy aircraft, and its robust qualities were proved almost beyond credulity by our CO, one bleak November afternoon, when he was leading us back from the target ranges in the Solent. Over Southampton we ran into low cloud, and when we emerged, Simon had disappeared. We flew back to Worthy Down and waited for him. Unbeknown to us, balloons had been hoisted over Southampton and Simon led us right through them in cloud. He was the only one of us who was unlucky: his port wings had struck a balloon cable and without warning he was swung round, one hundred and eighty degrees, in a turn of startling velocity, which must have frightened him out of his mind. When he recovered he found that he was flying in the wrong direction and had lost his squadron. When landed at Worthy Down we saw that his port mainplanes were partially severed and were holding together by the flying and landing wires between them, and a few feet of the trailing edge of both wings, which were still intact.'[21]

Another of the *Courageous* survivors, Lt-Cdr Hank Rotherham, found himself summoned to RAF Mildenhall in Suffolk, where he discovered that his advice and experience was desperately required. Bomber Command was about to launch a strike against German warships – namely the battleships *Scharnhorst* and the *Gneisenau* – in the Schillig Roads, which was to become known as the 'Battle of the Heligoland Bight.' Sadly, it was hardly a battle, more of a slaughter of the lambs for the crews of the twenty-two Wellingtons that were involved. RAF crews lacked experience of navigating over the sea, and Lt-Cdr Rotherham found himself volunteering to fly with the leader of the raid, Wg Cdr R Kellett of 149 Squadron RAF. The date was **18th December**:

> 'Eventually we reached the ETA for our turning point and headed south towards our target. Looking ahead with my binoculars (I had the only pair in the aircraft) I made out a coast ahead and asked what this would be. Our navigator, a young pilot with

about 60 hours flying time and no specialist navigation training replied confidently: "The coast of Germany". Looking again I could not see any low-lying land, just cliffs which made me think we were approaching Heligoland, which indeed we were. Instead of turning to the south of this island we were well to the north of it and as a result we sailed overhead at 14,000 feet in full view for all the world to see. So much for the element of surprise!

'We flew on across Schillig Roads, where there was nothing but a couple of merchant ships, towards the Wilhelmshaven dockyards where the *Scharnhorst* and *Gneisenau* were secured alongside. The pre-arranged signal that we were going to bomb was for the lead aircraft to dive 1,000 feet, and then level out and drop its bombs. This was a manoeuvre not calculated to improve the bomb aimer's accuracy. One of the aircraft had mistaken the merchantmen for naval vessels however, and dropped their bombs prematurely. Our aircraft had a good run in and when I had the battlecruisers nicely lined up in my sights I pulled the trigger. Nothing happened. As we turned away from the target I checked with the pilot, and I can still remember his exasperated gesture when he realised that he had not armed the master release switch in the cockpit. This was, to put it mildly, extremely frustrating. It meant that I lost my only chance of dropping a bomb in anger and thus I failed to settle my score directly.

'Ironically this blunder may have saved the CO from a court martial because the RAF was at that time still prohibited from bombing any target which might endanger civilians and the naval dockyard was embedded in a sizeable town. Furthermore he had been briefed to attack only warships in Schillig Roads and so the bombs dropped on the merchant ships were also "out of court". Although these rules sound totally ridiculous in light of all that followed, they were taken seriously at the time.

'The Germans, playing by a much more realistic set of rules, were pounding at us with anti-aircraft fire and their fighters were buzzing about. The Wellington next to us went down in flames, and in all we lost twelve of our twenty-two aircraft. Our squadron suffered the least because we were in the lead and our defensive fire was controlled by radio, but the rear aircraft took heavy casualties.'[22]

Unbeknown to the British, three test radar sites had been set up by the Germans on the islands of Heligoland, Wangerooge and Borkum, and these had given early warning of the approach of the raiding force. There was also a strong fighter defence in the area, and these combined with the heavy AA barrage encountered in the target area, devastated the Wellington formations. Twelve were shot down and six more crash-landed on reaching the English coast. Only three of the 22 returned unscathed. The Messerschmitt Bf109s and Bf110s initially claimed 38 victories, later reduced to 27. Three Bf109s were lost with two pilots killed, a fourth crash-landed with a wounded pilot, and a Bf110 returned with both crewmembers wounded. Others were damaged. Lt-Cdr Rotherham continued:

'I was very glad to see that my replacement, Lt-Cdr Phillimore,[23] was waiting when we returned to Mildenhall. At the debriefing I did my best to stop the man who had bombed the merchant ships from claiming credit for his attack since the photos taken at the time would show clearly that they were not warships. He persisted in his claim and in the end I had no choice but to leave him to his disciplinary fate which I presumed would follow. As far as I was concerned the entire raid was a black comedy of errors and I was so furious at this senseless waste of life and of opportunity that I decided to put my thoughts down on paper. They had failed in three functions: command, navigation and bombing technique. I had been horrified at their apparent lack of appreciation of the necessity for practice and for the development of high precision bombing methods.

'As the Royal Air Force as a whole had not appreciated their inadequacy, however, it is perhaps hard to put the blame on an individual squadron. They lacked any method of accurate wind finding, something which was critical to navigation over the sea where there are no visual clues to one's position, and essential for high altitude bombing. Indeed bombing without accurate wind information is mostly a waste of time. Individual bombing is similarly ineffective unless the crews are highly trained. Pattern bombing, on the other hand, provides a large spread of bombs and compensates for a multitude of errors. It is hard to think of circumstances where it is not the most effective form of attack on a ship or concentrated target. A close formation also improves the concentration of fire when defending against fighters. We did not consider that enemy anti-aircraft fire was sufficiently accurate to be given serious consideration when tactics were being decided.'[24]

A costly lesson that took the lives of so many young and inexperienced RAF airmen.

Even when faced with the possibility of being shot down by one's own side, there would often be a humorous side to what could have been a grave situation, as recorded by fellow Walrus pilot Lt-Cdr George Nicholl:

'Sub-Lt Johnnie Groves was detailed to fly a senior WRNS officer and her assistant from the Orkneys to the Shetlands on a recruiting mission. The first lady was indeed senior, for she had up her 1914-18 war medals, disposed, moreover, with dignity on a figure which made the use of a Mae West redundant and the fitting of a parachute impracticable. In all chivalry, Groves felt obliged to follow suit. They left in [Walrus] L2239 on an extremely murky November day. The distance between North Ronaldsay and Sumburgh Head is no more than fifty miles, with Fair Isle slightly east of the course, but soon after take-off nothing was to be seen but the grey and white-flecked waves a few hundred feet below. As time passed the senior officer, in her seat beside him, patently became sceptical of the pilot's navigational ability. "Have you any idea where you are, young man?" she interjected.

'After nearly an hour's flight against a head wind of unknown strength and still no sign of land, grave doubts were beginning to assail the pilot. However, looking down at the featureless waves beneath his wing he said with a display of confidence far from felt that they were "dead on schedule". Just then the weather lifted, and there was Sumburgh Head. Pointing away slightly to the west, Groves thankfully made for Sullom Voe. But his relief was short-lived, for a few minutes later the sky ahead became pock-marked with black smoke puffs. He suddenly realized they were under fire from the AA cruiser *Carlisle*.

"What are they doing, young man?" inquired his passenger. "Just practising,

Ma'am," Groves replied, frantically fumbling for the Very pistol and two-star identification cartridge: With the appearance of the correct recognition stars of the day, the firing ceased in their direction and concentrated itself on a stray He111 which had started strafing Sullom Voe simultaneously with the arrival of the Walrus. Groves put L2239 down on the water without further molestation and made fast to a buoy. The "skimming dish" from *Carlisle* came alongside and, before he had a chance to notice the female passengers, the coxswain said: "Cor, sir, laugh! They thought you was a fucking Jerry!" It then took Groves some embarrassed and apologetic moments explaining to "Ma'am" that she had actually been under fire. The recruiting drive apparently resulted in no more than the addition of one cook to HM Navy, and the Walrus returned to Hatston with her passengers the same evening.'[25]

The old training carrier *Argus* was now at Toulon where she could conduct training exercises for new pilots. One course comprised the RAFVR pilots, as Sgt Pickering recalled:

'One Sub-Lt pilot [Pike] spun in and was lost without trace. We – the RN ratings and RAFVR Sergeant Pilots – were lined up and were given a lecture. We were told that if we were so foolish as to follow the example of spinning in, that we would suffer an even worse fate than a watery grave! This materialised next day when we were offered commissions in the FAA so that we could continue to serve under the incompetent who had lectured us. Most of the RAFVR pilots were now disenchanted with Naval operations of aircraft, and with the obsolescent equipment available, and only two accepted the offer, Sgts Jack Marsh and Bernard Wigginton. It shocked the RN officers that we could be so foolish. Some of them even asked us why. One stuttered: "You are making a big mistake. We are shortly going to be re-equipped with Fulmars, which will be the best fighter aircraft in any service."

'But none of the FAA officers were interested in us. As far as they were concerned, we had failed their course. We were given rail warrants at Toulon railway station and told to find our own way back to England. This was no hardship. We all spoke some French – it would be three days before we got a train to Cherbourg and a boat to Portsmouth – and a good time was had by all.'

After a few days leave, the nine remaining RAFVR pilots who had been on the FAA course were ordered to report to No.3 Bombing and Gunnery School at Aldergrove in Northern Ireland, where they were employed as staff pilots flying Wallaces, Heyfords or Battles.

2. SOUTHERN WATERS

South Atlantic September 1939 – February 1940

'Exactly as the sun set behind her, a great volume of smoke billowed up and an enormous flash was followed in due course by the boom of a large explosion. So the 'Graf Spee' met her end.'

Admiral Sir Henry McCall, Naval Attaché in Buenos Aires, recalling the last moments of the *Graf Spee*

When war broke out the German Navy was well prepared and the dispositions of its major warships had been planned well in advance. Hence, the pocket-battleship *Admiral Graf Spee* commanded by Kapitän z.See Hans Langsdorff together with her supply ship *Altmark*, was roaming southern waters awaiting easy pickings along the main trade routes. They had departed Wilhelmshaven on 21st August 1939. The battleship carried an Arado Ar196 reconnaissance floatplane (T3+AH (0014) of 1/196). As part of the subterfuge, the undersides of the Arado's wings bore roundels in an attempt to deceive or confuse merchantmen that sighted her into believing it was a British or French machine – a flagrant breach of the international rules of war.[26] The floatplane's fuselage markings were also darkened to prevent recognition from a distance. U-boats also took up their stations. The Admiralty was only too aware of the havoc a German raider could inflict on the unarmed merchantmen plying these routes, and initially six hunter groups each comprising one battleship or cruiser plus destroyers were organised to meet the threat.

HMS *Sussex* (cruiser with two Walruses) off the Cape of Good Hope
HMS *Shropshire* (cruiser with one Walrus) off the Cape of Good Hope
HMS *Malaya* (battleship with one Walrus) in the Gulf of Aden
HMS *Ramillies* (battleship with one Walrus) in the Gulf of Aden
HMS *Cornwall* (cruiser with two Walruses) based at Ceylon
HMS *Gloucester* (cruiser with two Walruses) based at Ceylon

The carrier *Glorious* was attached to the Aden group, while *Eagle* was at Ceylon. The dispositions and compositions of these groups would vary as circumstances dictated. Since the carriers did not venture into the South Atlantic, *Sussex*'s and *Shropshire*'s Walruses in particular came into their own and three or four-hour air searches became routine for the crews. Additionally, the seaplane carrier *Albatross* embarked eight Walruses of 710 Squadron at Devonport and sailed for Freetown (West Africa), where some of these flying boats were to be stationed. A small detachment under the command of Lt-Cdr Herbert Hayes was also to operate from Dakar in co-operation with French aircraft based at Ouakam.

Other British warships were currently to be found in harbour at various South American and West African locations. One of these was the light cruiser *Ajax*, which departed Rio de Janeiro shortly before the outbreak of war and almost immediately intercepted the German freighter SS *Olinda* (4,576-tons) off the River Plate and sank her with gunfire just after 14:00 on 3rd September, barely three hours after Prime Minister Chamberlain announced that Britain was at war with Germany. Thus, the unfortunate *Olinda* became the first maritime casualty of WWII. Her crew had taken to their boats and were safely recovered by the British tanker *San Geraldo* – all bar one, that is. The *Olinda*'s quartermaster was a British merchant seaman, Joseph Barnard, who had been arrested and locked in a cabin when the ship's master heard the news of war. However, he managed to escape once the crew had abandoned the ship and, after a few hours in the sea, was eventually picked up by *Ajax*. A very lucky man. Next day, *Ajax* sank a second German freighter, the 6,594-tons SS *Carl Fritzen*, some 200 miles south-east of the Rio Grande do Sul.

A few days later, on 11th September, *Graf Spee*'s Arado piloted by Uffz Heinrich Bongardts with Oblt z.See Detlef Spiering as observer, sighted the cruiser *Cumberland* en route from Freetown to Rio, and they were able to warn their mother ship, which was engaged in refuelling from the supply ship *Altmark*, of its presence. The first victim of the German raider was the 5,051-ton Booth liner *Clement*, sunk on 30th September. Initially, it was assumed by Captain F C P Harris, the master of the *Clement*, that the warship sighted on the horizon was British or Brazilian, but when *Graf Spee*'s Arado suddenly appeared and Uffz Bongardts opened fire, slightly wounding Chief Officer Jones, he realised that his ship was under attack. Abandon ship was ordered and soon a launch from *Graf Spee* approached and took on board the master and chief engineer. The remainder of the crew, in two lifeboats, were allowed to make for the Brazilian coast some 75 miles distant. The *Clement* was eventually sunk by gunfire. Capt Harris, when finally released, said that he believed that he had been captured by the *Admiral Scheer*, *Graf Spee*'s sister ship unaware of the real identity of the warship. Two more British freighters were intercepted and sunk in the first few days of October, the 4,651-ton *Newton Beech* (with a cargo of maize) on the 5th, followed by *Ashlea* (4,222-tons, laden with 7,000-tons of sugar) on the 7th.

Ark Royal and battlecruiser *Renown* as Force K were ordered to provide additional support and en route to Freetown encountered a merchant ship on 9th October, which identified herself as the American *Delmar*. Lacking destroyers to close in, the merchant ship could not be boarded and she was allowed to go on her way. Later intelligence revealed that the genuine *Delmar* was in New Orleans and this was in fact the supply ship *Altmar*k. Meanwhile, the *Graf Spee* captured the 8,196-ton British cargo vessel *Huntsman* on the 10th, sinking her later. Another freighter, the *Trevenion* (5,299-tons) was despatched a few days later.

Force K reached Freetown on the 12th, where she replenished her stocks, and set sail again to join the search for the German pocket battleship two days later. Swordfish patrols enjoyed a little excitement on 18th October, one meeting a Norwegian freighter whose crew immediately took to their lifeboats. A weighted message bag was dropped with an explanation and apology, whereupon the crew re-boarded their vessel and continued on their way. Another Swordfish encountered a Belgian freighter and another weighted message bag was dropped to the crew, but this went straight down the funnel, causing the observer who dropped the bag to comment on his return to the *Ark* on his very good shot.

During the night of the 19-20th October, the 4,372-ton German steamer *Emmy Friedrich* departed Tampico, Mexico, to act as a second supply ship for *Graf Spee*. Allied warships began a search for her in the Gulf of Mexico, joined by the US aircraft carrier *Ranger*, as part of the Neutrality Patrol in the Caribbean. The light cruiser HMS *Orion*, which departed Kingston on the 21st and Canadian destroyer HMCS *Saguenay* sighted the steamer next day in the Yucatan Channel and she turned away, back into the Gulf of Mexico. The contact report from *Orion* enabled the old light cruiser HMS *Caradoc*, to intercept her early on the 23rd. *Emmy Friedrich* was scuttled and the cruiser picked up her crew of 33 and took them to Bermuda. Meanwhile, the *Altmark* frequently disguised her identity by repainting her funnel and topsides and pretended to be the Norwegian vessel the *Sogne*; thus avoiding immediate suspicion if intercepted or sighted.

Meanwhile, late on the afternoon of 20th October, the SS *Lindsay* radioed the *Ark* that she had been attacked by two U-boats but had beaten them off with her own guns. It was considered that with darkness rapidly approaching, it would be too dangerous to carry out an immediate search-and-strike as it would necessitate a night landing, so action was postponed until morning. At first light Swordfish and Skuas took-off but by then the U-boats had vanished and not even *Lindsay* was sighted. The crews returned to the carrier disappointed and frustrated. *Ark* now returned to Freetown to refuel, arriving on the 24th.

Ark Royal and *Renown* – now joined by a light cruiser and five destroyers – departed Freetown on 28th October, to rejoin the hunt. While searching further south on 31st October, *Sussex*'s Walrus L2261 failed to return, with Lt(A) Stanley Bird, Lt Cecil Osmaston RN and L/Air Bill Brown lost without trace. A subsequent three-and-a-half day search failed to find any sign of the missing aircraft. One of *Ark*'s Swordfish pilots later commented:

> 'An aircraft flying over the South Atlantic is the most solitary object in the world. It ranges the sky as lonely as a cloud, beyond the view of its fellows or parent ship. Hour after hour would go by without the sight of so much as a soapbox, yet each member of the crew had to keep constantly alert.'

Lt Bob Everett apparently used to shout down the Gosport tube to his Australian observer Lt Harrie 'Digger' Gerrett, 'Don't forget to talk to me now and again. It's the only way I'll be able to stay awake!'[27]

On 29th October, having refuelled from *Altmark* and having transferred her prisoners to the supply vessel, the *Graf Spee* forayed into the Indian Ocean to search for merchantmen plying the trade routes between Durban and Lourenco Marques (Portuguese Mozambique) but found no ships during her four-day patrol from 8-12th November. Moving further west to the entrance of the Mozambique Channel, she encountered the small, 706-ton oil tanker *Africa Shell*, which was duly sunk (on 15th November) after the crew had taken to their boats; with the exception of the ship's master Captain Patrick Dove[28] who was taken aboard the warship. Next day the Dutch freighter *Mapia* was stopped but then released to continue her journey. Making no attempt to cover her tracks and hoping to lead the searching warships into believing she was now active in the Indian Ocean, Kapt Langsdorff doubled back into the Southern Atlantic. Meanwhile, the *Ark Royal* had been ordered to investigate and rounded the Cape, while *Eagle* and her escorts had put to sea from Ceylon. One night a darkened ship suddenly loomed up and sent everyone aboard the *Ark* to actions stations. The vessel refused to answer signals, whereupon *Renown* trained her guns on the target, while *Ark* ranged six Swordfish armed with torpedoes ready for a strike. Searchlights were switched on – to reveal the New Zealand liner *Opawa*, whose captain thought he was about to be attacked by the German raider. The *Ark* suffered losses on 25th November, when two of her Swordfish from 810 Squadron collided in cloud while climbing away from the carrier. Both aircraft fell into the sea and two crewmembers (LAC Alan Lawson, RAF observer, and L/Air Edgar 'Ted' Shayler) were killed aboard Lt Arthur Pardoe's L2774/A2M while the pilot himself was rescued from the sea together with Lt Alex Stewart, LAC Leslie Lloyd (RAF) and Able Seaman W Freik from P4009/A2G.

The *Graf Spee* and her supply ship *Altmark* rendezvoused shortly after dawn on 26th November, the former taking on fuel and provisions. Captain Dove, who was treated exceedingly well by his captors, was allowed to exercise on deck and was permitted to witness the re-supply procedure. He also noticed much work being carried out on deck:

> 'Working parties started on their work of painting and entirely altering the appearance of the *Graf Spee*. Any British warship which had been given a description of her previous looks and expected to find her with a rusty sea-stained hull would no longer recognise her. Even her superstructure was radically altered. I walked round with Captain Langsdorff while the work was being carried on. He pointed out to me with obvious pride the dummy funnel which he was rigging up forward of his after gun turret ... As I continued my walk with him along the after-deck, I noticed two long strips of sheet metal about fifteen feet long and about a foot deep. On them I saw with a bit of a shock, the name *Deutschland* in large gold letters in German script. On the reverse side of the same strips was the name *Admiral Scheer*. "What's all this?" I asked Langsdorff. He smiled broadly. "Oh, that is for the benefit of neutrals. They are all looking for the *Scheer* or *Deutschland* and I am the phantom ship. These two ships are getting all the credit, but I am getting all the fun."[29]

The following day, some 50 British merchant navy officers from the various sunken ships were transferred to *Graf Spee* from the *Altmark*,[30] an indication that the warship was going to return home in time for Christmas. However events would soon overtake her, her crew and her prisoners. Captain Dove's narrative continued:

> 'We now noticed that every morning at daybreak the *Graf Spee*'s plane had her engine revved up and punctually at six o'clock she was catapulted into the air. Our cabin was immediately below the plane, and through a skylight we could see the catapulting gear swung round so that the machine was headed into wind. She went off with a loud roar and a hiss of compressed air. We sometimes wished it would take a nose-dive into the sea. On the morning of 2nd December, the plane flew away and, as usual, we wondered what sort of luck she was going to have. While she was still away the alarm buzzers started to sound all over the ship and our hearts sank. It was obvious that the ship had received a radio message from the plane and was hastening after some new prey.'[31]

Her latest victim was to be the British Blue Star liner *Doric Star* (10,086-tons, carrying a cargo of butter, cheese and frozen meat) that was sunk some 1,200 miles northwards off Walvis (Whale) Bay, South-West Africa. Meanwhile, Uffz Bongardts and Oblt z.See Spiering had sighted another merchant vessel, the large Shaw Savill freighter *Tairoa* (7,783-tons). They reported its position but had by then exhausted their fuel, Bongardts skilfully alighting the Arado on the sea to await rescue. *Graf Spee* arrived on the scene just as dusk was settling in, the floatplane being safely recovered together with its crew. *Tairoa* was intercepted and sunk the next day.

Force K had meantime arrived at Cape Town to take on fuel and supplies. Next day a message was received that a SAAF bomber had sighted a suspicious ship, which turned out to be the German 9,000-ton liner *Watussi*, but before *Ark*'s aircraft could become involved, her crew scuttled her and took to their boats. She was helped on her way by the 15in guns of *Renown*. Two days later *Graf Spee* caught and sank her last victim, the 3,895-ton British freighter *Streonshalh*, loaded with grain. As soon as Force K had refuelled, the ships departed Cape Town to hunt her down, and soon enjoyed a success when, on 5th December, some 300 miles west-south-west of Freetown, a Swordfish from the *Ark* sighted the German steamer *Uhenfels* (7,603-tons) that had departed Lourenco Marques, on her third attempt to escape back to Germany and had evaded the sloop HMS *Egret* patrolling off the port. When sighted she claimed to be Dutch but suspicion was aroused. The destroyer *Hereward* was detached from the screen to investigate and *Uhenfels* attempted to scuttle herself. However, the steamer was captured and on board was found a cargo of cotton and hides – and a quantity of opium valued at £250,000! Force K and their prize arrived at Freetown on the 6th, where she was renamed *Empire Ability*.

The *Ark* lost another aircraft on 8th December, when returning Skua L2880 of 800 Squadron missed all the arrester hooks and went over the port bow, killing the pilot Sub-Lt(A) Peter Bethell. However, the observer PO(A) G L Taylor was plucked from the sea. A success was gained on the morning of 9th December, when HMS *Shropshire*'s Walrus sighted the German merchantman *Adolf Leonhardt* (3,000 tons) off the Angolan coast. The Walrus, flown by Lt Anthony Kennard with Lt-Cdr Selwyn Harrison as observer, instead of attacking, signalled the ship to take an indicated course, but when the cruiser arrived on the scene three hours later, it was found the crew had scuttled their ship.

Three days later (11th December), Walrus L2273 of the *Albatross* detachment, flying a dusk patrol in the hands of PO(A) J G O Hofman, sighted a suspicious yacht and alighted beside it. His observer Lt Alan Gregory managed to board the craft only to find nothing untoward. *Graf Spee*'s Arado, on returning from yet another reconnaissance patrol suffered engine problems on alighting on the sea and, although, hoisted aboard, was now effectively out of action. However, its engine was removed to establish whether it could be for repaired; this was the spare, the original engine having been replaced earlier.

At dawn on 13th December, the *Graf Spee* was finally located by *Exeter*, *Ajax* and *Achilles* off the coast of Uruguay and pursued to the mouth of Rio de la Plata (River Plate), where battle commenced. Captain Dove, locked in the ship's prison with 60 other merchant officers, later wrote:

'The *Graf Spee*'s seaplane which had been revving up ready for the regular six o'-clock catapulting and reconnaissance, suddenly had her engine stopped. Then [via a spy hole] we saw the working parties of German sailors unloading shell after shell as they came up the electric hoists. I knew then there was going to be a battle. This was no preparation for taking on a harmless merchant ship.

'With a roar that nearly lifted us off our feet the *Graf Spee* fired off her first salvo [at 06:18]. I have never heard anything like it, nor had any of the other men with me. This was our first experience of fighting in a battleship. The armoured walls of our prison shuddered, clouds of dust floated down, the crockery rattled and several of the lights went out.

'The noise was so terrific that we could not at first distinguish the bursting of British shells from the *Graf Spee*'s own guns. 'We've been hit!' I called out to our crowd. But they wouldn't believe me. But the next shudder left no doubt. The whole ship seemed to stagger with the impact. We smelled petrol fumes and I guessed what had happened. A shell had struck the seaplane and shattered her tanks. That wasn't too pleasant. The seaplane with its load of petrol was almost directly above our heads ... To create a bit of a diversion and cheer ourselves, we started handing out bouquets to the British gunners. Every time the *Graf Spee* shuddered we would sing out, "Well hit, sir! or "That was a good one!" '[32]

During the exchange of gunfire, although outnumbered, *Graf Spee* inflicted heavy damage upon the *Exeter* (61 dead and 23 wounded), forcing her to break off the engagement, but not before an 8-inch shell from the British heavy cruiser had penetrated two decks then exploded in her funnel area – causing crippling damage to her boiler room. Both of *Exeter*'s Walruses (K8341 and K8343) had been damaged by shell splinters and were jettisoned, leaving just *Ajax*'s two Seafoxes for spotting duties, but one of these was soon rendered unserviceable due to gun-blast. The other (K8582) crewed by Lt Duncan Lewin and Lt Dick Kearney were strapped in, with engine running and ready to be catapulted. The crew had been awaiting orders:

'In *Ajax* the shape of the little Seafox aircraft was now clear against the sky, standing upon its catapult aft. The stars had gone. The observer, Dick Kearney, a big solid young man, was already in his seat. The catapult officer was chatting with him. The pilot, Duncan Lewin, grumbled under his breath as he swung easily into his seat. He fiddled a little, sighed and then said, "Morning, Dickie, 'morning, Monk." The night before had been a thick one in the wardroom. Kearney and Monk grinned at each other, and said sympathetically, "Morning, Drunkie." Lewin's name was Duncan, Duncan had become Drunken, and Drunken had become Drunkie, very early in his Navy career. It was to stay with him all his life, but there were some mornings when the nickname was harder to bear than others. The mechanic started his litany, and he gave the responses half-automatically. The mechanic swung the propeller, and at the third try the engine leapt into roaring life.'[33]

At 06:37 the order came to catapult the Seafox:

'... the after turret was firing forward so close to the catapult platform, that they were half-blinded by the red flash of the guns and could feel the heat of the cordite explosions. It seemed extremely likely that, as soon as they became airborne, they would be blown out of the sky by their own guns. But Drunkie Lewin couldn't have cared less. He waved his arm airily to the catapult officer and yelled, above the roar of the engine, "We'll have to stooge off between salvos! Stand by!" Monk shouted back, "You've only got a twelve seconds gap!" Kearney leant forward and tapped Lewin's shoulder. "With a six-inch shell up our tail, we'll really get some speed out of this old string-bag!"

'It was a spectacular take-off. They were enveloped in swirling smoke, the wind was whistling and shrieking through the stays and halyards. The aircraft roared, the guns crashed out, Lewin gave the signal. There was a flash and a bang from the catapult machinery and they were airborne! Lewin banked steeply. He had no time to gain altitude, and a few seconds later the after turret fired again. He nearly went into a sideslip, straightened out and started to climb. He headed towards the *Graf Spee*, and soon the whole battle area lay beneath him.

'The four ships were at maximum range, although the *Exeter* was closing with the enemy rapidly. She was already several miles away from the two six-inch cruisers, who were gathering speed to the northward. At this stage of the action, *Ajax* and *Achilles* had not concentrated their gunfire. On the alarm being given, each ship had gone into action independently with all guns at highest elevation, and they were firing rapidly and accurately at the enemy, who was replying with equal accuracy. His ack-ack guns opened up on Lewin, who was by now close enough overhead to see, with some discomfort, that the pocket battleship had two fighter aircraft [sic] and that one of them was already about to be catapulted – without even a six-shooter to defend himself, Lewin felt as naked as Icarus. He watched the fighter aircraft drawn back on the catapult, ready to be launched into the air against him, and decided, like the man who met the grizzly bear on the mountain path, that even a folded newspaper would come in handy.

'At that very moment, one of the six-inch cruisers scored her first hit, right on the catapult platform. The aircraft was wrecked. Lewin reported the successful hit to the Flagship and drew a deep breath. By now the ack-ack guns had found his range and he climbed higher. He looked around for cover. There was a thin ceiling of cloud at about 3,000 feet. According to his own account, he cruised along six feet under it, ready to pop through and put it between him and the enemy at the slightest encouragement, although it would have provided about as much protection as a transparent nightdress to a persecuted heroine.'[34]

The Seafox had sustained damage from AA fire. Returning to *Ajax*, Lewin made a skilful landing and the floatplane was quickly re-embarked.[35] Late in the exchange, one of *Graf Spee*'s shells caused four fatalities on the *Achilles*. In return, the *Graf Spee* was hit repeatedly by the 6-inch shells of the light cruisers, which could not penetrate her armour but nonetheless inflicted significant topside damage to the ship and also to the Arado, as Lewin had noted. It was during this strike that Uffz Bongardts, the Arado pilot, was killed.

With insufficient fuel to escape, Kapitän Langsdorff decided to enter the neutral port of Montevideo for repairs and to bury the ship's dead (36) and to receive medical aid for the 60 wounded on board. One of Langdorff's first actions was to release the crews of the merchant vessels he had sunk during her most recent voyage, and several of his former captives attended the burials including Captain Dove. Meantime, at the entrance to the Rio de la Plata, *Ajax* and *Achilles* were joined by the heavy cruiser *Cumberland* (with Walrus L2236 and pilot Lt(A) Glen Sedorski aboard) from the Falklands, to thwart any attempt of escape.

Under the terms of the 1907 Hague Covention, no foreign warship engaged in conflict was entitled to remain in a neutral port for more than 24 hours without risking internment. In addition, under the same convention, the *Graf Spee* had to give British merchant ships 24 hours start if they left port. The British Consul therefore cunningly organised for the merchant ships in port to sail at 24-hour intervals, effectively locking the *Spee* in the port whilst, at the same, time spreading propaganda about the vast fleet of British warships converging on the area. Eventually the Uruguayan Government announced that if the *Graf Spee* did not sail within 72 hours of its arrival it would be interned. Realising that he would probably lose his ship in any forthcoming battle and to avoid risking the lives of his crew unnecessarily, Langsdorff, after much deliberation, ordered the *Graf Spee* to be scuttled, but not before sending and receiving messages to and from Berlin:

> 'Strategic position off Montevideo. Besides the cruisers and destroyers, *Ark Royal* and *Renown*. Close blockade at night; escape into open sea and break-through to home waters is hopeless ... request decision on whether the ship should be scuttled in spite of insufficient depth in the estuary of the Plate, or whether internment is preferred. Langsdorff.
>
> 'No internment in Uruguay. Attempt effective destruction if ship is scuttled. Berlin.' [36]

On 17th December, the *Graf Spee* put to sea with a skeleton crew on board and when three miles out of Montevideo harbour, she stopped. In the evening, after the crew had abandoned the ship, a large explosion was seen on board. Among those to witness the epic event was Admiral Sir Henry McCall, Naval Attaché in Buenos Aires:

> 'Something extraordinary was about to take place. The great crowd immediately below us, denied their sight of a battle, was quite hushed. What was going to happen? Time passed in considerable speculation and suspense, but the truth, unlikely though it appeared, was beginning to dawn on some of us. Exactly as the sun set behind her, a great volume of smoke billowed up – and an enormous flash was followed in due course by the boom of a large explosion. So the *Graf Spee* met her end.'

Other witnesses included Lts Lewin and Kearney, who were up in their repaired Seafox at 3,000 feet and about two miles distant when the explosion occurred. At 20:54, Kearney signalled *Ajax* with the news. Admiral McCall continued:

> 'Darkness comes quickly in those latitudes, and as we watched the sky darkened into a black background against which huge flames licked up against the underside of dense rolling clouds from the burning fuel oil. The rumour spread that Captain Langsdorff had remained aboard and that some of his crew were trapped – and to the great crowd below us, which waited on and on through the night, this added a sense of tension and almost a sense of loss. He had made such an impression, even in those three short days. Next morning *Graf Spee* was still burning fiercely, and indeed it was not until four days later that all traces of fire had vanished. Gradually

we pieced together what had happened. Having turned his ship off the main channel, Captain Langsdorff had put her in shallow water and opened the sea cocks. Torpedo heads had then been suspended by ropes over open ammunition hatches which led straight down to the main magazines and petrol had been sluiced over the surrounding decks and set alight as the last of the party left the ship. In the fore part of the ship the flames burned through the hemp rope, the torpedo head fell, exploded in the fore magazine, and blew it up. Ironically enough, the enormous wave of sea water sent up flooded over the aft part of the ship and put out the flame; some weeks later Lieutenant-Commander Kilroy, a torpedo and electrical specialist, went aboard and found the aft torpedo head still hanging from a badly charred rope.' The British Admiralty had bought the wreck of the *Graf Spee* from Uruguay for, I believe, £14,000.'

Following the death of his ship, the honourable officer committed suicide three days later by shooting himself after writing to the German Ambassador to explain his actions:

'Your Excellency,

After a long struggle I have reached the grave decision to scuttle the Admiral *Graf Spee* in order to prevent her falling into enemy hands ... with the ammunition remaining any attempt to fight my way back to open and deep water was bound to fail. And yet only in deep water could I have scuttled the ship ... I have decided not to fight but to destroy the equipment and then scuttle the ship. It was clear to me that this decision might be consciously or unwittingly misconstrued by persons ignorant of my motives ... therefore I decided from the beginning to bear the consequences involved in this decision. For a Captain with a sense of honour, it goes without saying that his personal fate cannot be separated from that of his ship.

'I postponed my intentions as long as I still bore responsibility for decisions concerning the welfare of the crew under my command. After today's decision ... I can do no more for my ship's company. Neither will I be able to take an active part in the present struggle of my country. I can now only prove by my death that the fighting Services of the Third Reich are ready to die for the honour of the fray.

'I alone bear the responsibility for scuttling the battleship Admiral *Graf Spee*. I am happy to pay with my life for any possible reflection on the honour of the flag. I shall face my fate with firm faith in the Cause and the future of the nation and of my Führer. I am writing this letter to your Excellency in the quiet of the evening, after calm deliberation in order that you may be able to inform my superior officers, and to counter public rumours if this should become necessary.

Langsdorff.'[37]

The German freighter *Tacoma*, lying in the harbour, had sailed out in *Graf Spee*'s wake. The freighter had discreetly transferred the remaining crew during the day. Two tugs and a barge, called in from Argentina, took off the crew in neutral waters and made way for Buenos Aires. The crew were eventually interned in Argentina, where the majority remained until the end of the war. One who was released was the Arado's observer, Oblt z.See Spiering, who was allowed to return to Germany in June 1940.

By this time *Ark Royal* was at Rio de Janeiro, just over a day's sailing, and on hearing the news of *Graf Spee*'s demise she headed back for Freetown from where she continued to search the South Atlantic for any other raiders during the next six weeks before being recalled. The arrival at Rio of Force K was the subject of great interest, as recalled by L/Sea Tom Bailey aboard the *Renown*:

> 'In *Renown* we spent a whole day scraping the barnacles off the waterline, while being buzzed by a tiny aeroplane, a Pou-du-Ciel (the popular midget "Flying Flea"). The skipper did not think it worthwhile manning the guns!'[38]

One of the highlights of this period was the discovery by *Dorsetshire*'s Walrus of the German steamer *Waikama* out from Rio de Janeiro, The ship, intercepted by the cruiser, scuttled herself. On the other side of the South Atlantic, PO(A) Hofman's Walrus L2248 was signalled by *Albatross* to search for a neutral passenger ship known to be carrying German technicians. The vessel was located but ignored signals to head for Freetown. It was not until threatened with bombing – the Walrus being armed with 100lb bombs – that the ship obeyed and docked in Freetown next morning, when the Germans were removed. On 23rd December, a Skua of 800 Squadron from *Ark Royal* carried an all-Royal Marine crew in the guise of Capt Francis Bird (pilot) and observer Capt Keith Ford, of 810 Squadron (one of only two RM officers to qualify as an Observer). Their reconnaissance patrol proved uneventful. The damaged *Exeter* and her escorts meanwhile departed for England, the cruiser having taken *Cumberland*'s Walrus L2236 in place of her lost machines.

> 'Aboard *Ark Royal* on Christmas morning, in the blazing heat, the crew held a fancy dress parade on the flight deck, and Captain Power made the traditional rounds of the mess decks, which were gaily decked out with bright bunting and palm leaves. The ship had crossed the Equator several times during the hunt for the Spee, but there had been no chance of celebrating in the customary way. *Ark*, however, was not the sort of ship to miss a chance of fun like that, and in Freetown Father Neptune's will was at last served. There had been a song in one of the *Ark Royal* productions in which Lt Bob Everett, made up to look like Captain Power, had sung 'I'm a captain who has never crossed the Line!' Everett had been very doubtful about the wisdom of pulling the captain's leg in this way, but Commander Eccles had assured him, having heard the song through and laughed heartily himself, that the captain would love it. So he did, and it was strange, but true, that he had never been initiated. He appeared for the occasion dressed in a shirt and a pair of shorts, and was lathered, 'shaved' and most soundly ducked. Few of those present ever forgot the sight of the captain being christened by the full impact of the jet from a power hose.'[39]

On 4th January, *Ark Royal* arrived at Dakar and *Renown* at Freetown for refuelling. Departing on the 7th, *Ark* joined *Renown* off Sierra Leone on the 8th after she had left earlier that day with destroyers *Hero* and *Hasty*. They searched unsuccessfully for the German supply ship *Altmark* in the South Atlantic until arriving at Freetown on the 19th, before heading northwards for Gibraltar. The small force departed Gibraltar for home on 11th February and was ordered to help search for German ships that had escaped the blockade mounted at the Spanish port of Vigo, where they had been since the outbreak of war. Aircraft from the *Ark* sighted several of the German steamers and assisted in the capture of *Rostock* (2,542 tons) and *Morea*. The former was intercepted by the French sloop *Elan* and a prize crew put aboard and taken to Brest. She was re-named *Saint Maurice* but reverted to German service after fall of France. *Morea* was captured next day off the coast of Portugal by *Hasty*. She was placed with incoming Convoy *HG17* and arrived at Falmouth on the 17th (and was renamed *Empire Seaman*).

Meanwhile, the cruiser HMS *Cornwall* was also busy in the South Atlantic and was tasked to locate another raider, the 7,600-ton *Pinguin*, which the Germans referred to as a *hilfskreuzer* (auxiliary cruiser). The heavily armed ship, which carried two seaplanes (He114Bs of 5/196, one of which was a spare), had recently changed her guise from a black-painted 'Russian' ship fictitiously named *Perchura*, to a light-blue and white painted 'Greek' vessel, the *Kassos*. While scouring the southern seas for the raider, *Cornwall* had earlier intercepted a German supply ship, forcing her to scuttle, before capturing a collier and two tankers, these being despatched to Freetown, Rio de Janeiro and Bermuda respectively. By early May, *Cornwall* was patrolling just outside the three-mile national limit off Brazil, as recorded by one of her crew Ken Dimbleby:

> 'It was a particularly tedious time patrolling up and down the coast in the hope that enemy ships sheltering in neutral ports might come out and be seized. Every day when the weather was suitable, the Walrus aircraft were catapulted off the ship to carry out reconnaissance flights. The two pilots took turns and one morning Pilot No.1 [Lt(A) John Scott] decided to relieve the monotony of his morning flight by nipping inside the three-mile limit and flying over Pernambuco. When he returned to the ship he told Pilot No.2 [Sub-Lt(A) Frank Scott] that he had clearly seen lovely senoritas, and that they had waved to him.
>
> 'That was too much for Pilot No.2, who was by way of being a bit of a lady's man. When he took off for his flight, he also went inside the three-mile limit and flew over Pernambuco. But his luck was out. Before he had time to study the female population, he saw a Brazilian fighter plane diving at him.
>
> 'He turned and made for *Cornwall* as quickly as he could in the old Walrus with the fighter on his tail. He flew round and round the ship, cutting corners in the slow plane and the Brazilian could not stick to him as his fighter was too fast to turn quickly. Our pilot did not look at all happy, but eventually the Brazilian made off and he was able to land alongside the ship and be hoisted inboard. We had all collected on deck to watch the fun and thoroughly enjoyed the incident. I have an idea the Brazilian pilot did, too.'[40]

It is assumed that the Brazilian fighter from the 6th Air Regiment, had been scrambled from Recife airfield to chase the intruder out to sea. *Cornwall* would finally meet up with *Pinguin* a year later – and promptly send her to the bottom of the ocean.

3. NORTHERN WATERS 1940

'In theory [we were the] the fighter defence of Scapa Flow. That was the biggest laugh ever. The Skua was called a fighter-bomber, but in fact was neither.'

Naval Airman Alan Todd, 803 Squadron

When *Ark Royal* docked for her refit, the Skuas of 800 disembarked and joined 803 Squadron ashore at Hatston in the Orkneys, to help protect the nearby Home Fleet anchorage at Scapa Flow, in company with the Sea Gladiators of 804 Squadron, which had formed there some weeks earlier for that purpose. A sub-flight of three Skuas from 803 Squadron commanded by Lt Charles Evans was based at Wick; with him were rating pilots PO(A)s Dick Leggott and Arthur Johnson, known as 'Johnno'. After a five-week refit *Ark Royal* would sail on 20th March for the Eastern Mediterranean carrying only her Swordfish squadrons, which were flown ashore on reaching Alexandria to practice night flying over the desert.

Four months or so into the war and the FAA possessed just six fighter squadrons – all stationed at Hatston in the Orkneys, four of them – 800 (Lt-Cdr Geoffrey Torry), 801 (Lt-Cdr Peter Bramwell), 803 (Lt Bill Lucy) and 806 (Lt-Cdr Charles Evans) – equipped with Skuas and a few Rocs, the latter suited only to local patrols due to their lack of endurance. The other two squadrons – 802 (Lt John Marmont) and 804 (Lt-Cdr John Cockburn) – were still flying Sea Gladiators, which were suitable only for local defence.

There were currently 13 operational Swordfish squadrons, but only four of these were serving with the Home Fleet, either allocated to *Furious* or shored-based.

815 Squadron (Lt-Cdr R A Kilroy) was attached to RAF Coastal Command.

816 Squadron (Lt-Cdr H H Gardner) *Furious* but was currently shore-based at Campbeltown.

818 Squadron (Lt-Cdr P G O Sydney-Turner) *Furious* but was also currently at Campbeltown

819 Squadron (Lt-Cdr J W Hale) was shore-based at Ford.

Each squadron operated nine to twelve aircraft, while newly formed 826 Squadron had just received the first of the new Fairey Albacores, the Swordfish's planned replacement. The only aircraft carrier readily available to the Home Fleet, *Furious*, was undergoing a refit in the Clyde during this time.

Three serious incidents occurred during January, the first on the 11th, when Skua

L2946 of 803 Squadron, landing after a fighter patrol east of Orkneys, spun in at 500 feet due to engine failure and crashed at Tor Ness Point, Stronsay. Mid(A) John Barr and L/Air George 'Ginger' Uren both died of their injuries. A week later, the cruiser *Norfolk*'s Walrus P5648 crashed on landing at Cadder near Bishopbriggs, Glasgow. Lt(A) Edward Pope and L/Air John Baxter were killed. On 25th January, Sub-Lt(A) Gerald Williamson was killed when the 819 Squadron Swordfish he was ferrying from Silloth to Ford crashed south of Huddersfield. Newly trained 800 Squadron TAG N/Air Alan Todd laconically recalled:

> 'In theory [we were the] the fighter defence of Scapa Flow. That was the biggest laugh ever. The Skua was called a fighter-bomber, but in fact was neither. It did not have the proper engine, its Bristol Perseus sleeve-valve job being grossly underpowered. The RAF had all that was going in those days, the Navy got what was left. If it had had the proper uprated Perseus it would have been a faster and better fighter, with a better bomb load.' [41]

804 Squadron, also at Hatston, operated under the control of 13 Group, RAF Fighter Command. Newly qualified fighter pilot Lt Donald Gibson was surprised at the conditions on his arrival at Hatston:

> 'Eventually I arrived at Hatston. The short narrow runways and the hangars were finished but not the accommodation. I was shown to a Nissen hut, No.9 Hut of Fleet Air Arm fame, where lived thirty-two junior officers. If you wanted a bath, you put your name down in a book; there was only one lavatory, which was in a filthy state. When I arrived I said that I wanted a wash, which caused a sensation and a marine had to get me a portable wash basin, which we put in front of the stove.' [42]

A new carrier, HMS *Illustrious*, was completing in Vickers Yard in Barrow-in-Furness as the first of a class of carriers to be fitted with an armoured flight deck. At RNAS Worthy Down, 806 Squadron was formed on 15th February with eight Skuas and six Rocs[43] to provide the fighter component of the *Illustrious*' aircraft complement and was composed entirely of regulars, as recalled by Lt Desmond Vincent-Jones, Senior Observer:

> 'The Commanding Officer was [newly promoted] Lt-Cdr Charles Evans [ex-803 Squadron], also known as 'Crash' Evans or the 'Flying Christ' – and possibly one of the greatest FAA characters of all time, with his flaming red hair and pointed beard, and piercing blue eyes. The remaining pilots were reportedly handpicked from the best that the FAA could produce at the time – the section leaders being Lt Roger Nicholls, Senior Pilot, and Lts Colin Campbell-Horsfall and Bill Barnes. The remainder were junior lieutenants or sub-lieutenants, one Royal Marine and a few Rating Pilots [including newly qualified PO(A) Arthur Jopling]. The whole Squadron were regular RN entries. As Senior Observer, I flew in the CO's backseat. The three rating observers, the senior being PO(A) George Muskett, flew with the section leaders, and the remaining seats were occupied by TAGs. The ground personnel were a mixture of RN and RAF ratings with RAF flight sergeants predominating in the senior ranks. At the time the training of naval ratings as maintenance personnel was in its infancy.
>
> 806 moved to West Freugh near Stranraer at the end of March, one of the RAF's

Armament Training Camps. After two weeks of firing at drogue and ground targets, dive-bombing on the ranges off shore and other usual flying practices, the aircrew began to become reasonably proficient in the handling of their aircraft and the use of their weapons; only to be expected when taking into consideration the experience of the pilots concerned. At least the CO began to look fairly pleased and talk about the makings of a good squadron.

I remember well the wet afternoon, when no flying could take place, the CO sent for me to the draughty Nissen hut that served as the squadron office. He was standing beside the coke brazier, which provided the only means of heating, and gazing with horror at a message he was holding up to the light, as if he couldn't believe his eyes. He handed the offending message to me, saying 'I've got news for you, my boy!' The gist of the Admiralty signal was that all the Squadron aircrew except the four section leaders and their observers were to leave the following day and would be distributed amongst other squadrons then being formed, where they would be appointed for training duties. Their replacements would arrive two days later and consisted of three RNVR sub-lieutenants and five RNVR midshipmen, all of whom were coming directly from Flying Schools, together with eight Reservist Air Gunners, who had completed only a few months ab-initio training. At least I was happy to know that we would be retaining my excellent Petty Officer Observers to help get the other back-seat boys into shape.

I went with Charles Evans to Stranraer station to meet the new recruits, and seldom can a more motley or dejected collection of individuals been decanted onto a wet and windy platform. Their uniforms were obviously new, their caps were worn at odd angles and they barely knew how to salute! The look on the CO's face was unforgettable and horrific, but first impressions can often be deceptive. Little did we imagine what destruction this strange group would achieve in the months ahead. At least two of them hadn't started shaving!'

Mid(A) Graham Angus 'Gus' Hogg, who had not long finished fighter school, was one of the new arrivals. Prior to this posting, waiting for an operational unit, he had been told:

'You'll like Gladiators, but a cow could fly those. But, Hell, Skuas, it's no use trying to fly them, you'll just have to pray. They stall at 100 miles per hour and spin if you turn with the flaps down. They killed one third of our course.' I thought, at the time, that they must be clever pilots still to be alive but, later, at fighter school, I came to think that they and their dead friends must have been ham-fisted elephants. Nevertheless, there was a Skua in a hangar at Lee and the first time I saw it, I nearly deserted. The Hart had looked big after the Tiger Moth; this looked an impossible size. With its high undercarriage and cockpit windscreen it resembled some kind of bird, a crane perhaps. I sat in the cockpit and gaped at thousands of levers and dials, wondering how one possibly remembers the position and use of them all.'

On joining 806 Squadron, Hogg confided his first impressions to his diary:

'The CO expressed himself satisfied that we would not disgrace the Squadron completely. As for ourselves, we felt that we had landed in as fine a crowd of fellows as could be found anywhere. There were twelve of us: the CO; Nick [Lt Nicholls], senior flight commander; Bill [Lt Barnes], second flight commander; V-J [Lt Vincent-Jones] senior observer; Ivan [Lt Lowe] the adjutant, who had not long left Fighter School and the seven of us, Stanley [Orr], Eric [Buttle], Lew [Ayres], Daisy [Day], Jack [Marshall], Dick [Martin] and myself. All were doing their best to become smart and efficient, so that when the Squadron went into action, and it was coming soon, we should be ready for anything.'

Shortly thereafter, Hogg wrote in his journal:

'We commenced our aerodrome dummy deck landing, taking it in turns to fly the Gladiators, Skuas and Rocs. The whole essence of deck landing is to come in slowly with plenty of engine and doing this in a Skua scared the daylights out of me – and a few others. Should one come in too slowly accidents are likely to happen, as Daisy found out – to his cost.

He came in very neatly and, oh, so very, very slowly. At twenty feet he closed his throttle and came down like a brick, landing, or perhaps I should say arriving, with an almighty crash. The undercarriage gave way, the airscrew chewed grass, the engine came off and rolled onto the starboard wing. The tail and undercarriage oleo legs were left sticking vertically out of the muddy ground, completely separated from the aircraft. Daisy stepped out – 'She just came away in me 'ands' said he. That evening he was taken into Southampton (Stranraer) and filled up with liquor in celebration of his first crash.

On completion of our practice dive-bombing, during which we managed to score a direct hit on the married quarters, killing several chickens, we were ready for our real deck-landings.'

Lt Vincent-Jones added:

'The Admiralty graciously allowed us a further two weeks of armament training and every moment that the aircraft could fly was spent airborne, training the new boys how to use their weapons. After a few days of perilous manoeuvres and practice bombs falling anywhere but on the ranges, a very noticeable improvement became apparent and by the end of the fortnight several of these young pilots were achieving results in every way comparable with their more senior predecessors. Trying to teach them how to behave on ground was harder!'

Hogg's diary confirmed the successful training period:

'During our fortnight at West Freugh we continually practised dive-bombing and air firing. The CO warned us not to expect too many hits on the air-firing drogue. 'It's a very small target and the best score yet is eight points.' Lew [Ayres] and Dick [Martin] took off and returned with a score of twenty-four points apiece – they had proved our worth as pilots.'

Walrus L2296 of 700 Squadron operating out of Hatston was lost on **18th February**. On returning from patrol, short of fuel, and with the crew unsure of their position land was sighted, and Lt(A) Paul Woods decided to carry out a precautionary sea landing, following which the Walrus was anchored as close to shore as possible. On reaching shore they found out that they had arrived on the rocky island of Foula. Bad weather prevented Woods and his crew (Mid(A) Paul Furber and L/Sea Arthur Bell) from being picked up for some days, until the MV *Water Lily* arrived from Scalloway. But before the Walrus could be recovered from the north coast of the island, it was broken up by bad weather.

Blue Section of 803 Squadron enjoyed a little excitement of **12th March**, when Lt Bill Lucy and Lt Alex Fraser-Harris (a Canadian from Nova Scotia), flying Roc 8G with N/Air Ginger Hayman, sighted a submarine:

> 'Attacked sub. Sighted by Lt Lucy. He dived first. Did not see sub but dropped my bomb on his. Failed to fuse it! No results observed.'

At Hatston, Lt Donald Gibson of 804 Squadron also found some excitement a few days later, on **16th March**:

> 'There took place the first German air raid at night while we were there and I remember a Mr Isbister[44] had the misfortune to be the first civilian to be killed by the enemy. When this raid happened we were first sent to 28,000 feet but then to 10,000 feet. On the way down I turned off my oxygen at 15,000 feet and passed out. I found myself, when I came to, doing stall turns in the dark over Hatston. This raid was notable for the fact that one of our pilots, in the middle of the battle, in the dark, landed and urinated on the runway, thereafter taking off again and rejoining the fray. This was probably caused by the barrel of beer from which we helped ourselves in No.9 Hut – we had not been expecting the enemy! I bet the RAF could not cap that story.'[45]

Lt Fraser-Harris of 803 Squadron added:

> 'Air raid at 1940. Fourteen aircraft over, bombs dropped on aerodrome. No damage. *Norfolk* slightly damaged, houses bombed at Stennea [*sic*]; one killed, seven wounded. Seven Naval personnel casualties. One raider brought down by AA [*sic*]. No fighters engaged. All Gladiators up, no Skuas airborne. Attack was very well timed at dusk, but bombing was lousy.'

In this raid, carried out by 21 He111s from I/KG26 and 18 Ju88s from I/KG30, the heavy cruiser *Norfolk* at anchor in Scapa Flow was damaged at 1959. The bomb passed through the upper, main, lower decks and exploded near Y shell room. This blew a hole in the starboard side below the water line. A fire was started and X and Y magazines were flooded. Four officers were killed, four officer and three ratings wounded. In the same attack, the old battleship *Iron Duke* (being used as a depot vessel) was near missed by three bombs. Two bombs exploded astern of battleship *Rodney* causing no damage. Returning German crews claimed hits on three battleships and one cruiser. Most of the Home Fleet was at Scapa Flow at this time and this prompted the Admiralty to order Admiral Forbes to take his fleet to sea during the next moonlight period between 19th and 26th March.

On the evening of **20th March**, Lt Teddy Taylour (L3028/6B) was leading Green Section (two Skuas) of 800 Squadron on convoy patrol just south of Orkney when he spotted a formation of He111s:

> 'While acting as leader of Green Section, escorting Convoy *ON21*, Kirkwall portion,

I sighted about ten He111s approaching the convoy from the north-east. I immediately put my section into line astern and attacked the nearest enemy machine. I succeeded in getting a good shot – beam attack with full deflection to stern chase with no deflection from under enemy's tail 200 – 150 yards. Enemy aircraft climbed into cloud. After expending all ammunition, I carried out dummy attacks to confuse enemy bombing. Own aircraft hit by seven bullets. No real damage. No visible damage to enemy.'

Taylour's observer Lt Robert Bostock (known as Robin) also got in on the action and fired a pan of .303 from his Lewis gun. The second Skua (L3025) was flown by PO(A) Eric Monk and had become separated from the leader during the initial dive. He therefore attacked independently four Heinkels in succession, commencing with the fourth in line. Although he was unable to bring down any of them (one gun failed to fire), they jettisoned their bombs at random and made for the clouds. Monk's gunner N/Air Len Hills also fired at the fleeing bombers, using half-a-pan of ammunition. The returning Skua crews reported seeing one ship on fire, and indeed the Heinkels – from II/KG26 – managed to inflict damage on five ships despite interception by the Skuas and a Hurricane of 43 Squadron, whose pilot claimed one shot down. The aircraft of 6 Staffelkapitän Hptm Otto Andreas crashed into the sea with the loss of the crew. This was possibly the same aircraft as that attacked by Lt Taylour. Some 40 minutes later, 803 Squadron's Blue section was more successful east of Copinsay, one of the islands to the east of the Orkney mainland, as Lt Bill Lucy (L2925/8F) reported:

'Returning from convoy escort, my observer noticed firing to port. We investigated. A single enemy aircraft, pursued by three Hudsons, were seen some way away. We gave chase but lost the enemy just before we were in range. We chased it into the clouds, and Blue 2 parted company. Returning towards base, we observed an enemy aircraft front-gunning merchant ships. I got into position above the enemy before he spotted me and delivered an attack. I overestimated the enemy's speed and closed to about 50 yards, being then thrown off my sights by the slipstream. I turned and then delivered another attack. Again I closed too rapidly, firing short bursts, and was finally smothered in oil from the enemy. The enemy was still climbing slowly with undercarriage down when he disappeared into the clouds. I fired 400 rounds from each gun. Short bursts on each attack.'

This aircraft, a Heinkel from 2/KG26, was hard hit and was obliged to crash-land near Duhnen, west of Cuxhaven, the radio operator (Gfr Hans Bähr) having been killed in the action. The aircraft was classified as a complete write-off. On reading subsequent copies of the combat reports for this action, the Director of Naval Air Division commented:

'Undoubtedly a fine effort but it is considered that the two aircraft of 800 Squadron would have had a better chance of shooting the enemy down if they had their guns lined up as directed in Admiralty Letter A/NAD876/39 dated 2nd February 1940. Against an enemy aircraft taking avoiding action, a pattern of six feet square at 300 yards as being used on this occasion would reduce the chance of bringing down an enemy aircraft.'

Of Bill Lucy,[46] Capt Birdy Partridge RM (who was posted to command 800 Squadron at Hatston on 1st April), wrote:

'Bill and I were great friends and had shared many happy days in *Glorious* in the Mediterranean in those halcyon pre-war days of 1937-38. He was a most competent pilot and not prone to 'split-arse' manoeuvres so often associated with fighter pilots! He was steady and reliable and his deck landings both by day and night were a joy to watch. I was at Eastleigh at the outbreak of hostilities and during some of the so-called Phoney War. We were getting a lot of routine flying, mostly giving trainee air gunners rear-gun practice at drogue targets over the sea at Littlehampton. The start of the Norwegian campaign in the spring and early summer 1940 put a sudden end to our Phoney War and I parted company with Bill to find myself first at Wick in northernmost Scotland and, then, at Hatston in the Orkneys.

'It was at Hatston that Bill and I met up again, he as CO of 803 Squadron and myself as CO of 800. Both squadrons were equipped with the fighter/dive-bomber Skua. Up in the Orkneys in those early war days we were doing a lot of flying, mostly defensive patrols over the sea, out of sight of land, and lasting four to four and a half hours. Occasionally one came across a lone merchant ship being attacked by a Heinkel 111. We were usually able to chase it off, but due to lack of performance we were unable to catch it. It was rewarding, however, to return low to the ship to be greeted by the crew on deck wildly waving their thanks.

'Bill seemed to be more successful than the rest of us and already was able to claim two He111s shot down and another possible. I questioned him about his success and he explained that he always patrolled either at 12,000 feet or as high as the cloud base would allow, so that, hopefully, he would have a height advantage over any enemy aircraft and catch up with it in the ensuing dive. He then added quite casually that he never opened fire until he was just about to collide with the enemy's rear turret! This sounded a very hazardous form of attack to me and when I suggested to Bill that one day the rear gunner was going to get him first, he smiled, shrugged his shoulders and said he was sure it was the best way of "blasting the buggers out of the sky". Any suggestion of opening fire with a short burst at about 300 yards, closing in with short bursts until the final kill, cut no ice with Bill. Nor would he concede that the enemy rear gunner's aim and peace of mind might be affected by the sight of tracer coming towards him!'[47]

806 Squadron was also put on alert, on **26th March**, causing Mid(A) Gus Hogg to write:

'The Squadron was in a terrific flap. It was to fly North to the Orkneys as soon as possible to join *Glorious*. No one thought much of the idea; we were obviously going to assist in the Norwegian campaign, which probably meant landing on a frozen lake or something equally frightening. It was impossible to get near a telephone for officers saying good-bye to their wives and families. I bid my farewells lying on a stretcher in the sick bay, using the doctor's telephone. On all sides of the wardroom, pilots and observers were writing last letters and composing heart-rending telegrams. The ground crews and equipment were sent off that night by special train, the aircraft having been left ready for a hurried take-off. We 'stood by'.

'Scottish weather, however, ordained that we should not take off until two days later [**28th March**]. When we did, the clouds were only at about 1,500 feet, which is not great height when aviating in the North of Scotland. We took off singly and joined up on the CO as he became airborne. I was flying a heavily loaded Roc on the left of the leader, which was about the best position I could have been considering the flight that followed. We flew up the west coast, finding it extremely bumpy, until we reached the Caledonian Canal, up which we headed. The clouds were down on the mountainsides and we were flying up a natural tunnel. The Squadron went into sections, in line astern stepped up, the leading section being fairly low. The air was full of pockets and sometimes we would rise or fall 300 or 400 feet, stopping at the denser air with a body-shaking crash. If the cloud had come down to sea level there would have been no turning back, the mountain enclosed us on both sides. The last sections spent a large part of the trip in the clouds. Everyone was extremely thankful when we emerged from the mountains and saw Inverness ahead. A short trip over some small hills and we were at Evanton, where the CO had decided to land for the night. The sections broke up and came in to land independently.'

The Rocs were giving 806 Squadron lots of problems, PO(A) Arthur Jopling experiencing electrical fires in the gun turrets of L3102 and L3105. On the first occasion, the fire broke out when five miles from base and although he managed to land safely, his TAG N/Air Pat Bolton was recovered from the turret almost unconscious. The same pair escaped injury four days later during another training flight.

During the morning of **3rd April**, several reconnaissance He111s from 1(F)/122 were sent out to search the area between the Orkneys and the Firth of Forth, and at 12:40 one of these reported the presence of a convoy to the east of Peterhead. One of the Heinkels was intercepted off Kinnaird Head near Fraserburgh at 09:50 by a pair of 803 Squadron Skuas, but no damage was inflicted. Lt Ned Finch-Noyes, on sighting the aircraft, opened fire at 250 yards range with a snap shot two-seconds burst with full deflection, but lost it as it climbed into clouds. His No.2, Lt James Rooper opened fire from 600 yards, and commented: 'Owing to inferior speed of Skua it was not possible to close to effective range before Heinkel reached the clouds.' Three more inconclusive engagements were reported by the Navy pilots some 40 minutes later. A further interception was made by an RAF Gladiator from the Sumburgh Flight, Shetland, but with no better success.

The Home Fleet, on standby and warned to anticipate early action, set sail for the Norwegian coast in two separate flotillas – the main force, commanded by the Commander-in-Chief Admiral Sir Charles Forbes aboard HMS *Rodney*, comprising four battleships, three heavy cruisers, seven light cruisers and 14 destroyers was ordered to approach Bergen, while to the north-west lay a force of four light cruisers and seven destroyers under Admiral Layton. The operation started tragically when on 9th April an 803 Squadron Skua (L2948) stalled whilst joining up with the convoy escort and crashed near the aerodrome. PO(A) Bill Chinn and N/Air Tom Burgess were both killed.

The expertise of Lt-Cdr Geoffrey Hare RN, currently attached to HMS *Sheffield* for observing duties, was called upon to assist the RAF, as he recalled:

'On the night of **8-9th April**, I was flown from Lossimouth to take off next morning

> in a Blenheim for a recce of Bergen and the adjoining fjords. The Blenheim squadron [254] had never flown any distance over the sea and neither had they any training in ship recognition. Three or four RN observers were required to navigate and identify any enemy ships [between] Stavanger and Bergen. My Blenheim flew to Bergen where we sighted three enemy cruisers and reported them. On the way back we passed over the Home Fleet and signalled our sightings to C-in-C by Aldis lamp.'

Lt-Cdr Hare flew with Flt Lt H M Mitchell aboard Blenheim IV L8786 for the sortie to Bergen (10:25–15:10), while Sub-Lt Charles Joy carried out a similar mission, but to Stavanger, with Plt Off Beal in L8840 (10:38–14:50), both aircraft returning safely.

Two Walruses were launched from *Rodney* to carry out reconnaissance of the Norwegian coastline near Trondheim, but neither gave the C-in-C Home Fleet further news of the German movements. At 18:43, Walrus P5649 was again despatched:

> 'The Commander-in-Chief was by this time so certain that the Germans were about to invade Norway that he personally told the pilot of this Walrus [Lt Bateman] that he was to allow himself enough fuel to land in Norwegian waters and then give himself up; that he would be free next day since Germany was going to war with Norway, when he was then to get hold of enough fuel to take him back to the Shetlands. All of this he did.'

Running low on fuel, the Walrus alighted in Kristiansund harbour and Lt Clem Bateman and crew including Lt Conway Bush as observer, were interned. Here they joined the crew of a Luftwaffe Ar196 floatplane that had earlier alighted at Kornstadfjord, also out of fuel, having flown from the damaged cruiser *Admiral Hipper*, which had been rammed by the British destroyer HMS *Glowworm*. The German crew, Oblt z.See Werner Techam and Ltn z.See Hans Polzin (pilot), had approached locals trying to purchase fuel for their aircraft but were apprehended and handed over to the police. Norwegian airmen Lts Kaare Kjos and Magnus Lie of the Trondelag Naval District were despatched in Høver MF11 floatplane (F342) to Kornstadfjord to take control of matters.

The Phoney War ended abruptly on **9th April** when news came through that Denmark and Norway had been invaded. The first German troop transports had set out for Norway on 3rd April on the commencement of Operation *Weserübung* (Weser Exercise), the invasion of Denmark and Norway, and four days later covering warships and others carrying further troops followed suit. Copenhagen was soon occupied and Denmark surrendered. In Norway, seaborne troops landed at Oslo, Kristiansand, Egersund and Bergen in the south, Trondheim in the centre and Narvik in the north.

The British Fleet was soon spotted by German reconnaissance aircraft, following which X Fliegerkorps ordered an attack by its prepared and waiting coastal bomber component – He111s from I and II/KG26 and all three Gruppen of Ju88-equipped KG30, while Ju87s of I/StG1 were ordered to make the first assault. However, due to the distance the British ships were from the coast, the Stukas were forced to turn back. The first bombers to make contact were therefore Ju88s of KG30, and these promptly sank the destroyer HMS *Ghurkha* and inflicted minor damage to the cruisers *Southampton* and *Galatea*. A second wave of Ju88s and Heinkels damaged the heavy cruiser *Devonshire*,[48] with near misses inflicting slight damage to the light cruisers *Sheffield* and *Glasgow*. These successes were achieved at a cost, however, four Ju88s falling to intense AA fire from the ships, including that of Hptm Siegfried Mahrenholtz, Gruppenkommandeur of III Gruppe. The Germans also suffered losses to their naval forces, the heavy cruiser *Blücher* having been sunk by Norwegian coastal guns and torpedoes, with the additional loss of her three Ar196s, while the cruiser *Karlsrühe* (and her Ar196) fell prey to RN submarine HMS *Truant*.

Following the unwelcome but not unexpected appearance of the British Home Fleet, ten He111s of KGr.100 were sent out on the morning of **10th April** on an armed reconnaissance east and south-east of the Orkneys and Shetlands, followed by an He111P of 3(F)/ObdL. Immediately behind this reconnaissance screen came 35 He111s of KG26 to respond immediately to any targets spotted. As the reconnaissance aircraft approached the Scottish coast, it was intercepted by seven Hurricanes of 43 Squadron, then based at Wick, Caithness, which were flying out to sea towards Ronaldsay. Against such opposition Oblt Karl Heinz's aircraft had no chance; shot to pieces, it flopped onto the sea and broke in half. Three men were seen swimming, but were too far from land for there to be any chance of being picked up before they succumbed to exposure.

The KGr.100 aircraft subsequently reached the area and reported that two convoys had been seen off the Moray Firth, and heavy naval units south of the Orkneys. These reports referred to two cruiser flotillas and a French force, which were now retiring to Scapa Flow, and at once these became the prime targets. The first attacks began when the KGr.100 aircraft found shipping off Kinnaird Head, but their bombing caused little damage. Numerous interceptions by defending fighters then followed, and some heavy fighting ensued. The first such engagement occurred during the afternoon when a Hurricane of 605 Squadron, also based at Wick, on convoy patrol, spotted a German aircraft at 15:45; this was a Heinkel of 1/KGr.100. Two attacks were made, but the bomber slipped away in cloud, returning with the flight engineer (Obfw Richard Roder) dead, and a second crewman (Uffz Alfred Traupe) wounded, but with only minor damage to the aircraft.

Almost an hour later, two He111s were seen at 14,000 feet by another section from 605 Squadron. The three Hurricanes climbed to the attack and one of the bombers was shot down, only two members of the crew being seen to bale out, but in fact Oblt Harald Vogel and all his crew in this 4/KG26 aircraft survived and were rescued by a Royal Navy trawler. However it was not just the RAF defenders that were involved in repelling these raids. The Sea Gladiators of 804 Squadron had a very active time, as remembered by Lt Donald Gibson:

> 'In our Gladiators we had several alerts after German reconnaissance aeroplanes; there was an RAF Hurricane squadron at Wick, which had success and our own first blood was partly by courtesy of this squadron. I think we both intercepted more or less together and somehow we became involved and shot it down.' [49]

The successful pilots were Sub-Lt Michael Fell (N5510), PO(A) Geoff Peacock (N5538), and PO(A) Bert Sabey (N5509) of Yellow Section who opened the scoring for 804 Squadron when they shot down one of the Heinkels, as recorded by the unit's diarist:

> 'A tremendous day for HMS *Sparrowhawk* [RNAS Hatston], the first and we hope by no means the last. 804 began their fun at 1605hrs when Yellow Section flew off to Copinsay. There were a great many plots on the board, the weather fine with

layers of cloud varying in density up to about 10,000 feet. About 16:40hrs Yellow 3 saw a Do17 [*sic*] and the Section gave chase. Sub-Lt Fell got in a burst at about 500 yards as the Do17 disappeared into the cloud: but followed him in. Yellow 2 went in above the cloud and as he came out so did the Do17 some 400 yards away. Peacock got in a burst before the e/a dived away back into the clouds. We were later informed that Do17 was crying SOS with a leaking petrol tank and did not reach his base.'

There were no Do17s involved in these actions, only He111s and it seems probable that their victim was a Heinkel from 1/KG26 that crashed into the sea off the island of Sylt on return, in which Oblt Otto Houselle, Uffz Franz Gruber and one other member of the crew were drowned.

'At 16:45hrs Red Section were sent to patrol between Copinsay and Burray. As soon as they got there Red 1 saw a He111 about ten miles east going north-east. Hot pursuit was begun and as the Section followed, Hurricanes could be seen gathering on the cloud-dodging Heinkel's tail. After a few minutes the e/a began climbing, twisting and diving. By the time Red Section arrived and got within range No.43 Squadron had done their job. The e/a's motors were idling and he dived down to 20 feet over the sea. For two or three miles he held at 20 feet with a dark oil streak trailing behind him on the sea and finally flopped port wing first. Six Hurricanes and Red Section flew around the wreck as 'Nifty' got the position and saw the fuselage break in half, the port wing come off and the remainder sink as three of the crew swam for it.'

This was 43 Squadron's victim, the Heinkel was from 3(F)/ObdL. Meanwhile, following the reports of the British shipping, a heavy raid had been prepared, and this came in at dusk once again, when about 40 bombers approached, comprising 19 Heinkels of I/KG26, followed by 19 Ju88s from I and II/KG30, the latter crews briefed to bomb naval oil supplies at Scapa. Ten Hurricanes from Wick-based 43, 111 and 605 Squadrons were scrambled, as were a dozen Sea Gladiators from 804 Squadron:

'At 20:45, the evening blitzkrieg began. Red Section was scrambled to Copinsay and 15–20 enemy aircraft were reported approaching from the east at 20,000 feet, so Red patrolled at 18,000 feet between Copinsay and Burray. By 21:00hrs all Sections were in the sky and the party had started, the guns putting up an ugly barrage. Yellow had the first chase after an e/a, which was in a long dive towards Kirkwall and which peppered Kirkwall and Hatston with front guns. Yellow Section unfortunately could not keep pace though the optimistic Yellow 3 [PO(A) Geoff Peacock] gave the e/a a burst at a very long range in order to ease his repressed fighting spirit.'

Lt Rodney Carver was at the head of Red Section, with Lt Donald Gibson and Sub-Lt David Ogilvy:

'At 21:10, Red Section dived down to 11,000 feet about four miles east of Burray, (an island between Kirkwall and South Ronaldsay.) Unfortunately Red 2 was left behind in the dive. As soon as they flattened out a bomber crossed 200 yards ahead from port to starboard, Red 1 and Red 3 turned and pursued and loosed off nearly all ammunition, gradually closing in from 300-200 yards. The enemy fired back narrowly and finally turned and dived away to the south-east with smoke coming from his starboard motor. During this party Blue Section [Lt Smeeton N2275, PO(A) Stockwell, PO(A) Theobald] were lurking further west and came galloping up on seeing the shooting. Plenty of e/a were coming in and so Smee chose a back one and stuffed himself under its tail. He and his section rattled away with such good effect that the e/a was last seen in a flat right hand spiral going down towards South Ronaldsay. Unfortunately no wreckage was found and so the very probable result could not be confirmed.'

Their victim was possibly an aircraft from 2/KG26 whose crew reported that their aircraft had been very badly damaged by fighters before it crash-landed at Marx, where it was a total loss although Ltn Hubert Schachtbeck and his crew survived.

'By 21:50hrs the party was over and 11 Gladiators had returned. The 12th was Blue 3 [PO(A) Theobold] who shortly afterwards could be heard calling "Where am I?" Nifty told him and led him back to Wick where he spent the night.'

One Gladiator was claimed shot down by the crew of a returning Heinkel. The Hurricanes meantime had accounted for a He111 from Stab I/KG26 (Fw Busaker and crew which included Oberstlt Hans Alefeld, the 45-year-old Gruppenkommandeur), and two Ju88s – flown by Obfw Walter Brünn and Ltn Hans Hohendahl – fell to Scapa's AA defences. A costly intrusion. A German report of this action revealed:

'At 12:40, ten aircraft of KGr.100 are sent out on an armed reconnaissance searching for shipping off the Shetlands and Orkneys. Between 16:17 and 16:40 east of the Orkneys in the Moray Firth two convoys are spotted consisting of 14 steamers, 10 destroyers, two cruisers and four individual steamers. The convoy and steamers are heading on a westerly heading, the warships on a northerly heading. At 17:40 off the southern tip of the Orkney Islands two battleships, three cruisers and six destroyers are spotted on a north-north-westerly heading. This fleet was attacked without recognizable success. Throughout the flight Spitfire [*sic*] and Hurricane fighters and shipborne flak harass the unit. In an air battle a Hurricane fighter was shot down.

'At around 12:50, six aircraft of 1(F)/122 take off for a reconnaissance mission in the northern area of the North Sea. At 17:00, one battle-cruiser (*Hood*?) with four cruisers as well as several destroyers are spotted on a course steering north-west off the Orkney Islands. Concerns raised that this may be the same fleet as reported by KGr.100. Aircraft have a short encounter with two Lockheed [Hudson] aircraft with no result.'

The report carried on:

'At 11:00 an He 111 of 3/ObdL is sent on a reconnaissance mission to Scapa Flow. The aircraft is shot down with the loss of all crew.

'Between 12:38 and 12:39 II/KG26 take-off for operations over the North Sea. On the basis of information supplied the Gruppe heads towards the Orkneys. Due to bad weather attacks were limited. At 18:40 from 700 metres, coming out of cloud, a surprise attack was launched on a destroyer with two SC500 bombs. At 18:50 an attack on a cruiser was unsuccessful. The attack had to be called off due to worsening weather. (Cloud base had dropped from 700 to 500 metres and visibility was less than a kilometer). Two aircraft were lost, while one other crash landed at Stavanger.

'Nineteen aircraft of I/KG26 – taking off about 18:20 – head out to attack the reported naval forces east of the Orkney Islands. Due to worsening weather and the approach of nightfall many crews did not find their target. Of those that did some were unable to attack due to being blinded by floodlights carried by the ships. Those aircraft that did bomb could not observe their results because of the blinding effect, though a large warship was probably hit with one SC250 bomb. During the attack three floodlights and some flak was knocked out. The defence of the ships was an unknown quantity of flak and about 200 floodlights. In addition Gladiator fighters also tried to intercept the bombers. One of these was shot down.

'Nineteen aircraft of KG30 take off at 18:37 to attack the enemy naval forces in Scapa Flow. Seventeen aircraft were able to attack. Several near misses on the tidal walls and one SD500 hit on a cruiser were observed. Within the area 2 cruisers and several destroyers were noted. In the northern part of the bay two cruisers with some destroyers and steamers were also spotted. Defence of Scapa Flow was provided by floodlights and ground and ship based flak. One aircraft was lost in the attack.'

Another success was claimed by the FAA during the day when a Walrus of 700 Squadron out from Hatston on an anti-submarine patrol, P5655 crewed by newly promoted Lt Johnnie Groves, observer Lt-Cdr Archie Fleming and TAG L/Air Frank Smith, attacked a submerged submarine about ten miles east of the Orkneys. Oil, rising from the surface before the attack, increased in quantity, and the destroyer HMS *Hero* was called in to complete the work, the kill being jointly awarded, the first such kill being claimed by a FAA aircraft. It was believed that their victim was *U-50* (Kaptltn Max-Herman Bauer), which went missing in the North Sea at about this time, although the Germans accepted that the submarine had fallen victim to British Mine Field No.7 laid by four destroyers on 3rd March. Alternatively, it may have been the wreck of HM submarine *Tarpon* (Lt-Cdr Herbert Caldwell RN), also lost on this date. German records show that *Tarpon* had attacked the Q-ship *Schiff 40* at 07:24; the first torpedo missed, as did a second. The Q-ship picked up the *Tarpon* on her sonar and her periscope was sighted, following which depth charges were dropped. The counter attack went on most of the morning until finally at 12:52 a pattern of depth charges brought wreckage to the surface. The Q-ship remained on the scene until 05:00 the next morning secure in the knowledge that she had sunk the submarine. Lt-Cdr Caldwell and all 54 members of the crew were lost.

4. 'THIS RAMSHACKLE CAMPAIGN'[50]

German invasion of Norway and Denmark – April 1940

"Our Fleet Air Arm aircraft are hopelessly outclassed by everything that flies in the air – and the sooner we get some different aircraft the better."

Admiral Sir Charles Forbes, C-in-C Home Fleet

Originally called operation *Studie Nord*, the proposed German invasion of Norway was later renamed operation *Weserübung* and planning had started in early February 1940. Later that month, General von Falkenhorst was given command of the operation and on 1st March, Hitler signed a directive on *Weserübung*. The objective being; 'preventing British aggression in Scandinavia, secure iron ore from Sweden and the setting up of naval and airbases for the war on Britain.' By 20th March, the plans were complete and General von Falkenhorst reported that everything was ready for *Weserübung* to go ahead. On 3rd April, German supply ships left harbour and headed for Norway. The warships would be at their predetermined positions on the Norwegian coast by 04:15 on 9th April. The task force was split into six groups.

Group I Narvik: Ten destroyers and 2,000 men commanded by General Dietl. The Norwegian warships *Eidsvold* and *Norge* were sunk and Narvik captured.

Group II Trondheim: The *Admiral Hipper* and four destroyers carrying 1,700 men approached Agdenes coastal fort at about 03:00. The ships had already passed before the batteries opened fire. Trondheim was taken three hours later.

Group III Bergen: The two light cruisers *Köln* and *Königsberg*, the training ship *Bremse*, with several smaller craft carried 1,900 men past Bergen coastal fort at 02:15. The batteries around Bergen scored several hits but did not sink any of the German vessels, although the *Königsberg* was damaged. They continued to fire until the German commander threatened to bomb Bergen if they did not ceasefire.

Group IV Kristiansand: The light cruiser *Karlsrühe* and several smaller vessels carried 1,100 men. The coastal battery there opened fire as soon as they were within range, at about 05:00. The ships went back to sea and tried again at 09:00, only to fail yet again. Later that morning, the battery received orders not to fire on allied ships, which they thought were coming to help. Only when the ships had passed did they notice their flags were German not British or French.

Group V Oslo: The heavy cruiser *Blücher* and pocket-battleship *Lützow*, (ex-*Deutschlend,*) light cruiser *Emden* and the flakship *Brummer*, with several smaller vessels carried 2,000 men and staff. At 23:00 hours April 8th, the Norwegian guardboat *POL III* fired a warning shot and coastal batteries fired off a couple of shots with the help of spotlights. The Norwegian minelayer *Olav Tryggvason* fought with German ships while the *Blücher* was sunk after being hit by two torpedoes from the Oscarsborg battery. The remaining German ships left Oslofjord and landed the troops at Son later that morning.

Group VI Egersund: The town was captured by some 150 German troops without resistance. These had been landed by minesweepers.

Meanwhile, German paratroops (*Fallshirmjäger*) were dropped at Sola, Stavanger to capture the airfield there. The same thing happened at Fornebu (near Oslo). Both fields were captured by the afternoon and the first troops arrived in Oslo from Fornebu at about 15:00 that day. The invasion was almost a complete success for the Germans but they had not captured the King or the Government, who had won precious time when *Blücher* was sunk. Thus, they were free to choose and refused German demands of surrender.

While 804 Squadron's Sea Gladiators were involved in the defence of Scapa, 800 and 803 Squadrons' Skua crews found themselves engaged in one of the FAA's greatest single successes – the sinking of the damaged light cruiser *Königsberg* in Bergen harbour on the morning of **10th April**. This was not an officially planned operation but one devised by Lt Bill Lucy and carried out by the Skua crews, as recalled by the new CO of 800 Squadron, Capt Birdy Partridge RM:

> 'On the not-too-frequent occasions when I could take a day off and hand over the running of my Squadron to my senior pilot, I used to relax as best I could; sometimes by strolling round Kirkwall or gently exploring the surrounding countryside, anything in fact that was peaceful and in no way connected with flying and the war. But not so my friend Bill Lucy. As far as I could make out he spent all his off-duty time in the operations room, studying the reports coming in and hoping always that he would find some new target that he and his squadron could attack.
>
> 'I was having a quiet and peaceful lunch when Bill burst in excitedly, saying, "There's a German cruiser alongside in Bergen harbour and the Met men say the weather will be clearing shortly." I had a horrible feeling that Bill had in mind something I wouldn't approve of or like very much – and I wasn't far wrong. "Let's take both squadrons over and dive-bomb the cruiser at dawn tomorrow morning," said Bill airily. My quiet, peaceful lunch in ruins, I pointed out to Bill that in still air, Bergen was two hours' flying away and two hours back and that the Skua's endurance was only four hours and 20 minutes; a head wind, a forced diversion or a tangle with enemy fighters and we would never get back. Bill would have none of this and merely said that even if some of us had to ditch on the way back it would be worth it if the raid was successful. Though not a fire-eater like Bill I was certainly prepared to take reasonable risks for myself and my squadron, and obviously such an attack could not possibly be expected by the enemy and would therefore have that greatest advantage of all surprise. But was this a reasonable risk?
>
> 'My next observation was that there were long-range German fighters, Me110s, at Stavanger and that we would be sitting targets for them. Not, Bill said, if we carry

out a surprise attack, straight in and out; they will not have time to get up from Stavanger and intercept us. I then asked him how the hell we carried out a surprise attack on a target that lay 30 to 40 miles up the Bergen Fjord; to which he replied that we should take off at night at a time that would allow us to arrive over Bergen at sunrise. Non-fire-eater Partridge then played his trump card by saying that though such a raid might just be possible the Station CO [Captain C L Howe RN] would never authorize such a risky undertaking; but Bill's reply was that he had already discussed it with the CO and that if I agreed we had authorization to carry it out tomorrow. I must admit that on my own I don't think I would even have thought up this plan and all credit for its inception must go to Bill Lucy. His enthusiasm and confidence was however having an effect on me and I was beginning to think it might, with luck, be possible. After a little further discussion I agreed and we reported to the Station CO who gave us the order to go ahead.'[51]

Sixteen aircraft were thus assembled from the two squadrons, all that were available. Each was to carry one 500lb SAP (semi-armour-piercing) bomb and eight 20lb Cooper anti-personnel bombs. Capt Partridge's usual observer Lt Robin Bostock was currently on loan to the RAF, as were several other experienced naval observers at this time, whose expertise was required to instantly recognise and identify the plethora of British and German warships operating in Norwegian waters. To replace Bostock, Lt-Cdr Geoffrey Hare was ordered back to Hatston to navigate the strike. Partridge continued:

'I watched my aircrews' faces when I told them what we were going to do. If their reactions were the same as mine originally were they didn't show it; they took it calmly and magnificently. There were a few questions and answers and then I warned the pilots to take extra care about the take-off and forming up in the dark. The Skua with full armament and fuel was not very nice or easy to fly.'[52]

'The 16 crews selected to participate in the operation were:

	800 Squadron		**803 Squadron**
Yellow Section		**Blue Section**	
L2940	Capt R T Partridge RM	L2925	Lt W P Lucy
	Lt-Cdr G Hare		Lt M C E Hanson
L2934	PO(A) H A Monk	L2881	Capt E D McIver RM
	L/Air L C Eccleshall		L/Air A A Barnard
L2900	PO(A) J Hadley	L2910	Lt A B Fraser-Harris
	L/Air M Hall		L/Air G S Russell
White Section		**Green Section**	
L3028	Lt E W T Taylour	L2903	Lt H E R Torin
	PO(A) H G Cunningham		Mid(A) T A McKee
L3001	Lt J A Rooper.	L2918	Lt L A Harris RM
	PO(A) R S Rolph		N/Air D A Prime
		L2931	Lt W C A Church
			PO(A) B M Seymour

Spare Section
L2933 Lt K V V Spurway
PO(A) C J E Cotterill
L3037 PO(A) J A Gardner
N/Air A J Todd

Red Section
L2923 Lt B J Smeeton
Mid(A) F Watkinson
L2991 Lt C H Filmer
N/Air F P Dooley
L2915 PO(A) T F Riddler
N/Air H T Chatterley

PO(A) Eric Monk was down to fly in 800 Squadron's Yellow Section:

'None of us had ever flown with a 500lb bomb and the trip was near our endurance limit. Final note at briefing was, "If you have less than 60-gallons of fuel after the attack, fly on to Sweden, destroy your Skua and try to get back." Not a very good sleeping draught. I went to bed shortly after briefing and my chum Ron Lunberg came along to wish me luck in the morning.

'The shake at 03:00 was a relief but the thick corned-beef sandwiches we were offered at briefing remained untouched. Going out to the aircraft I had mixed feelings and wondered if my kite would fail to start. It was then I found out that once I was strapped into my familiar L2934 it was just another flight, no more worries. All was ready, bomb on, safety pin for my bomb in my pocket in case it was not dropped, Colt .45 in my flying overall pocket alongside the compass, and L2934 started up first cartridge. Warm up the engine, check boost and revs, throttle back to check the magnetos and check that the tanks are full. It was a fine morning as we climbed up to 16,000 feet, heater on, and doing 140 knots. Eventually the coast came into sight, the sun was up, the sky blue, the hills topped with snow, lower down the pine trees and then the water of the fjord. Wonderful, except that there was a war on.' [53]

PO(A) Dickie Rolph, flying with Lt James Rooper in L3001, recalled:

'The Skua, when fully loaded, needed all the runway that Hatston could provide and once airborne it behaved like a pregnant porpoise, so it needed some flying ... it is about 325 miles from Hatston to Bergen each way, and the maximum range of the Skua was about 675 miles, so there was no room for mucking about ...' [54]

All 16 aircraft were safely in the air shortly after 05:00, Lt Lucy leading the two squadrons, which became separated in the darkness and heavy cloud that covered the path of their flight. Capt Partridge wrote:

'Then it was my turn. Followed by my pilots, we gingerly flew round above the airfield in the dark as we gradually joined up in formation at 3,000 feet. Then Bill swung round on a course for Bergen, climbing slowly to reach 10,000 feet. We levelled out at that height and settled down to our most economical speed of 140 knots. It was important that leaders should keep a constant speed and that followers should not drop astern; excessive use of throttle to catch up or slow down meant more fuel used, and we didn't have any of that to spare! I settled down 200 feet above and a few hundred yards out on Bill Lucy's starboard quarter. For some reason I always preferred flying on the right when in formation, I don't know why. It was a dark night but there were stars, which helped, and I had no difficulty in keeping the other squadron in view, unless we ran into cloud. More time, of course, to think now and

I felt sorry for the back-seat crews who had even less to do than the pilots; at least we had our instruments to check, our formation to keep and could curse at the aircraft which refused to stay trimmed fore and aft.

'My observer [Lt-Cdr Hare] called me up on the intercom and told me that he reckoned we had just passed the halfway mark and were well set to arrive on time. He also pointed out the wispy clouds that were beginning to form and said that he thought they might increase. I had already noticed them and told him that if I lost contact with the other squadron I would climb to 12,000 feet and he would have to navigate me to the target. He seemed very calm and happy about this. The cloud was increasing: it was now almost three-tenths and occasionally I would lose sight of Bill Lucy's squadron. But on we went as smoothly as ever, both squadrons in fairly open formation. I was beginning to lose sight of them more often now and began to climb to 11,000 feet so that there would be a vertical separation between us. Suddenly I knew I had lost them and in the dark it was most unlikely I would pick them up again. I told my observer that I was out of contact with 803 Squadron, that I was climbing to 12,000 feet and would be carrying out an attack independent of the other squadron. This separation of the squadrons would mean that instead of the continuous surprise attack of 16 diving Skuas, one squadron or the other was probably going to attack after an interval, thus minimizing the effect of surprise and certainly alerting the defences. There was nothing to be done about it and we had discussed and recognized this possibility.' [55]

Feint signs of the approaching dawn were now showing and details of the nearest aircraft could be made out. It was 06:40:

'Shortly before 06:55 we both spotted the island just off the Bergen Fjord fine on our port bow. I glanced around and below for the other squadron, hoping that I could rejoin, but although the cloud had cleared away as we approached the coast there was no sign of them. The sun was just beginning to rise in a bright golden ball above the mountains, which we knew cradled Bergen down to the waterline. Calm, precise instructions were now coming from the rear cockpit over the intercom Suddenly, ahead of us was Bergen, looking quiet and peaceful in the sparkling, early morning sunlight. To port were three large fuel storage tanks and ahead and to starboard ships, but merchant ships only – no cruiser. There was no sign of activity of any sort, no enemy fighters and no AA fire. We were almost down to 8,000 feet when we spotted her, a long, thin, grey shape lying alongside a jetty. I pulled away to port in order to make a great sweep up to the mountains and over the town of Bergen itself and so attack out of the rising sun. Now I was heading back towards the German cruiser and concentrating hard to get my Skua and those following me into the correct position for starting our dive.' [56]

The majority of the Skuas went into the final 60-degree attack dive from a height of 6,500 feet, releasing at around 2,000 feet altitude. This gave the bomb time to arm itself on the way down and to have sufficient terminal velocity to penetrate the decks of the target and do meaningful damage to her innards. There were obviously a number of variations to this average, with some pilots releasing at 2,500 feet, and two of them, Lt James

Rooper and Lt Les 'Skeet' Harris RM, recording bombs away at 3,000 feet. In Rooper's aircraft was PO(A) Rolph, who remembered:

> 'We formed into attack formation when crossing the mountains just north of Bergen, before turning towards the target, our diving point, and the harbour. My pilot said, "Keep a good lookout for the bomb." Now, I ask you, diving at 65-70-degrees, 290 knots and then pull out!' [57]

PO(A) Eric Monk recalled:

> 'As I stall-turned to enter my dive the shell bursts covered Bergen like a black lace curtain. The *Königsberg* had been damaged by the Norwegian coast batteries but there were still quite a lot of shell bursts on the way down. Steady on the target, offset turret, no mistaking the Köln-class cruiser, 5,000 feet, check bomb is armed, 3,000 feet and release, down to sea-level, weaving away down the fjord.' [58]

Other pilots elected to press on further down in order to ensure hitting, with both Lts Lucy and Ken Spurway releasing at 1,500 feet. Capt Partridge continued:

> 'Having reached a suitable position, I did a 90° turn to port, eased back on the stick, flaps down, further back on the stick, a half stall turn to starboard and then I was in a well-controlled dive with the cruiser held steady in my sights. I was losing height and down to 6000 feet with the target still held steady in my sights when to my astonishment ahead of me in the dive I saw a Skua release its bomb and go racing away at water level. I later found out that this was the last aircraft of 803 Squadron so, quite fortuitously, we were going to carry out our planned continuous raid with all 16 aircraft!
>
> 'I was attacking the ship from bow to stern and the only resistance being offered was coming from a light Bofors type AA gun on the fo'c'sle which kept firing throughout the engagement; tracer bullets were gliding past on either side. My dive was still firm and controlled with the ship held steady in my sights and I could see water and oil gushing out of her below the waterline and guessed that she had already been damaged. Down to 3,500 feet now and beginning to watch my height; mustn't lose accuracy by releasing too high and mustn't release too low and risk blowing myself up – 3,000 feet, 2,500, 2,000, and at 1,800. I pressed the release button on the stick and let my bombs go, turning violently away to starboard and then down to water level when well clear. As we raced low down the fjord at full throttle Hare was telling me that he reckoned we had had a near miss on the ship's starboard bow when he suddenly said "MTB travelling fast ahead of us", and there was a motor torpedo boat, at full speed with decks crowded with servicemen. I turned towards her and as we got near gave a long burst with my front guns and saw men jumping off and into the water.' [59]

Lt Kik Filmer's TAG, N/Air Fred Dooley also fired at the MTB, as did PO(A) Dickie Rolph (in Lt Rooper's aircraft) who recalled:

> 'Flak opposition was not very heavy, and we did our getaway at about 50 feet. I was able, to my satisfaction, to machine-gun a boatload of German soldiers crossing the fjord. I believe I scored a few hits.'

Capt Partridge:

> 'We were being fired on now by AA batteries in the woods on the steep side of the fjord and in this mad dash we were making I was tempted to have a go at them too. Sensibly, I resisted this rash impulse and continued to climb to 5,000 feet over our rendezvous. There I saw the glad sight of Bill Lucy with all his squadron but one, and I was soon joined by mine. Circling, waiting for Bill's straggler, was bad for my nerves as the excitement of the attack and getaway began to wear off. As I sat there jittery in my cockpit imagining hordes of Me110s arriving at any moment I was vastly relieved to see a single-engined monoplane approaching; Bill's missing Skua. We learnt later that this aircraft had dived with 803 Squadron but had had a hang-up and couldn't release its bombs. The pilot [Lt Church], determined not to jettison them, had laboriously climbed back to 8000 feet, circled over Bergen again, and carried out a lone attack after we had all gone. This time the AA gun on the fo'c'sle was no longer firing.' [60]

During his initial dive Lt Bill Church (flying with PO(A) Brian Seymour, who had shot down the first German aircraft way back in September) found himself out of position and, rather than waste his bomb, took the calm decision to go around and try again. This he did, making his second run from stern-to-bow of the target in a shallower, 40-degree attack. He dropped his bomb at just 200 feet through considerable flak as the *Königsberg*'s gunners were, by this time, wide-awake. He escaped unscathed for his audacity and clawed his way back up to 3,000 feet with bursting shells following his track. Church was later to report that his Skua suffered nothing more than, '... one large hole in main plane close to fuselage'. The last pilot over the target was Lt Teddy Taylour, making his lone assault well after the rest having become separated. Arriving some ten minutes late, he found the target shrouded in smoke, but nonetheless made his 70-degree attack dive from 6,500 feet, releasing his bomb at 2,000 feet. He scored a close miss on the mole alongside. The smoke cleared long enough for him to get a good look and he reported that the cruiser was badly hit. There was a fire amidships, she was listing to port and oil was leaking from her tanks staining the water alongside.

On the receiving end of the Skuas' attack the *Königsberg* soon became enveloped in the smoke and flames of explosions as the 500lb bombs rained down in quick succession. None went wide; every bomb was a hit or a very near miss, either in the water astern or on the mole close alongside. The resulting clouds of smoke, dust from the rubble and the fires aboard the target were intense and made observation of results difficult. Few of the pilots could get a clear view of results. One of those who did, PO(A) Tom Riddler, confessed his bomb had missed the ship but started a large fire in a warehouse on the jetty alongside. L/Air George Russell stated that his pilot, Lt Fraser-Harris, quite definitely hit fair-and-square on the cruiser's forecastle, punching through and leaving a large black hole from which vomited flames and white smoke. He noted in his logbook: 'Got in at 800 feet and attacked. Lt Spurway noticed his bomb detonated inside the ship, and resulted in clouds of debris and smoke. Finally, Capt McIver RM scored what was probably the decisive hit of the attack, amidships between the *Königsberg*'s two funnels, which penetrated her engine room and blew open her hull on the port side, lethal damage that was almost immediately compounded by a near miss just a few feet away. Birdy Partridge continued:

> 'Sixteen aircraft into the attack and sixteen out! It seemed too good to be true: and we had certainly damaged that ship, perhaps we had even sunk her. We were now on course for home and had been airborne for some two and a half hours with the best part of another two hours flying ahead of us. It would be touch and go, and should a head wind get up it seemed extremely likely that some of us at least would get very wet feet. After ten minutes on our homeward course – disaster! The outer aircraft on my starboard side suddenly went into a vertical dive and hit the sea under full power; all that remained was a large circle of disturbed water and a few pieces of wreckage. There was nothing that could possibly be done save to continue on our long flight home. It was never possible to discover what had happened but it seemed likely that either the aircraft had been hit and succumbed to elevator control failure or the pilot had been wounded, held out so far, and then suddenly collapsed.'[61]

The unfortunate crew were Lt Bryan Smeeton and his observer Mid(A) Fred Watkinson in L2923/8P. Their bodies were not recovered. Birdy continued:

> 'I landed at 09:45, having been in the air for four-and-a-half hours. Some of the aircraft clocked up five minutes longer, depending on the order in which they had taken off and landed. Some marvellous stories ran round the squadron for days afterwards among the ground crews – "He didn't have enough petrol in his tanks to cover a penny"; "As he taxied in towards me his engine cut dead, his tanks were completely dry"; "His engine cut out as he touched down" – a certain amount of exaggeration no doubt, but it was assuredly true that we had mighty little to spare.'[62]

PO(A) Monk remembered:

> '80-gallons indicated in the tanks, then out to sea into formation for the two-hour flog back to Hatston. We checked for signs of oil or fuel leaking on any of the aircraft in the sub-flight, and kept a constant check on my oil pressure. The leader's observer "zobbed" (Morse code by waving hand) "Report fuel remaining." I reply: "75". I was feeling rather hungry now. Two hours later we landed at Hatston with almost empty tanks and taxied in feeling tired but elated. On the way to the mess I passed the Captain who asked if I was ready to go again and I am pleased to remember that I replied, "Not till I've had my breakfast."'[63]

Capt Partridge's final comment:

> 'There was great excitement, congratulations and euphoria whilst we were being debriefed before going off to breakfast. General opinion among the naval pilots and observers was that our target had been a Köln-class cruiser and we were all certain that she had been badly damaged, perhaps even sunk. This was confirmed later by a report from RAF reconnaissance flights and photographs, which showed that the ship was sunk alongside the jetty. Later, intelligence from Norway established that she was in fact the cruiser *Königsberg*.
>
> 'Bill Lucy's rash, mad plan had worked and for the loss of only one aircraft, which seemed a small price to pay; and so I suppose it was except to those directly con-

nected: sorrowing mums and dads, brothers and sisters, fiancées perhaps and girl friends. They had received a blow that for some might last a lifetime but which we, distressed as we were at the loss of good friends, had to put as soon as possible from our minds, or accept as the fortunes of war in the full knowledge that it might be anybody's turn next. Grieving over losses is bad for morale and efficiency and from now on our losses were to mount rapidly: it was not long before the only surviving officer of my squadron was myself. The sinking of the *Königsberg* was a historic event, demonstrating for the first time the effectiveness of the dive-bomber against major warships.'[64]

The action reports indicate that the first wave scored two direct hits (Lt Alex Fraser-Harris being the third to dive and Lt Kik Filmer, eighth to dive) and the second wave one, (Lt Ken Spurway). The final witness of *Königsberg*'s ultimate demise proved to be none of her assailants, but came from the captain of the American tanker *Flying Fish* anchored in the harbour, who had a grandstand view. According to this eyewitness the German cruiser began sinking by the bow, with flames soaring up to 100 feet into the sky and she went deeper and deeper. Eventually, her stern rose up and her screws could be seen. Some 50 minutes after the departure of the last dive-bomber, the *Königsberg* rolled over and capsized. The cruiser had taken three direct hits and two near misses, the latter causing more damage than the former. As the hull ruptured, water poured in and, at 10:51, she sank with the loss of 18 dead and 24 wounded. With her went her Ar196 of 4/196, T3+HH. One bomb, which had missed the target, destroyed a Ju52/See floatplane of KGrzbV.108. Not a bad return for a 15-minute action in which a light cruiser and two enemy aircraft had been destroyed.

Captain A V S Yates (a cousin of Admiral Somerville), who happened to be at Hatston that day, recorded in his diary:

'What a day! I awoke at 04:30 to the roaring of the Skuas as sixteen of them took off for Bergen, and I was on the aerodrome to welcome them as fifteen out of sixteen returned soon after 09:00. Brave gang in old aircraft, which cannot catch a modern bomber, let alone escape from fighter, they all attacked the one German cruiser in Bergen. They estimated three if not four hits and of course hits on the jetty alongside may well have been effective. Anxiously we counted as they came back, most in perfect formation, two with crumpled wings, the last one very groggy, banking widely as he came into land and having to make a second shot at it. No heroics, no press photographers here as in the RAF. They fell in outside Headquarters and as they were dismissed, I heard one sailor chuckle to another "What do we do now mate? Bomb up again?" "Shouldn't be surprised", came the answer. As they walked away little Dick Bell-Davies, their Admiral with a VC ribbon on his breast, said, "Well done" to one or two of them. That was all!'[65]

Nonetheless, Lt Bill Lucy and Capt Birdy Partridge RM were each subsequently awarded the DSO for their leadership, while Lt Teddy Taylour received two DSCs (one for the 20th March action), and single DSCs were awarded to Lt-Cdr Geoffrey Hare, Lts Harry Torin and Michael Hanson, and Mid(A) Tom McKee. DSMs were announced for PO(A)s Eric Monk and Cuts Cunningham. Others received Mentions in Despatches.

One recorded accolade emanated from the office of Vice-Admiral, Orkneys and Shetlands (Vice-Admiral Sir Hugh Binney) who remarked:

'This was, I think, the first occasion on which Skuas had been used in action for the real purpose for which they were designed, viz a dive-bombing attack on an enemy warship. The ship was sunk, the attack was a complete success and I consider it was brilliantly executed ... the distance to Bergen and back is 560 miles, not greatly inside the maximum endurance of the Skua.'

Of this early period HMS *Glasgow*'s senior Walrus pilot, Lt Johnny Ievers, remembered:

'On the day Norway was invaded *Glasgow* was patrolling off the Norwegian coast. I was then the Flight Commander of the Walrus flight on board and was flown off to look for a German pocket battleship reported to be nestling in the fjords there. After three hours' fruitless searching we returned to *Glasgow*'s last position to find she had left in a hurry under German air attack. We flew back to Molde and taxied up to the jetty where we were met by the harbourmaster. Having told him our problem he said 'Oh well, you're in good company because *Rodney*'s Walrus is here already and we also have a German floatplane which landed here this morning and which we have captured. They are up the fjord some fifteen miles'. We took off and flew up the fjord, where we found not only the *Rodney*'s Walrus and its pilot, Lt Clem Bateman, but a very modern looking Arado floatplane and a very antiquated Norwegian seaplane sheltering under the lee of the fjord out of the incessant stream of German aircraft flying overhead. We eventually managed to get in touch with the Admiralty on the Walrus's radio at night and were able to tell them where we were and what we were doing – we must have used a code of some sort.' [66]

The captured Ar196 (ex-*Admiral Hipper*), now bearing Norwegian markings, was flown to Aandalsnes by a Norwegian pilot, where it joined the two Walruses and a Norwegian NAS Høver MF-11 floatplane, to form the Romsdalfjord Flying Group, carrying out valuable local reconnaissance for a few days.

The Home Fleet had by now been joined by *Warspite* and the *Furious*, the latter the only carrier immediately available. *Ark Royal* and *Glorious*, both currently in the Mediterranean, were on their way to Gibraltar at best speed in order to rejoin the Home Fleet. Unfortunately, *Furious*, which had been in the Clyde, only had time to embark her two Swordfish Squadrons, 816 and 818, each with nine aircraft. Her presence with the fleet being considered a necessity, the ship did not close the Orkneys to embark the Skuas of 801 Squadron, then at Evanton. RAF reconnaissance reports placed the *Admiral Hipper* in Trondheim and plans were immediately drawn up for *Furious*' squadrons to make a dawn torpedo attack. This was to be the first aerial torpedo attack of the war to date. All 18 aircraft were to participate, 816 Squadron being led by Capt Dick Burch RM (with the CO Lt-Cdr Henry Gardner as his observer) in P4169/U4A, and 818 Squadron by Lt-Cdr Pat Sydney-Turner (P4212/U3A).

Take-off commenced at 04:00 on **11th April**, with the entire force taking its departure at 04:19, the squadrons proceeding independently to attack from different directions. Climbing to 8,000 feet en route, 816 Squadron sighted Trondheimfjord at 05:14, the roads being entirely obscured in cloud. Hoping to surprise the Germans, the formation commenced a diving attack at 05:19. Emerging from the clouds at 3,000 feet, the *Admiral Hipper* was nowhere to be seen – having departed the previous evening for Stavanger. Flying towards Skjorenfjord, the Swordfish crews sighted a destroyer at anchor and opted for her, the attack commencing at 05:22. All nine aircraft made good drops, but to their utter disappointment, about 500 yards from the target, all the torpedo tracks ended, four of the nine exploding. Not equipped with proper maps, the attackers had not realised the target was protected by shoals. Meanwhile, 818 Squadron had sighted a destroyer in Trondheimfjord heading towards the harbour. Opting for her, eight of the nine attackers were able to release their torpedoes. Two exploded prematurely, the other six being avoided. It was a very disheartened band that returned to the ship at 06:30. Flying with Sub-Lt Peter Roberts in P4163/U3G was L/Air Jack Skeats:

> '816 and 818 gaily left *Furious*, flying just above sea-level (flying at sea level tends to rip off the undercarriage), passing over some skerries where the families came out to cheer and wave. We felt good although I for one had only a hazy idea what we were about. Air-gunners were not allowed to attend briefings – after all, we were only passengers. The approach to Trondheim was made at low height, with a short encounter with a flak ship and then a slow climb to top the mountains that surround the harbour and slide down the other side on our bottoms to the harbour itself and smite the Hun.
>
> 'Alas, the Hun was a damn sight smarter than we were and had left three days earlier, leaving lots of Swordfish sculling around without a target. Not dismayed, we proceeded to seek out a lone German destroyer making its way up a neighbouring, narrow fjord flanked by pines. The approach was made by side-slipping down over the pines, levelling out and then pressing the button after sighting. I am not quite sure of the pecking order but several kites preceded us in dropping their tin-fish and as we reached our drop position the bed of the sea came up to greet us in one big gout of sand and spume. And then another and yet another right underneath us flying as low as we dared. Damn fine gunners, these Germans, I thought before realization struck me. The depth of water was such that the torpedoes of the aircraft in front of us were blowing up on sandbanks in the fjord. Nevertheless, I saw at least two plumes of water rise up at the stern of the target and two hits were accredited.
>
> 'Back home to Mother [*Furious*] who turned out to be Mother Hubbard. The mess-deck was empty when I reached it, lunchtime was long gone and the cupboard was as bare as a baby's elbow. Cold and hungry I made my way to the Main Galley and did my Oliver Twist bit. The Chief Cook had obviously not read his Dickens, and said with deep emotion and great sympathy "Serves you bloody well right. You should have been here when the meal was served." '[67]

Later that morning, *Furious* despatched two Swordfish of 816 Squadron – P4167/U4B flown by Sub-Lt(A) Nigel Ball and U4H piloted by Lt(A) John Read – on an armed reconnaissance over Trondheim. After completing the main task, they decided to dive bomb the

German destroyer still anchored in Skjorenfjord at 12:20. Unfortunately, all the six bombs dropped fell wide of the mark. As U4H departed the area it was chased by a German floatplane but escaped by flying low. Both aircraft returned safely at 13:45.

Following the highly successful attack on Bergen by 800 and 803 Squadrons, Captain Howe at Hatston decided that another attack on the harbour was in order. The previous day 801 Squadron had arrived from Evanton, sizably increasing the number of Skuas available for the strike. A total of 20 Skuas was thus assembled. The first wave, seven from 803 was led by Lt Bill Lucy (8F) and took-off at 14:05 on 12th April; next came six from 800 Squadron led by Capt Birdy Partridge RM (L3025), some 15 minutes later, and finally seven from 801 led by Lt-Cdr Peter Bramwell at 14:30. Each Skua was armed with a single 500lb SAP bomb.

803 Squadron arrived at 16:15, approaching the target at 5,000 feet. Many ships were in harbour. Bombs were released at 2,000 feet but only near misses were reported although a lone E-boat, *S-24*, was strafed and damaged by Green Section (Lt Harry Torin (8A), Lt Skeet Harris RM (8B) and Lt Bill Church (8L) during which three German sailors were wounded, but L3037/8Q failed to return. PO(A) Jimmy Gardner's TAG was N/Air Alan Todd, who remembered:

'On 12th April, my mother's birthday, I was shot down over Bergen. We went across the hogwash to attack general shipping, and in the dive we caught one. The engine just faded away, we heaved ourselves over a small hill and went straight down into the fjord at 100-120 knots, just slithered along the calm water and came to an almighty splashy stop. We got the dinghy out of the tail stowage and got ashore. We made our way to a little house, where the family dried us off, then their local Dr Hansen took us down to the fjord to the US tanker *Flying Fish*, but they threw us off as soon as they found out who we were, fearing the hostility of the Germans. The skipper said, "Give yourselves up. They'll look after you."

'Ashore again, we stumbled along a little track we'd found and bumped into the doctor again, on his rounds. He was taken aback but led us to a little lodge in the woods belonging to Nurse Emma, a little old lady who hid us for several days until the hunt died down, then arranged for a boat to take us up the coast. We were then handed on from person to person, crossed a fjord to Aalesund, and after four weeks tracking caught up with the evacuation, and I recognized men and marines off the old *Barham*, dug in there to hold off the German Army. A coastal steamer took us back to Scapa, where we found out that the Squadron had been practically wiped out.'[68]

This was the only loss suffered by the Skuas during the attack. PO(A) Eric Monk of 800 Squadron recalled:

'Petty Officer Gardner failed to return, but he sailed into Kirkwall Bay two weeks later in a "borrowed" boat and still had a small bottle of Pusser's rum in his pocket. When the Captain sent to see him in the afternoon, the rum was in his tum and the Captain had to wait till next day! These raids continued for quite a time with 800, 801 and 803 Squadrons taking part.'[69]

Meanwhile the Home Fleet made its way northwards from Trondheim and, late on the

12th, reached a point 150 miles from Narvik. Here two waves of Swordfish totalling 16 aircraft, nine from 816 and seven from 818 Squadrons were readied for a bombing strike, the latter unit taking-off at 16:15.

818 Squadron
U3A Lt-Cdr P G O Sydney-Turner. Lt W Kellet. PO(A) W H Dillnut.
U3B Lt P C Whitfield. Lt D J Godden.
U3C Sub-Lt(A) K H Appleton. L/Air T G Cutler.
U3F Lt(A) G Smith. Lt R Dyer. L/Air D C Milliner.
U3H Sub-Lt (A) G R Hampden. L/Air H H Simpson.
U3K Lt(A) S Keane L/Air J G Skeats.
U3L Sub-Lt(A) S G J Appleby. L/Air E Tapping.

Snow and sleet hampered visibility, with cloud ceiling down to 1,000 feet. Led by Lt-Cdr Pat Sydney-Turner, the seven Swordfish attacked shipping in the port, claiming direct hits on two destroyers. One bomb hit the destroyer *Erich Köllner Z13*, a member of the crew being killed and five wounded, while the Norwegian fishery protection vessel *Senja* was also hit and severely damaged. A second destroyer, *Erich Giese*, suffered minor damage and three small Norwegian craft including the sloop *Michael Sars*, taken over by the Germans, were sunk, while the captured Dutch steamer *Bernisse* (951-tons) was scuttled during the attack. A hail of anti-aircraft fire from I/Flakregt 32 and warships shot down the CO's aircraft (P4212/U3A), which ditched in Ofotfjord from where he and his crew, Lt Kellet and PO(A) Dillnut, were rescued by the destroyer *Punjabi*. U3L flown by Sub-Lt(A) Sid Appleby was also shot down and he and L/Air Ernie 'Hoss' Tapping, both wounded, were picked up by the destroyer HMS *Grenade*. A third Swordfish, U3K flown by Lt(A) Stan Keane, was set on fire, but his TAG L/Air Jack Skeats, although wounded, managed to dowse the flames with his hands – a feat for which he subsequently received the DSM. One of his friends, L/Air Harry Simpson later recalled:

> 'My pilot, who had been promoted from Midshipman the week before, was Sub-Lt (A) Hampden, and when we were clearing the target area he called to me over the Gosport tube, saying, very languidly, "Air Gunner, did our bombs come off?" In the excitement I hadn't noticed, but, leaning back in my cockpit to look under the wing, I confirmed that the fins were still there. There was only one thing to do – off G-string and climb over into the empty observer's cockpit to check the fuse box on the starboard side. Climbing over and hanging on was terrifying in itself, but, after doing repairs and reporting to Hampden, I was even more terrified when he informed me that we must go round again. My God! That boy – he was about three months my junior – was brave. I don't know whether he was decorated or not as he was killed the next day going up to Narvik, ahead of *Warspite*, with Ray Dale as TAG. But he should have been given a VC – and I should have definitely got something for not baling out on the spot!
>
> 'Anyway, round again we went, mixture as before, but this time the bombs came off and fell close enough to a merchantman for its bows to be lifted out of the water. I remember seeing a man jumping over the side and thinking how cold it must have been in the sea at that time of year. Clearing the target area again and exchanging

chummy remarks with my pilot, we joined up with two other Swordfish for the run back to *Furious*, and here we come to the hero of the saga. In one of those aircraft was Jack Skeats. I think he was flying behind Lt Stan Keane and their Swordfish was a mess. No sign of Jack but there was a hell of a hole in the underbelly – it later transpired that most of this flooring had wrapped itself around Jack's buttocks and legs.

'The air gunner in the other aircraft, Doug Milliner, and I exchanged conjectures by hand signalling as to whether he was a 'goner' or not, as he should have been. We came to no real conclusion. By this time it was getting really dark and murky and it was with some relief that *Furious* was sighted after she had been forced to show us the way with a short searchlight display – not really allowed in wartime, but I will be eternally grateful for the gesture. Joining circuit, the lame ducks landed first and there was some slight delay because of an undercarriage collapse by one of them, but finally it was our turn.' [70]

Apart from the two missing aircraft, the surviving Swordfish got down safely including Lt(A) Keane's damaged machine U3K with the wounded Jack Skeats in the back, but that was not the end of the story for L/Air Simpson:

'In our initial briefing before take-off we had all been informed that there was likely to be little ground opposition but there might be enemy fighter activity. Accordingly, on the way back, Doug and I kept our Lewis guns ready to defend ourselves and the other aircraft from any such attacks and my 97-round pan was still on after a successful landing. During the push for'ard to the lift I took this pan off and stowed it away on its peg. On the way down in the lift, I saw that all the activity was around Jack Skeats' aircraft. Sick berth tiffies were lifting him from the cockpit and he was limp. While we waited, he was placed on a stretcher, which just happened to be directly behind my aircraft. I watched things very sympathetically, thanking Providence it wasn't me and thinking, in a desultory kind of way, "Poor sod". I really did like the chap. I pushed the Lewis gun with a thump back into its stowage. The gun went off. I had committed the cardinal sin in not clearing the gun and leaving one up the spout-and there was Jack's head all nicely lined up.'

'The noise and the tumult died away for what seemed an eternity and everyone's eyes turned in my direction. Someone in the vicinity – I think it was Paul Whitfield – said, "Was that you?" There was no need to answer: my white face must have told it all. However, tumult returned, the sick berth lads lifted up the stretcher and away they went. No sign of additional damage which rather surprised me in a piqued kind of way, as I was usually quite a good shot at shooting a sitting bird. Then I remembered hearing a buzz at the same time as the incident of the shot and suddenly noticed there was a jagged hole in the corrugated flooring of my cockpit. It hadn't been there on the way back to the ship, so ...?! Yes, the round up the spout had gone good until it got mixed up with an obstruction. Not Jack's head, but the tail oleo, or something technical like that. It then ricocheted off the iron deck and, being deflected somehow through 180-degrees, finished up in the deckhead and, on the way, making a jagged hole just one inch from my right foot.' [71]

The second wave of Swordfish,[72] 816 Squadron led by Capt Dick Burch RM (with Lt-

Cdr Guy Hodgkinson, the CO, as his observer in P4169/U4A), had meanwhile become lost in a snowstorm, and returned later to make the first night deck landings. An aircraft landing from this group, K6002/U4L piloted by Lt(A) Marcus Donati,[73] plunged off the flight deck of the carrier and landed upside down in the freezing waters. Donati and his TAG L/Air Frank Smith scrambled clear to be rescued by HMS *Hero* after 45 minutes with only their life vests for support, their liferaft having gone down with the plane. On his eventual return to the carrier Lt-Cdr Sydney-Turner remarked that his attack:

> '... was carried out in conditions of which the squadron had had no previous experience and without a reconnaissance, which would have been extremely valuable in deciding tactics of approach. The only maps available were photographic reproductions of Admiralty charts, which showed no contours.'

On the morning of **13th April**, in support of Admiral Whitworth's battle group, three Swordfish from 818 Squadron flew anti-submarine patrols, while ten more from 816 and 818 Squadrons again headed for Narvik, led by Capt Dick Burch RM in P4169:

816 Squadron
U4A Capt A R Burch RM. Lt D Sanderson. L/A L A Webber.
U4C Mid(A) C D Livingstone. N/Air J R Bristow.
U4G Lt(A) K G Sharp. N/Air S M Oliver.
U4H Lt(A) J Read. N/Air G N Thompson.
U4K Lt(A) F Whittingham. Lt O M Cheeke. L/Air F White.
U4M Sub-Lt(A) P J Broughton. L/Air A J Atkin.

818 Squadron
U3B Lt P C Whitfield. Lt D J Godden.
U3C Sub-Lt(A) G R Hampden. N/Air R Dale.
U3F Lt(A) S Keane. Lt D Langmore. L/Air L O Clark.
U3M Mid(A) D H Dammers. N/Air A J Sturges.

The attack was not successful, near misses again being all that could be achieved against the destroyers *Bernd von Arnim* and *Hermann Künne*, although the Norwegian patrol vessel *Kelt* was sunk. Gunners on the former warship shot down one Swordfish in which the pilot 19-year-old Mid(A) Denis Dammers suffered a severe wound to his left leg but managed to crash-land the aircraft (L2810/U3M) in a snowdrift on the coast at Emmenes. Dammers[74] and his TAG L/Air Alex Sturges were picked up from the side of the fjord by the destroyer *Punjabi*. A second Swordfish (U3C) was brought down by the guns of the *Erich Giese* and the harbour defences jointly, Sub-Lt(A) Grenville Hampden and N/Air Ray Dale losing their lives when it crashed into Ofotfjord.

Meanwhile at noon, a Royal Navy destroyer force led by the battleship *Warspite* entered Ofotfjord to flush out German destroyers there. *Warspite* launched her catapult Swordfish floatplane L9767/L for Lorna, flown by PO(A) Ben Rice with Lt-Cdr Walter Brown (CO 701 Squadron) as observer, and TAG L/Air Maurice Pacey, and armed with two 250lb high-explosive, two 100lb anti-submarine and eight 40lb anti-personnel bombs. Their instructions were:

1. Carry out a general reconnaissance for the squadron advancing on Ofotfjord, with

particular reference to the presence of German warships inside the fjords, the movements of German forces, and the positions of shore batteries
2. Bomb any suitable targets.

A German destroyer was seen and soon afterwards a U-boat – *U-64* (Kapltn Wilhelm Scholz) – was spotted anchored near a jetty in Herjangsfjord. Rice dived on the submarine and released his two 250lb bombs from between 200-300 feet, while Pacey sprayed the conning tower with his guns. The first bomb hit the bows of *U-64*, which sank within half a minute. Some return fire had been received and the Swordfish returned triumphant with nothing worse than a damaged tailplane. Rice recalled:

'I couldn't see the bombs fall as we pulled out, but Pacey saw the starboard bomb fall close alongside and the port one hit just abaft the conning tower; the U-boat was already sinking when I could see her again. She hit us in the tail with one shot. I think it was from her 37mm gun.'[75]

U-64 was unable to resurface and the surviving members of the crew escaped using escape apparatus. One man, who was unable to find his, managed to reach the surface without it. Fortunately, the men were only in the icy water for a few minutes before being pulled out by German soldiers in rowing boats. Eight men were lost, the commander and 37 surviving the ordeal.

That night (**13/14th April**), the RAF despatched six Wellingtons of 38 Squadron to carry out a reconnaissance of the aerodrome at Vaernes. One of these (L4339) crashed into the sea 22 miles north of Whitby just after midnight with the loss of the crew, which included observer Sub-Lt(A) Lionel Franklin, attached from 771 Squadron for duties with Bomber Command. It seems that the Wellington had been intercepted and shot down by a Bf109 from II/JG77 flown by Ltn Heinz Demes operating from Kjevik airfield at Kristiansand.

Six Skuas from 800 Squadron led by Capt Partridge RM (L3025) set out from Hatston at dawn on 14th April, followed 50 minutes later by nine from 803 Squadron led by Lt Lucy, to attack the port of Bergen once again. The first strike bombed large freighters alongside the quay, and also machine-gunned two submarines – *U-7* and *U-60* (Kapltn Georg Schewe) – and two E-boats, *S-23* and *S-25*. By the time 803 Squadron arrived, the weather had closed in with 10/10th cloud over the target area. The sections became split up in cloud and Green and Red Sections aborted the mission, but Lt Lucy led Blue Section (Capt Eric McIver RM and Lt Alex Fraser-Harris) through the cloud, emerging at 400 feet into clear sky and carried out an attack on the 7,560-ton German freighter *Barenfels*, which was loaded with war supplies including guns. Lucy's attack resulted in a near miss, which nonetheless, caused the freighter's hull to stave in. She sank stern first, taking her cargo down with her. A flying boat identified as a Dornier was then sighted moored in the harbour, the Skuas carrying out a strafing attack but were greeted by a wall of flak from the guns of defending Flakregt.33, which claimed two of the attackers shot down. One Skua (L2881/8H) crewed by Capt McIver and L/Air Bert Barnard was indeed lost, as were the crew. The 'Dornier' was in fact a He115 floatplane of 1/KüFlGr106, which was severely damaged and subsequently written off.

Next morning (**15th April**) at 05:00, two Skuas flown by Lt Bill Lucy (A8F) and Lt

Harry Torin (A8A) of 803 Squadron departed from Hatston to undertake an armed recce of the outlaying defences of Bergen, at the behest of Captain Howe. On reaching the Norwegian coast they split up and made individual approaches to Bergen, Lucy sighting a German patrol boat, the *Tarantel-18* (a captured Norwegian coastal vessel) targeting this with his single 250lb and eight 20lb bombs, gaining hits. It was believed that the vessel sank immediately but was in fact only badly damaged. Meanwhile, Lt Torin sighted a surfaced submarine *U-58* (Oblt Heinrich Schonder), which he claimed was hit by one of his 20lb bombs, but little if any damage was inflicted. Both Skuas returned safely to Hatston.

The Fleet returned to Scapa during the day, leaving *Furious* and her escorts anchored in Tromsø harbour due to bad weather and the need for oiling. During the day her reconnaissance Swordfish flown by Sub-Lt Peter Roberts of 818 Squadron spotted some aircraft on a frozen lake. His TAG in U3B was L/Air John Blain:

> 'Suddenly, we noticed a group of German aircraft lined up on a frozen lake below us. We dived down to examine them, and flak came up, followed by a Dornier. I fired at the Dornier, but with the diving and twisting of the Swordfish I am quite sure that my efforts were purely token. We decided to return to the carrier, and I sent a radio message giving the position of the lake. On reaching the carrier we found that the radio operators had not received the signal, and my maintenance was suspect. However, the remainder of the two squadrons took off to bomb the lake.' [76]

There were eleven Ju52s dispersed on frozen Lake Hartvigvann.[77] They had arrived the previous evening carrying an alpine battery. At 1726, a strike of eight Swordfish from 816 and 818 Squadrons was launched to undertake the first dive-bombing attacks to be made by such aircraft:

816 Squadron

U4A	Capt A R Burch RM	Lt-Cdr H H Gardner	N/Air G N Thompson
U4B	Sub-Lt(A) J N Ball	Lt A S Marshall	N/Air R Pike
U4C	Mid(A) C D Livingstone	N/Air J R Bristow	
U4F	Lt A T Darley	Lt D Sanderson	N/Air T P Dwyer
U4K	Lt(A) K G Sharp	Sub-Lt (A) M St J Cardwell	L/Air F White
U4M	Sub-Lt(A) P J Broughton	Mid(A) W A B Bland	L/Air A J Atkin

818 Squadron

U3F	Lt(A) G Smith	Lt R Dyer	L/Air C D Milliner
U3K	Lt(A) S Keane	Lt D Langmore	L/Air L O Clark

Returning crews claiming two direct hits and others damaged by near misses. During this raid Capt Burch RM collected a large splinter from his own bomb in his starboard upper plane. Four of the Swordfish also carried out a strafing attack. Two Ju52/3ms of 3/KGrzbV.102 were totally destroyed and most of the others suffered blast damage. Two of the Swordfish did not reach the designated target and attacked a Do26 in nearby Beisfjord instead, where two of the flying boats from KGrzbV.108 were offloading supplies when the Swordfish attacked. One of the biplanes, P4167/U4B, was shot down by gunners of I/Flakregt.32. Sub-Lt Nigel Ball managed to force-land in the fjord, he and his crew (Lt Marshall and N/Air Pike) being rescued by the destroyer *Zulu*. The second Swordfish,

U4H, was also hit by flak, having both mainspars broken, but nonetheless managed to reach *Furious* and land safely. U4F, U4K and U4M also received minor shrapnel damage. L/Air John Blain added:

> 'They had not returned when darkness fell, so the captain decided to light up the flight deck for the returning aircraft to land on. They all returned safely.' [78]

The first Allied landings were well under way by now. In the north, British troops occupied Harstad in preparation for an attack on Narvik, and were later reinforced by French and Polish units. As the Harstad-bound troopships approached their destination, escorting destroyers located and sank *U-49*. British troops also went ashore in the Aandalsnes area to try to hold Central Norway with the Norwegian Army.

It was decided that the Skua squadrons at Hatston would continue the armed reconnaissance sorties to Bergen. Working under the same plan as before, two aircraft from 800 Squadron were despatched in company around 09:45 on **17th April**, some four-and-a-half hours later than intended due to weather. Each carried a single 250lb SAP bomb and eight 20lb Cooper bombs. Again, the actual reconnaissance was carried out at low level, from 5,000 feet to 1,000 feet. Lt Ned Finch-Noyes sighted a small warship, identified as *Bremse*, tied up at the Dokajeer jetty and dive-bombed her at 11:50, but no results were noted. Photos were taken and both aircraft headed back, Finch-Noyes making it to Hatston, but Capt Birdy Partridge RM, caught by a 180-degree shift in the wind direction, made a forced-landing at Sumburgh, his aircraft L3025/6A being seriously damaged when it overturned on the soggy ground.

Before dawn, at Stavanger, an RAF Hudson from 233 Squadron dropped flares and incendiaries over the airfield, one of these setting fire to a Ju52/3m hack of Stab/KG30, while the cruiser *Suffolk* shelled the area for some 80 minutes. As dawn crept over the area the Hudson was attacked by a Ju88C of Z/KG30 (4D+BH), Obfw Martin Jeschke identifying his opponent as a Blenheim in the gloom, and claiming to have shot it down. According to the Hudson crew however, their attacker had broken away and caused them no further trouble. As the Hudson departed, it passed a Walrus that had been launched from *Suffolk* to spot for her guns. Flying the Hudson was Flg Off Gron Edwards, who later wrote:

> 'The day before the operation there was a long planning session in the Operations Room. *Suffolk* was to shoot off one of her Walrus amphibians to spot for the gunfire, and if there was any difficulty; "i.e. when the poor sod is shot down" muttered Bill [Tacon] – a second Walrus would take over, and if he had any difficulty, then we would take over, Hudson No.2 taking over if we got the chop. Perhaps sensing a certain amount of unease, the Ops Room Controller added "We might be able get a fighter Blenheim over to give you backup." "How many 'lls' in bullshit?" muttered my navigator. 'A Mark IV Blenheim with enough petrol to get to Norway, have a scrap with a Hun, and still get back!!'
>
> 'If they were laying on four spotting aircraft they obviously considered that a few of us were going to cop it. We were to carry a load of incendiary bombs, the idea being – in the pre-dawn light – to start a fire of some sort on which *Suffolk* could sight her opening salvo. With a Naval lieutenant commander [Lt-Cdr Archie Fleming] to spot for the fall of shot, and a Naval signaller [N/Air Rine] on board we took

off just at 01:15 hours and circled Leuchars with our navigation lights on, waiting for our No.2 to join us. But could see no sign of him, so after a few minutes we switched off our lights and set off for Norway without him. We'd miss his backup. On our return, we learned he'd had complete electrical failure, so had had to go back.

'Having made our landfall and met up with *Suffolk*, we ran in on the aerodrome. Some anti-aircraft hate came up at us, but after we released our incendiaries we carried on and dropped a flare over the centre of the aerodrome as a further mark for *Suffolk*. I took up my spotting line just out to sea, saw the first four gouts of ruddy flame as *Suffolk* fired one gun from each turret, and handed over the direction of things to the Navy, being now fully occupied with anti-aircraft lookout. Also wishing that my No.2 would appear to give me support if I was jumped by anything.

'The gunner came up on the intercom. "Aircraft coming up astern. Looks like a fighter Blenheim." So they'd kept their promise ... Tracer smoke streaked six feet beneath me and spiralled ahead. I went into an immediate steep turn, slamming open the throttles. Then the gunner's belated "He's opened fire. It's a Junkers 88," came over the intercom. It was a forgivable error: in the still poor light before sunrise the frontal views of the Blenheim and the Ju88 were much the same. But it had enabled an aircraft of similar performance to get on my tail, and the pilot soon proved that he was no tyro. Try as I might, he remained on my tail, and I just couldn't get on his.

'A bullet going through the cabin of a metal aircraft makes a noise like cracking a whip and smashing a window at the same time, and they were now coming at depressingly close intervals. Then, as I looked over my left shoulder, I saw some of McAdie's bullets going into the region of his port engine. It looked as though he'd connected. Either that, or he had shot off all his ammunition, for he broke away and vanished to the south. Apart from the holes in the metalwork all seemed well with our Hudson. We'd kept no navigation log during the scrap, so it took a bit of time to find ourselves – about 20 miles south of Stavanger. Hurrying back to the shooting match, our reward was that *Suffolk*, apparently thinking that the Ju88 had won, let fly at us with her anti-aircraft guns. We fired off a recognition flare, indicated our profound displeasure on our Aldis signalling lamp, and carried on with the spotting. We got home in time for breakfast.'[79]

Suffolk had, in fact, launched both of her Walruses, the undercarriages of which had been removed to increase their endurance. They were launched at 45-minute intervals, the pilots Lt(A) Bob MacWhirter and PO(A) J McG Elliot (with Lt Hugo Bracken, the flight commander, as observer) being instructed to fly back to Aberdeen on completion of task. MacWhirter was launched in L2284 at first light, only to find conditions appalling and Stavanger airfield covered in snow. An aircraft initially identified as a Bf110 – presumably Jeschke's Ju88 – was sighted at 6,000 feet and N/Air Stanesby prepared his gun for action, but on re-sighting a twin-engined aircraft it was found to be a Hudson, obviously Flg Off Edwards' machine. On completion of his duty, MacWhirter as instructed set course for Scotland, reaching Aberdeen after flying for three and three-quarter hours, leaving sufficient fuel for just a further half-hour's flying – a close run call. They were followed in by the other Walrus, which also landed safely in Aberdeen harbour.

Her duty done, *Suffolk* – unaware that her shelling of the seaplane harbour at Sola had caused the total loss of four He115s of I/KuFlGr.106 and five He59s and a Bv138 of KGzbV.108 See – headed away from the danger area with her escort of destroyers as the daylight spread, but the ships soon came under attack as Luftwaffe bombers searched for them. First off were ten He111s of I/KG26, which departed from Sola at 08:15. Four of the bombers succeeded in finding the British units as they fled at high speed and *Suffolk* was hit twice by bombs, which did little to reduce her speed. The Heinkels were followed by shadowing Do18s, one of these (M2+KK) reporting three cruisers and four destroyers heading away west. More bombers were already airborne, a dozen Ju88s from II/KG30 finding the fleeing *Suffolk*, and she was hit again and severely damaged. At this point fate took a hand when a dozen RAF Blenheims arrived to attack Stravanger and these prompted the Ju88s to break off their attacks on *Suffolk*, allowing her to escape further damage. At noon, as *Suffolk* and her cohorts came within range of fighter protection from the Orkneys, word was received at Hatston requesting air cover. 803 Squadron was placed on alert to fly fighter patrols over her throughout the remainder of the day. Two Skuas of Green Section (Lt Harry Torin and Sub-Lt Ian Easton) were despatched immediately, meeting her 150 miles off the coast. Several German bombers were sighted at 13:40, but the duo was able to break up their attacks, one Do18 being claimed badly damaged. This may have been M2+KK of 2/KüFlGr.106, which had made the first sighting of *Suffolk* earlier in the day. The flying boat suffered engine damage, forced-landed at Haugesund in damaged condition, and sank; the crew got out safely and were rescued.

An hour later, six Skuas of 803's Blue Section (Lt Bill Lucy/Lt Alex Fraser-Harris/Lt John Christian) and Yellow Section (Lt Skeet Harris RM/Sub-Lt(A) Guy Brokensha/Sub-Lt(A) Freddy Charlton) arrived to relieve Green Section. At 1440, both sections shot up a He111 – obviously a straggler from a force of 22 Heinkels from I/KG26 that had again found the ships but made only ineffectual attacks. The Skuas claimed strikes on the Heinkel, Lt Harris (L2991) noting:

> 'With Sub-Lt Brokensha drove off several German aircraft – one He111 retired with white smoke pouring from both engines. Possible. Score No.1.'

Of this combat, his first, Sub-Lt(A) Brokensha (L2905/8K) wrote home to his parents in South Africa, describing the action in the main for the benefit of his two younger brothers:

> 'Skeet and I had one grand battle with one of those 111K jobs and vented our spite in an ugly rattle of musketry by pumping lead into his guts. No flames, no rubber dinghy in the sea, no visible blood, Hell! But I bet he had a sticky trip back home – if he made it.'

The third member of the section Sub-Lt Freddy Charlton managed to get in on the action:

> 'Lengthy chase by six Skuas on a He111 when only the fastest and most persistent got in stern attacks. After losing it in cloud, it was reported by another aircraft to have crashed in the sea.'

Despite this report, the 1 Staffel machine suffered only minor damage although a crewmember was wounded. Blue Section also chased away a shadowing Ju88. Lt Fraser-

Harris of Blue Section in (L2910/6H) noted:

'Engaged He111. Lost the swine in cloud. Think he was pretty full of lead.'

About 30 minutes later two sections of 801 Squadron arrived overhead. Red Section, led by Lt Robert Strange, chased off a snooper at 15:20. Red 2 (PO(A) Henry Kimber with N/Air Lionel Miles in L2912) in fact claimed the Heinkel shot down.[80] At 15:33, Yellow Section – Canadian Lt(A) Bill 'Moose' Martyn (L2917) and L2912 flown by Sub-Lt(A) Bernard Wigginton (ex-RAFVR) led by Lt-Cdr Peter Bramwell (L3005) – encountered a flying boat identified as either a Do18 or Do26, which they promptly shot down. This was in fact Do18D (836) K6+FH of I/KuFlGr.406 flown by Fw Karl Petersen. Another Do18, K6+HM, later landed to rescue the shot-down crew but found that they had drowned.[81] This particular flying boat was obliged to force-land on the sea a little later due to engine failure, but succeeded in taxiing to Lista. Later still, after refuelling, 803's Yellow Section and Blue Leader returned, this time leading a section of Gladiators from 804 Squadron and they covered *Suffolk*'s arrival at Scapa without further action. With her stern awash, the battered cruiser barely made it. A further force of Heinkels from III/KG4 that had been sent out to attack *Suffolk* found not the battered cruiser, but Admiral Layton's battle group returning to the Shetlands from the Aandalsnes area. Their attack on these warships proved no more successful.

Sheffield's Walrus was also active during the day, Lt Johnnie Groves with Lt-Cdr Geoffrey Hare (now returned to his normal duties) as his observer, having been launched in P5670 on a photographic reconnaissance of Trondheim and the surrounding fjords prior to planned army landings in that area. While flying over the town they spotted a number of He115s on the water, and the eager pilot shouted, with rather more enthusiasm than sense, "Look, sir – let's go down and beat them up." This produced the laconic reply from Hare: "Be your age, J. Groves, be your age. We're here to photograph them, not machine-gun them."

A reply hardly uttered when they saw fighters taking off from Vaernes airfield and the Walrus accordingly fled at her top speed low over the hills towards Namsos, so low that they carried away their trailing aerial on the pine trees. Three hours' flying, much of it at high speed, left them with barely any petrol by the time they made a water landing at Namsos, then in British hands. After interrogation by an intelligence officer, they poured a few cans of benzene, which they found, into the tanks and taxied off in darkness down the fjord. Hare believed *Sheffield* would be somewhere off the entrance, which in due course proved to be the case, although they reached her not without an altercation with a belligerent British trawler en route. After being out of radio touch with the ship for seven hours, the relief with which they were received was tempered not a little by annoyance on the part of the handling party who, after a full day at action stations, were called from their hammocks at 23:00 to hoist the Walrus aboard.[82]

Having taken aboard enough fuel at Tromsø to again steam, *Furious* sent off three aircraft at midday on **18th April**, one Swordfish to search seaward of the carrier to ensure that she could depart safely. A second was despatched to the Narvik area with orders to locate the Flag Officer Narvik – Admiral Lord Cork[83] – for further communication, while a third was sent to Narvik to photograph the area. At 13:50, while transiting the narrowest part of Grotsundfjord in company with two destroyers, *Furious* was surprised by a single FW200 of I/KG40, which dropped two 250kg bombs. One landed very close, badly whipping the hull, and stripping some of her turbine blades. Although she was able to continue operations, this damage would soon force her home for repairs. She recovered two of her aircraft but the third failed to return. P4214/U4K, returning to the carrier at low level after completing the photographic mission, hit a power line across the Kvalsund. In the resulting crash Lt(A) Frank Whittingham, the pilot was killed, while Lt(A) Ossie Cheeke and L/Air 'Pinky' White were both seriously injured, though quick action on the ground saved their lives.

Help would soon be on the way however, with the arrival at Scapa Flow of *Glorious*, to be followed three days later by *Ark Royal*. Both carriers were hurriedly re-stocked and re-provisioned in preparation for almost immediate operations with the Home Fleet off the Norwegian coast.

Next day (**19th April**), whilst on a reconnaissance sortie in Swordfish U3K of 818 Squadron, Lt(A) Stan Keane could not find *Furious* again due to thick fog. The aircraft was directed to Harstad but the weather was so bad it crash-landed at Skogsfjordvannet, Ringvassöya (an island near Tromsø). During the landing the left wheel broke through the ice of the frozen lake, which resulted in damage to the propeller and left wing. Lt(A) Keane and his crew, Lt Marshall and N/Air Les Clark, decided to wait for help. The aircraft was later dismantled by Royal Norwegian Navy air mechanics and transported to Skattøia seaplane base near Tromsø. A second Swordfish from 818 Squadron – P4163/U3G – also failed to return, having been shot down north of Narvik by German AA fire. The pilot, Sub-Lt(A) Peter Roberts was wounded, but rescued from the fjord in which the Swordfish crashed by the light cruiser HMS *Aurora*. The other two crewmembers did not survive. Observer Lt Charles Messenger RN succumbed to his injuries soon after being picked up, while TAG L/Air Tom Cutler was killed in the crash.

This day also witnessed the captured Arado Ar196A floatplane (ex-*Admiral Hipper*) touch down at Sullom Voe without challenge.[84] At the controls was Norwegian NAS pilot Lt Kaare Kjos, who had been ordered to fly to Scotland from Romsdalfjord, in company with the two Walruses – *Rodney*'s L5649 and *Glasgow*'s L2311, and the Norwegian MF-11 floatplane (F-346), although varying speeds meant that the formation had become split. Flying *Glasgow*'s Walrus was Lt(A) Johnny Ievers:

> 'After four or five days there was a favourable easterly wind and we set off for the Shetlands, which was the nearest point in the United Kingdom. The Arado was sent off ahead with *Rodney*'s observer [Lt Conway Bush] in the back. It was twice as fast as we were, and there was no point in keeping him with us doing 80 knots. Shortly after departure the wind went round to due west and started to blow Force 6 to 7. We went down lower and lower on the water until we were flying at about 100 feet to lessen the wind effect. After some three and a half hours with no Shetlands in sight, we decided to ask Hatston for a D/F bearing which was immediately forthcoming and told us 'You are bearing 090', which meant that not only had we missed the Shetlands but we were about to miss the Orkneys as well.
>
> 'After some four-and-a-half hours airborne and with fuel gauges showing virtually empty, out of the sky came a flight of three Sea Gladiators from 804 Squadron [Yel-

low Section comprising Lt-Cdr Cockburn, Lt Alex Wright RM and PO(A) Bert Sabey in N5509] which had been scrambled to investigate the bogeys approaching from the east! They proceeded to riddle the wretched Norwegian seaplane full of holes. Besides the Norwegian pilot there were three or four of his countrymen crowded in the back seat but mercifully none of them was hit. I decided the best thing was to get down on the water, which we did, being by then in the lee of the islands, and we taxied the last three or four miles rather ignominiously and beached the aircraft. The Arado meanwhile had flown straight into the Shetlands and landed at Sullom Voe without being challenged at all, with German markings [sic] and the lot. It always struck me as wonderful the British get shot down and the German comes in unscathed!' [85]

The next day Lts Bateman and Ievers were flown to London in the back seats of two Ospreys and spent the day being debriefed on the situation in southern Norway, culminating in a session with Winston Churchill, as Ievers recalled:

'I did not endear myself in replying to his question about the Norwegian reaction to how things were going by saying very tactlessly that all they wanted was to see a lot more British soldiers on the ground.' [86]

Skuas from 800 and 801 Squadrons individually raided Bergen on **20th April**, where E-boat *S.22* was sighted, attacked but not damaged. Capt Birdy Partridge noted: 'L2940. Attack on enemy warships at Narvik. No targets found. Attacked MTB at Bergen.' One Skua and crew was lost when Mid(A) John Crossley's 800 Squadron machine L2999 crashed between Lerwick and the Orkneys, his observer TAG L/Air, Maurice Hall also losing his life.

Allied ground forces in the Aandalsnes region now found themselves under severe air attack and called for assistance, feverish efforts being made to provide air support. On 19th April, the Gladiators of 263 Squadron RAF were ordered to Scapa Flow, there to embark aboard the carrier *Glorious* which had just arrived from Gibraltar. *Ark Royal* followed on her tail. The RAF Gladiators were flown aboard by FAA pilots from 802 and 804 Squadrons, much to the chagrin of the RAF pilots, one of whom, Flt Lt Stuart Mills, recalled:

'We were warned at short notice to move to Prestwick from where we should be embarking on an aircraft carrier. We guessed this meant Norway. Only minimum kit and equipment could be taken. Ground personnel, under Flt Lt Tom Rowlands, the squadron's other flight commander, departed for Rosyth, while we flew up to Prestwick. There I was able to buy one *Daily Telegraph* war map, which included part of Norway. We had no other maps of the country. We boarded *Glorious* off Prestwick on 22nd April. Much to our annoyance, Fleet Air Arm pilots, some of whom had had only limited experience of Gladiators, were detailed to fly our aircraft onto the carrier. One landed in the sea and was lost.'

Among the Gladiator pilots posted to *Glorious* was Lt Donald Gibson of 804 Squadron, who wrote:

'Our bliss was ended by the German invasion of Norway. We arrived above *Glori-*

> *ous* and I made my first operational deck landing. The Gladiator was one of those aeroplanes where the view ahead, when approaching the deck, was poor. I landed and was surprised not to feel the comforting deceleration of an arrester wire and I put this down to some error of mine in failing to pick one up. I was so astonished at having arrived at all that I relaxed, being brought to by the Flight Deck Officer, one 'Queenie' Easton, beating me over the head with his red and green flags, which I was supposed to be obeying. I had arrived in *Glorious* and, unknown to me, the war was getting rather more serious. I taxied on to the forward lift and beside me were two dead bodies of sailors, these poor men, goofing as we called it, had got in the way of the aeroplane before me which had taken a wave off.' [87]

Also joining the carrier were PO(A)s Dick Leggott and Johnno Johnson, who had been flying with 803 Squadron's sub-flight at Wick. Leggott recalled:

> 'Lt Charles Evans asked us to join him on *Glorious*. However, Evans didn't join *Glorious* [he had been given command of 806 Squadron] and this rather upset us. We had heard a few rumours about *Glorious* and soon we learnt that things were not at ease between the captain [Captain D'Oyly-Hughes] and his air staff, his Commander Flying, Commander J B Heath and Lt-Commander Flying [Lt-Cdr E H P Slessor].' [88]

However, on arriving aboard the carrier the two pilots were warmly greeting by Captain D'Oyly-Hughes:

> 'Captain D'Oyly-Hughes greeted us very kindly indeed. He liked his fighter squadron. There was never a difficult word between the fighter squadron CO (Lt Jack 'Ginger' Marmont) and D'Oyly-Hughes; Lt-Cdr Slessor and Commander Heath were also on the bridge, standing on one side. "I'm very pleased to see both of you," D'Oyly-Hughes said to us: "I know you've had a certain amount of experience in an operational squadron and have seen something of the enemy. You two will be much more valuable than those two standing there". He pointed at Slessor and Heath. I thought he was joking! I was about to give a polite social laugh when I saw Heath and Slessor looking so hangdog and dejected. I thought, Christ, what's going on? I was amazed Heath didn't say to the Captain, "Hey, steady on," or something. But he didn't. He just stood there, like a small boy. They were extremely nice people, both of them, Heath and Slessor. Maybe they were too nice to be in a situation like that.' [89]

Old hands aboard *Glorious* included Mid(A) Roy Hinton who had joined 823 Squadron as an observer in November:

> 'In 823 in *Glorious* we had a marvellous crowd. They accepted us, although when we were sent out we had very, very, very little experience; in fact it horrified the senior officers in *Glorious* when they heard how very little experience we had. We were shoved out there because they wanted people desperately, even though we were only half-trained. In those days you had literally, the two services, the Fleet Air Arm on one side, the RN executive types on the other. They certainly weren't the closely-knit service, that it subsequently became.' [90]

Fellow observer, 812 Squadron's Lt Alfie Sutton added:

'*Glorious* had a tremendous spirit, marred only by a growing apprehension as to the stability of the new Captain. But whilst I was in the ship there were enough of the old commission to hold us all together. We were front line squadrons and we reckoned that we were the elite of the Navy on whom the brunt of the war would fall in the early stages.'[91]

But when *Glorious* sailed on **22nd April**, her Swordfish squadrons were left ashore and she was carrying not only the 18 RAF Gladiators (including one Sea Gladiator to replace the lost Gladiator) but also 18 Sea Gladiators of 802 and 804 Squadrons, plus 11 Skuas of 803 Squadron. A twelfth Skua had been lost, as noted by Lt Skeet Harris RM: "Hatston to *Glorious*. Red Leader. Midshipman Griffith (Red 3) crashed landing on." The Skua (L2915/8R) skidded over the port side of the carrier, and although Stephen Griffith was recovered his TAG, L/Air Ken Brown,[92] was lost. *Ark Royal* followed *Glorious* with 21 Swordfish (810 and 820 Squadrons), 18 Skuas (800 and 801 Squadrons), five Rocs and one Walrus. 801 Squadron had a new CO, Lt Colin Campbell-Horsfall from 806 Squadron, although the former CO Lt-Cdr Bramwell was also aboard the carrier. Flt Lt Mills continued:

'The crew of *Glorious*, which had been hurriedly recalled from a long spell in the Mediterranean, was in a poor, even mutinous mood. They had had no shore leave with their families after a protracted absence abroad. D'Oyly-Hughes, the ship's captain, wanted the squadron to take off on 24th April at a point about 300-350 miles off the Norwegian coast and fly in from there to Lake Lesjaskog. He knew we had no maps of the landing area. We felt this to be quite unreasonable. Baldy therefore asked the captain if we could be put off much closer in - 150 miles off Norway. Because we had no maps, he also asked that two Navy Skua aircraft be put up to lead us to the frozen lake.'

The next 24 hours saw the arrival at Aandalsnes of an RAF advance party, whose job it was to unload servicing equipment for the RAF Gladiators, which were to operate from the frozen lake at Lesjaskog. Towards the end of the afternoon of **24th April**, the Gladiators began taking off from *Glorious*. In two flights of nine, they were led to the lake by Skuas flown by Sub-Lt(A) Guy Brokensha and Lt Harry Torrin, landing at 18:00. Of the epic flight, Brokensha later wrote home:

'I led the Gladiators to their frozen lake on account of their having no navigation. The weather was foul, snow, high wind and the most evil unfriendly sea I have ever seen – and cold, cold. After a bit of dithering we reckoned we could get through so off we went. Gosh, it was a grand sight – me leading and the Glads in perfect formation all round me. We went through the first few storms but it started getting worse, so because old arse-end Charlie was having a tricky time – visibility being practically nil in snow storms – I went round the rest and that called for some pretty handy navigation from my observer (a grand old Petty Officer who has been flying for 15 years, and with me since I got my section). My course steering must have been better than usual for we hit the coast bang where we aimed for – not bad after 150 miles of twisting and turning and changing winds. I climbed to 10,000 feet and then had to start map reading to find the lake. Our first sight of Norway, when we crossed the coast, was lovely.

'Everything looked peaceful, the fjords were as still as glass and the reflections of the snow-capped mountains, fir trees and small villages and fishing boats have to be seen to be believed. The country looked like a lovely chocolate cake with lots of icing on it, yet I couldn't help thinking it would be a tricky place to be shot down, force-landing grounds being just 'no-est'. However, after a little anxious milling around I found the lake and signalled the Glads into tight formation and we went screaming down all our 10,000 feet in a glorious hell dive. There was no sign of life when we first stuffed our noses down, I expect the poor troops thought it was the Prussians and made a quick dive for the bushes, but about halfway down the skating rink – that's what it looked like – suddenly became alive with figures.

'Down we roared and broke up at practically nought feet, the Glads zooming straight up again in a frenzy of upward rolls, loops and roll-offs. I can't compete in that line in our present cabs so we flogged round and watched the first few land accompanied by cheering troops leaping into the air frantically waving. I felt good. Andy, my observer, and I then slid down the valley and back to our old floating 'drome. On the way out of the valley we spent all our time waving and trying to show our roundels to terrified Norwegians, children included, who were running as though possessed or throwing themselves flat as we approached, obviously expecting to be gunned.'

Flt Lt Mills was leading the Gladiators:

'After one-and-a-half hours flying, the Gladiators were landing on the ice. I flew on for another 60 miles or so to Dombas rail junction to reconnoitre the area. The main road and rail track between Aandalsnes and Dombas had recently been heavily bombed.'

Two patrols from 803 Squadron were airborne from *Glorious* to provide cover for the RAF fighters, Lt Bill Lucy leading Blue Section in 8F, and Lt Skeet Harris RM leading Red Section in 8P.

Blue Section		**Red Section**	
L2925	Lt W P Lucy	L2881	Lt L A Harris RM
	Lt M C E Hanson		PO(A) K G Baldwin
L2910	Lt A B Fraser-Harris	L2991	Lt C H Filmer
	L/Air G S Russell		N/Air H Pickering
L2924	Lt J Christian	L3010	Sub-Lt I H Easton
	N/Air S G Wright		N/Air A J Hayman

At 17:55, a number of He111s were sighted, Red Section engaging one, as Lt Harris RM noted:

'Patrolled over Aandalsnes and Gladiator Lake [Lesjaskog]. Attacked several He111s. All dropped bombs and retired. One Heinkel severely damaged. [Victory] No.2?'

Having received attention from all three Skuas, the badly damaged 9/KG4 Heinkel

5J+JT managed to reach Oslo/Fornebu, where it crash-landed and was written off. The crew survived. At 18:20, Lt Bill Lucy and Blue Section spotted another German aircraft, identified as a Do17 but was in fact another Heinkel of 9/KG4. Although out of ammunition, Christian joined in the attack, allowing his gunner N/Air Gordon Wright to let loose with his Lewis gun. Their victim was 5J+AT flown by Uffz Schultz, on board of which were Staffelkapitän Hptm Martin Schumann and the Gruppenkommandeur of III Gruppe, Major Ernst Kusserow. The Heinkel belly-landed on fire south-east of Romsdalfjord. The burning aircraft skidded into a farmhouse before it came to a halt. Major Kusseow, who had been wounded during the attack, was strapped in securely and was fortunately rescued by people from the farm, while the remainder of the crew escaped safely from the burning aircraft, only to be taken prisoner.

Ark Royal also contributed two sections of Skuas to this duty, one from each of her squadrons, but two of these, L3050/6M piloted by Mid(A) Chris Treen (with N/Air Doc Goble) and L2877/7K flown by Lt Colin Campbell-Horsfall (with PO(A) Eddie Suggett), ran out of fuel on the way back and had to ditch. Both aircrews survived the icy water, although Campbell-Horsfall suffered injuries, were plucked out of the sea by escorting destroyers and later returned to their carrier, very much the worse for wear. Of the ditching, Doc Goble recalled:

'Our patrol area was over Namsos, then occupied by our troops, who were having a very bad time of it due to the absence of air cover. Our orders were to stay over Namsos as long as possible, and as air time at an economic speed was estimated at a maximum of five hours, we would be able to stay for no more than three hours. Namsos was, as expected, a shambles of fire and smoke and there seemed to be fighting to the south-east.

'Aircraft flying in tight formation require quite a lot of juggling with the throttle and, towards the end of the patrol my pilot, Midshipman Treen, was obviously getting rather anxious, as there were several calls to the flight leader, giving him our fuel state. Eventually, we left the area and made for the *Ark* and, as usual being the "tail end Charlie", we were the last to land. As we turned into the final approach, the engine just died and down we went into the drink. For all her many faults, the Skua did float, giving us ample time to get the dinghy out; alas, "it came away in me 'and, Sir," was ever the excuse, as I yanked on the release wire, only to find it dangling in my hand without freeing the dinghy, and so we had to scramble up toward the tail as the aircraft sank. We saw a destroyer approaching at speed and she swung to a halt with such a dramatic flourish that her wash drove our poor old Skua under and we had to swim for it. However, they launched a boat very quickly, and within ten minutes we were being helped over the side of the destroyer.

'The first person I saw was a Chief Petty Officer who had been my PO when I was a boy seaman on HMS *Danae* in 1935. He said that the bottle he offered me contained neat rum, but I was so cold that I neither tasted nor felt any effect from this 96 proof spirit. I was given the, then, standard treatment for hypothermia – although we called it something a lot more Anglo-Saxon than that. I was dunked alternately in hot and cold baths – if it didn't kill you, you were deemed to be cured!'[93]

Lt(A) Tom Gray only just reached the *Ark* in time to avoid a similar fate:

> 'My hook broke first go. Landed, no hook, but sand on deck [assisted landing]. About a gallon left. Panic!'

With Lt Campbell-Horsfall's brief command of 801 Squadron abruptly ended, Lt Robert Strange assumed temporary command. Meanwhile, 700 Squadron lost a Walrus during the day, L2316 operating out of Hatston on an anti-submarine patrol in the area of Fair Isle, (between Orkney and the Shetland Ilses), failing to return. It is believed the Walrus encountered a Do18 (probably from KüFlGr.406) and was shot down. PO(A) Cyril Smeathers, Mid(A) Paul Furber and N/Air Ed Adams were all reported missing. While searching for the missing aircraft, a second Walrus, P5660 flown by PO(A) Fred Thomson (with Sub-Lt(A) Fred Holmes and N/Air Harry Barrett) sighted another Do18, or possibly the same machine, which they decided to investigate. The Dornier, K6+GH of 1/KüFlGr.406, suddenly carried out an attack, getting on to the tail of the Walrus, which hastily jettisoned its bombs and dived for the sea. Barrett returned fire and after four minutes the Dornier broke off the action. Thomson manoeuvred the Walrus in an attempt to shadow the departing Dornier but owing to its superior speed contact was soon lost. The Walrus suffered no damage in the exchange.

25th April was anticipated to be a big day, as the arrival of the two additional carriers, this time carrying fighters, was expected to greatly assist the Army and Navy units operating in northern Norway. The big effort was to occur in and around Trondheim (where the Germans were), and Aandalsnes to the south and Namsos to the north (the British landing sites). By 03:00, the two carriers were in position. In an overcast sky, a Force 2 wind and 35-foot swells, the strike force went in several waves. With pairs of 802 and 804 Squadron Sea Gladiators providing cover in two-hour shifts, the first wave of Swordfish departed at 03:10, *Ark Royal* commenced launching 14, each armed with 4x250 lb GP and 8x20 lb Cooper bombs. Three of the five section leaders were Royal Marine pilots.

820 Squadron

A4A	Capt A C Newson RM	Lt-Cdr G B Hodgkinson	L/Air R H McColl
A4B	Lt(A) G R Humphries	L/Air C Pendleton	
A4C	Lt(A) D J Gudgeon	L/Air J Watson	
A4F	Lt B E Goulding	Lt A W N Dayrell	N/Air R Finney
A4G	Lt H de G Hunter	L/Air S Smith	
A4H	Lt R S Beveridge	L/Air T A Baker	

810 Squadron

A2A	Capt N R M Skene RM	Lt J E Smallwood	L/Air J Wayles
A2B	Lt A W Stewart	L/Air H W V Burt	
A2C	Sub-Lt(A) R C Eborn	L/Air P W Clitheroe	
A2P	Lt D F Godfrey-Faussett	Sub-Lt H E H Pain	L/Air T E Wibrow
A2Q	Sub-Lt(A) R B Pearson	N/Air J G Ellis	
A2R	Capt W H N Martin RM	Lt R A Crawford	L/Air H G Edwards
A2G	Lt AA Pardoe	PO(A) L M Lloyd	
A2K	Lt N R Corbet-Milward	L/Air J F Black	

At 03:30, L2768/A2K crashed on take-off, Lt Neville Corbet-Milward and L/Air Joe Black, being promptly rescued by the plane guard destroyer. The others set course for the airfield at Vaernes, Capt Alan Newson RM (with Lt-Cdr Guy Hodgkinson the CO as observer) leading six of 820 Squadron's Swordfish while Capt Nigel Skene RM, leading seven of 810 Squadron's machines, headed for Lake Jonsvatnet outside of Trondheim, where many German transport aircraft had been observed the prior evening. They had orders to switch to Vaernes if no enemy aircraft were found. At the same time, *Glorious* despatched five Skuas of 803 Squadron's Blue and Red Sections to attack shipping and seaplanes reported to be in Trondheim harbour. From there they were to shift to the lake and cover the slower Swordfish during their attack. The Skuas, being faster than *Ark Royal*'s Swordfish, arrived over Trondheimfjord at 04:40 and commenced their attack on nine He115s and six ships sighted in the harbour. The pilots from Blue and Red Sections were:

Blue Section

L2925	Lt W P Lucy
	Lt M C E Hanson
L2910	Lt A B Fraser-Harris
	L/Air G S Russell
L2924	Lt J M Christian
	N/Air S G Wright

Red Section

L2881	Lt L A Harris RM
	PO(A) K G Baldwin
L2991	Lt C H Filmer
	N/Air H Pickering

Lt Skeet Harris RM leading Red Section in 8P noted:

'Trondheim! Hit port oleo leg on arrester gear when taking off. Decided to carry on with raid with one leg flapping. Dive bombing attack by Blue and Red Sections on nine He115 floatplanes. Then escorted nine Swordfish, who bombed airbase. Returned and carried out low machine-gun attacks on floatplanes. Heavy AA fire encountered. Seven floatplanes sank. Remaining two damaged. Landed on OK on starboard wheel and port wingtip. Eight galls of petrol left!'

Actual losses were four He115s of I/KüFlGr.506 sunk and three more damaged. One Skua, L2910/8G, was hit by AA fire and forced-landed in Sorfjord in shallow water near a village. Lt Alex Fraser-Harris later reported:

'The water was extremely cold, and we had great difficulty in walking up the beach to a group of Norwegians. They were very unfriendly, but had mistaken us for German airmen, two of whom they had killed the day before. As soon as our identity was established, their attitude changed completely and we were given warm clothing and food. We were only a short distance from the German forts, and German patrols were on the roads. So, dressed as Norwegians, we were led by a guide to a small farm in the mountains. Shortly after our arrival several Norwegians came in from the vicinity of the German forts and also from Trondheim. From them I collected what appeared to be valuable and urgent information and decided to try to get through to British Headquarters forthwith. We travelled in Norwegian dress. A guide who spoke English and knew the way to the British lines arranged the journey. We left at 22:00 and walked to the head of the valley, where we got a sleigh from a farm. On this we travelled for 5 miles up to a lake in the mountains. Here we left the sleigh and at 03:30 set off on skis up a river valley to the north. Our efforts at this art were not a success, and we finally walked, going being fairly good on the frozen snow.'

After an eight-mile slog, they had breakfast in a farmhouse, boarded a second sleigh at 08:00 hours and finally reached another fiord where they boarded a small boat, which transported them to Folafo. Here, the obliging Norwegian police hired them a taxi, which carried them the final short distance to the British Brigade Headquarters. They had travelled a total of 69 miles in 24 hours. They finally rejoined the squadron aboard *Glorious* courtesy of the anti-aircraft cruiser HMS *Calcutta*.

Meanwhile at 04:50, 820 Squadron commenced its diving attack on Vaernes from 5,000 feet and in the face of intense AA fire. Three hangars were destroyed, some small buildings damaged and one or two large aircraft claimed destroyed. One of these was a Ju52/3m of KGrzbV.107. Meanwhile, having discovered no aircraft on Lake Jonsvatnet, 810 Squadron diverted to Vaernes, and at 05:25 they gave the airfield its second attack within an hour. Apart from the Ju52/3m, German losses included seven Ju87Rs of 1/StG1, which had just arrived at Vaernes. AA fire accounted for three Swordfish, 810 Squadron's K8879/A2R ditched near the destroyer HMS *Maori*, which quickly picked up the crew, of Capt Norrie Martin RM, Lt Crawford and L/Air Edwards; the same destroyer also picked up Capt Newson RM, Lt-Cdr Hodgkinson and L/Air Bob McColl from 820 Squadron's A4A, which ditched nearby, but L2790/A2G could not be found although *Ark Royal* received a signal from the crew about their predicament and an aerial search was sent off to lead a destroyer to them; Lt Arthur Pardoe and PO(A) Leslie Lloyd (ex-RAF) were lost. These two had survived a collision between two Swordfish back in November when hunting for the *Graf Spee* in the southern seas, but this time their luck had run out.

With the survivors of the first wave retiring, the Skuas of the second wave arrived. Between 04:15 and 04:30, *Ark Royal* had despatched nine Skuas (seven from 801, two from 800) under Lt-Cdr Peter Bramwell's command, while *Glorious* sent the remaining six Skuas of 803 Squadron's Green and Yellows Sections. Each aircraft was armed with a single 250lb GP bomb and 8x20lb Cooper bombs, and had orders to proceed independently to the various fjords surrounding Trondheim harbour and attack any enemy shipping sighted. The Skuas were unable to locate any warships in the harbour, so released their 250-pounders on two 5,000-ton merchant vessels and their 20-pounders on floatplanes, claiming one hit on a ship and many near misses. One section sighted a Ju88 on a frozen lake, which two strafed while the third attempted to bomb it as it prepared to take-off. Its gunner fired in defence of his aircraft and received a burst of fire in return from one of the strafing Skuas, which was believed to have silenced him and badly damaged the bomber.

803 Squadron's Yellow Section – Sub-Lt(A) Guy Brokensha (L2905/A8K), Sub-Lt(A) Freddy Charlton (A8M) and PO(A) Johnno Johnson (A8L) – meanwhile dive-bombed two oil tankers located in the harbour and set them on fire. 803's Green Section – Lt Harry Torin/Mid(A) and Tom McKee (A8A), Lt George Callingham and N/Air Des Prime (A8B) and Sub-Lt Ian Easton/N/Air Ginger Hayman (A8C) – having bombed a ship at Trondheim, ran into an impenetrable weather front while returning to the ship, and ultimately all three returned to the area of Namsos and made successful force landings. While orbit-

ing in an effort to find the carrier, a He115 was sighted and Lt Callingham attacked it at once, but his port guns jammed, although he was able to silence the rear gunner with only those in the starboard wing working. The floatplane (2248 of 2/KüFlGr.506) climbed for cloud and reached it, but was beginning to emit smoke. Seconds later it fell out of the cloud and crashed into trees on a mountainside near Størdalsøren, on the south-west bank of Trondheimsfjord; the crew baled out and were rescued by German troops.

Lt Callingham did not have enough fuel left to return to the carrier, so forced-landed A8B on a sand spit. He taxied along this until all his fuel had gone, but some French soldiers then appeared and helped pull the aircraft to safety. It could not be recovered however and was later destroyed by British troops. Meanwhile, Lt Torin in A8A came down on shore near Roan, south-west of Namsos, while Easton came down at Osen in A8C, neither he nor his New Zealand-born TAG being hurt. Fortunately, all three crews quickly linked up with Allied forces, though it would be some time before they got home.

At 04:55 and again at 05:55, *Ark Royal* launched sections from 800 Squadron to provide fighter patrols cover the Allied landing site at Namsos. The first patrol, Red Section (led by Lt Ned Finch-Noyes), intercepted another He115 but lost it in cloud. They then chased a big, four-engined aircraft identified as a Ju89 – probably one of KGrzbV.105's Ju90s – but could not catch this either before returning at 08:50. The other section returned at 10:15 having made no contact. By that point the weather had closed in and further flying was suspended.

Altogether, 34 Skuas and Swordfish had taken part in the morning's operations. Norwegian sources later reported that six seaplanes had been destroyed or damaged beyond repair, and five aircraft destroyed at Vaernes. However, the arrival of the RAF Gladiators at Lake Lesjaskog had not gone unnoticed and, during the afternoon, they were bombed and strafed by Ju88s and Bf110s, 13 aircraft being destroyed or damaged. The five surviving Gladiators flew over to the airstrip at Aandalsnes.

Early next morning (**26th April**), six 801 Squadron Skuas were launched from *Ark Royal* to patrol over the little port at Aandalsnes, and these were soon in action. Three He111s from 5/KG54 and three from 4/KG54 had been despatched on armed reconnaissance over the Otta-Loma Grotli area. Both formations were spotted by the Skua pilots at about 11:45, and the 5/KG54 trio was intercepted over Lesjaskog, one flown by Fw Richard Gumbrecht being attacked by Lt(A) Moose Martyn and N/Air Reg Davies in A7C. His fire mortally wounded Fw Willy Stock, the belly gunner in 5J+CN (1526), and also struck the starboard engine. Lt-Cdr Peter Bramwell and Lt John Collett in A7A then attacked. It was believed that he damaged the Heinkel's other engine although it seems that this had already been hit by a splinter from an AA shell, and lacked sufficient power to keep the aircraft in the air. Lt-Cdr Bramwell's aircraft was then hit by return fire from the defiant gunner, Bramwell sustaining a minor wound that compelled him to break off the attack.

With the bomber sinking rapidly, and unable to avoid crashing into a mountain now looming ahead, Fw Gumbrecht put the Heinkel down on its belly in the snow on the mountainside at Digervarden. The three survivors, Gumbrecht, Obfw Günther Hölscher and Fw Karl Stolz (who had been wounded), climbed out as the Skuas thundered overhead. The survivors' consolidated account revealed:

'During the attack Stolz was hit three times and Hölscher escaped death by a miracle; he had just gone back to see what had happened to Stock when a neat row of bullets punctured the fuselage exactly where he had been sitting. In the meantime, Gumbrecht struggled to keep airborne. The starboard engine had overheated and had to be stopped while the other was running – just. Gumbrecht considered it was time for baling out, but both Hölscher and Stolz disagreed since it would mean leaving the presumably unconscious Stock in the crashing aircraft. Unable to keep the bomber in the air Gumbrecht was left with no alternative but to try a belly-landing somewhere among the snow-covered mountains. They hit the ground just short of the highest mountain top and the bomber skidded along on the snow for some 300 metres before it finally came to a rest.' [94]

The German airmen set out in deep snow, hoping to reach German forces at Kvam, but after three days they were captured.[95] A second Heinkel was attacked by Sub-Lt(A) Bernard Wigginton (A7B) and this was last seen losing height and pouring smoke, being claimed as a probable.

As the KG54/801 Squadron combat had been taking place, *Glorious* was launching three more Skuas from 803 Squadron, and somewhat later at 13:08 these also intercepted He111s, part of a force of ten from II/LG1, fourteen from III/LG1 and eleven from I/KG26, which were undertaking a concentrated attack on Aandalsnes and Lesjaskog, where they claimed one Gladiator destroyed on the ground. The bomber crews reported having seen the two other Gladiators, which had got into the air, attempting to catch them, but without success. Three of the I/KG26 bombers were attacked over Storfjord by the Skuas flown by Lt Bill Lucy in A8F, Lt Kik Filmer in A8Q and Lt John Christian in A8H. The windscreen of A8F was at once covered in a film of oil and Lucy had to break away to clean it before returning to the fight. Filmer meanwhile made an individual attack, damaging one bomber:

'At about 13:00, flying at 8,000 feet, I observed three Junkers 88s [*sic*] travelling in the opposite direction, to the southward. I immediately rocked my wings to draw the leader's attention and set off in pursuit. The enemy aircraft were about to make a bombing attack on Aalesund and were flying fairly slowly, so I caught up with them in about five minutes. As I got within range and fired a burst they turned, still in formation, down to the right and in the opposite direction. I followed, firing all the time at the left-hand aircraft until I was within less than 100 yards range. As I broke away to the left and downward I felt my aircraft being hit. Petrol flooded the cockpit, getting in my eyes before I could pull my goggles down, and there appeared to be an oil leakage somewhere. The aircraft I had attacked was by this time losing height rapidly with smoke pouring from the starboard engine. The other two machines were circling over it.'

Lucy and Christian resumed the attack from the beam, but the bombers then began to draw away from them, one apparently dropping out of formation as they went. In fact two Heinkels of 2 Staffel had been damaged, though neither was very badly hit. In one, a member of the crew was killed, and in the other two were wounded. Lucy and Christian then attacked an aircraft identified as a Do17, before sighting another He111 below, this time L1+KT of 9/LG1. Several passes were made on this latter, and it lost height pouring smoke; the undercarriage came down and the stricken aircraft finally pancaked into the eastern end of Romsdalsfjord sinking after three minutes. Some members of the crew were seen swimming to the shore as the two Skuas, both of which had been damaged during the fight, headed back for their carrier. Uffz Theodor Mertens and his crew were all reported missing; in fact two died in hospital (Ltn Eberhard Kahl, the observer, and air gunner Gfr Heinz Föhr), one became a prisoner (Mertens) and one (Fw Gerhard Rein) was freed later by German troops. Lt Filmer, meantime, realised that he was going to have to crash-land his damaged aircraft, L2991/8Q:

> 'My engine suddenly began to run very roughly indeed; so much so that I thought the engine would tear away from its mountings. The throttle was useless, moving the lever either way made no difference to the revolutions. I then saw smoke coming from beneath the instrument panel so I switched off the ignition. No more smoke issued, but the airscrew continued to turn at 1,600 revs. until I was down to 4,000 feet, when it suddenly stopped completely. At about 1,000 feet, I switched on the ignition momentarily, but the smoke appeared once more so I switched off finally.
>
> 'During this time I had tried to obtain an answer from my observer, Acting Petty Officer [Ken] Baldwin, but with no success. Looking through my rear window I could see him lying on his back so assumed he was either killed or wounded. I could see no fields below large enough to have made a good landing, so decided to force-land in the sea in Aalesund harbour, near enough to the jetty to enable my observer to be rescued quickly. I pancaked on the water with the undercarriage up, undid my straps and climbed aft to help Baldwin. He was dead however, having received a burst in the head. I then pulled the dinghy release grip, but no dinghy appeared and before I had time to lever open the compartment the nose sank quickly, air pouring out of the flotation tank in the port wing, which had been hit. I was now in the water holding on to the fuselage, and tried to put more air into my life-saving jacket, but found this impossible as the coldness of the water had taken my breath away. I then tried to climb onto the tailplane, but this was also impossible as the fuselage was too slippery and my legs and arms were paralysed by the water. I hung onto the parachute release wires until help came. I was taken to hospital and was very kindly treated.'

During the mid-afternoon period, three 800 Squadron Skuas led by Capt Birdy Partridge RM attacked one of two He111s from 5/KG54 which were bombing the sloop HMS *Flamingo*. No obvious effects of this interception were seen, but return fire wounded PO(A) Jack Hadley in A6C and, indeed, the gunner of one of the Heinkels submitted a claim for a Skua shot down. Despite wounds to his face and head, Hadley believed he shot down the Heinkel and was able to reach the carrier and land safely. Armourer Ron Jordan recalled:

> 'Hadley got shot through the nose and another bullet in his head rest. His nose swelled up, it closed his eyes, and he half crashed on landing. He skidded one way, then across, zigzagging down the flight deck. We were ready to leap up and unload the guns and we didn't know which way to run.' [96]

The final engagement of the day occurred during the evening when six Skuas of 800 Squadron, launched from *Ark Royal* two hours earlier, attacked an He115 of l/Kü-FlGr.506 and undertook a running battle with it. Lts Ned Finch-Noyes (L3000), Ken Spurway and James Rooper all exhausted their ammunition before the floatplane escaped, believed to have been very badly damaged and streaming fuel from both floats. In fact, it had suffered only minor damage, although the radio operator was wounded.

Furious was at long last ordered to return to Scotland, having been operating non-stop off Norway for the past two weeks. Two days previously she had reported two propeller shafts out of action, as a result of the earlier near miss. One of her wounded airmen, N/Air Jack Skeats commented:

> 'The old *Furious* and her aircrews almost burned themselves out with the tremendous pressure of operations. Her machinery badly needed rest and repair.' [97]

As did her aircrew. The carrier was safely berthed in the Clyde by 07:00 on 29th. Her captain, Captain Troubridge, made a general signal that:

> '... since leaving the Clyde on 8th April, *Furious* aircraft have flown 23,870 miles, dropped eighteen torpedoes, 15½-tons of bombs, lost 50 per cent of planes, and had seventeen hit by enemy fire, taken 295 photographs. Casualties – three killed, seven wounded, two missing feared dead.'

The ship well deserved the commendatory signals from the Fifth Sea Lord, from Churchill and from the Chief of the Air Staff, and her air group in particular merited their Captain's comment in his report:

> 'It is difficult to speak without emotion of the pluck and endurance of the young officers and men who flew their aircraft to such good effect. All were firing their first shot in action – whether torpedo, bomb or machine-gun; many made their first night landing [on a carrier] on April 11th and, undeterred by the loss of several of their shipmates, their honour and courage remained throughout as dazzling as the snow-covered mountains over which they so triumphantly flew.' [98]

The remaining handful of RAF Gladiators, by now at Setnesmoen, were now forced to cease operations due to lack of aircraft and fuel. In two days 49 sorties had been made, resulting in 37 interceptions and claims for six aircraft shot down, with numerous others damaged. The following evening the last three Gladiators were destroyed by the unit's ground personnel, who then embarked on the French freighter *Cap Blanc*, where they joined the pilots. There seems little doubt that, but for the weight of Luftwaffe bombing, the Allied forces at Namsos and Aandalsnes could have held on for much longer but, with the virtual destruction of the RAF Gladiators in such a short period however, the C-in-C of the Expeditionary Force decided that Central Norway would have to be abandoned and the Allied fortunes pinned on the north. Consequently, during **27th April**, withdrawal was planned – and the evacuation of Aandalsnes and Namsos soon got under way. Meanwhile in the north, reinforcements of French Alpine troops, Foreign Legionnaires and Polish infantry began arriving at Harstad for the proposed capture of Narvik. The abandonment of the Trondheim area would leave the Luftwaffe free to operate from Vaernes airfield, from which they would be able to operate over Narvik; thus an urgent search for possible fighter airfields by the Allies was begun. The Norwegian Air Force bases at Bardufoss and Banak offered themselves, whilst undeveloped ground at Skaanland also appeared promising.

Over Aandalsnes the Fleet Air Arm redoubled its efforts to provide air cover and combats were frequent throughout the day. In the morning two Do215s of 1(F)/ObdL and a He111 of 1(F)/122 undertook reconnaissances to the north, spotting the warships of Admiral Wells' force, including the carriers identified as *Ark Royal* and *Eagle* [*sic*]. Meanwhile, *Glorious*' Sea Gladiators got their first chance against the Luftwaffe at 09:35, when three 804 Squadron aircraft and one from 802 Squadron were scrambled, catching the reconnaissance Heinkel (2117) ten minutes later. The intruder was low over the water some 20 miles from the fleet when engaged. Lt Richard Smeeton (N2275) led the section (including T/Lt(A) Bill Taylor, an American[99]) down to attack, the Heinkel making off at top speed and gradually drawing away, although it was seen by Sub-Lt Rod Lamb to touch the wave-tops three times. The bomber had been badly damaged, and forced-landed on a frozen lake at Storvatnet, well to the north-west of Trondheim, 65% damaged, the crew claiming that they had shot down one of the Sea Gladiators in return.

The main target for the German bombers remained the southern arm of the British pincer movement on Trondheim. Heinkels from KG26, KG54 and LG1, and Ju88s of KG30 attacked Aandalsnes town and harbour, shipping in Molde and Romsdalsfjord, and ground targets to the south. Four waves of bombers were sent out from 12:00 onwards, the first comprising six He111s from 4/KG54. These were followed, an hour later, by 18 He111s from III/KG 26, which were intercepted by three 800 Squadron Skuas flown by Capt Birdy Partridge (A6A), Lt Teddy Taylour (A6B) and Sub-Lt Bas Hurle-Hobbs (A6C). The fighters had taken off soon after midday and caught a Heinkel of 9/KG26 bombing HMS *Flamingo* off Aandalsnes. The bomber, 1H+CT (3178), commanded by Ltn Horst Schopis, forced-landed south of Grotli, with Uffz Hans Hauck killed in the attack, and Uffz Josef Auchtor wounded. Capt Partridge later wrote:

> 'I saw a Heinkel carrying out a bombing run on the sloop HMS *Flamingo*, which was lying fairly close in just off Aandalsnes. The Heinkel was 1,000 feet higher than we were and I was now climbing flat out to try to get above him, but before we could get anywhere near he dropped his bombs, which missed and was away to the south with a good two miles lead. Now the chase was on! After ten minutes with throttles jammed wide open I was at the same height as my quarry and gaining slowly but surely on him. 600 yards astern of him now and his rear gunner started firing at me, though I was hardly within his range for accurate shooting, but the thought did cross my mind that he might have a lucky shot! Being the leader of my flight I was obviously going to arrive ahead of my other two aircraft who were also flat out and trying to keep up with me. I held my fire until I was about 400 yards astern when I opened up with a long burst, closed in to 300 yards and let him have the rest of 600 rounds per gun. I was now out of ammunition but the Heinkel had smoke pouring from his port engine and was being attacked from below by one of my other Skuas. He was also losing speed and there was no fire coming from his rear gunner. My observer asked me to pull out on the beam of the enemy so that he could have a go with his rear gun, and I started to do this, then decided against it. The Heinkel was losing

height rapidly so further attack was unnecessary and seemed to me too much like kicking a man when he was down. I was later told not to be so chivalrous and that I should have blown him out of the sky: I'm still glad I didn't. Instead I called my other two aircraft off and when they had formed up on me asked my observer for a course back to the ship. There wasn't much time left for us to continue the patrol and I was of no use without front gun ammunition.' [100]

His observer Lt Robin Bostock added:

'I managed to get in a couple of bursts with my gun and Birdy (my pilot) got in several good bursts. We saw our Heinkel go down and crash-land on the side of a hill. We felt rather elated and started to look for another suitable victim when I heard a shout from Birdy that something was wrong with the engine, and, sure enough, within a few minutes it started to cough and splutter. The Heinkel must have hit us somewhere.' [101]

Capt Partridge:

'Then suddenly, as I was swinging round onto our new course, my engine cut dead without warning and we were surrounded by a shattering silence ... I had often thought about what I would do if I found myself in a really desperate situation. Sometimes I imagined I would panic, or perhaps even die of fright; but now that it had happened, to my astonishment I was in a mood of fatalistic calm with no panic whatsoever. I was to experience this same reaction on later occasions, but I think it would have been more creditable if my calm had been more aggressive and less fatalistic. Outwardly, however, I appeared to be completely in control and unperturbed. Our long chase lasting about 26 minutes had taken us inland in a southerly direction and certainly well out of gliding distance of the sea where there would have been a reasonable chance of a wheels-up crash landing and getting away with it. We were down to 11,000 feet now and gliding ever so silently, too silently! Below and around us there was nothing to be seen but snow and mountains, the most inhospitable and impossible terrain for a forced-landing, and also impossible for baling out. Not much use to land by parachute on top of a snow-covered mountain and be subsequently frozen to death.' [102]

Lt Bostock:

'I hurriedly looked around for a nice soft spot to land, but all I could see was miles of snow with great jagged rocks sticking up. At last we saw what appeared to be a road running round the bottom of a hill and, as by this time the engine seemed to have completely seized up, Birdy tried to put her down there. Actually he pulled off a very good forced landing, but unfortunately, what we had thought to be a road was in actual fact a sort of moraine [a ridge of rock]. The appearance of a road had been given by the small stones and mud underneath the snow brought to the surface by the sun's heat. Of course, the landing made a mess of our aircraft. We were both unhurt, and after climbing out we looked around and decided that the only thing to do was to burn the aeroplane and then try to find some sort of shelter. The weather was fair, in that it wasn't snowing. But as usual it was bitterly cold.

'I took my navigating instruments and confidential books out of the aircraft and Birdy took a few things from his cockpit. Then we set fire to the aircraft. It burned beautifully, and having seen it well alight we set off. I soon found that walking through six or eight feet of soft snow – looking like a Christmas tree, with our chart-boards and other instruments – was not altogether as easy as it had seemed. In fact I soon decided to get rid of my encumbrances. We buried everything except the confidential stuff, and just about this time we saw a small hut towards the top of the hill, near where we had crashed. We decided to make for this, not only to get some shelter but also to give us a chance of seeing where we were. I knew we could not be very far from Aalsund.

'After what seemed to be a very long time – and it is amazing how the clear atmosphere deceives one in estimating distances – we arrived very hot, very tired but triumphant, at the top of the hill and the hut. There was no door and absolutely nothing at all inside. It was just a log box. It was of course better than nothing, particularly as it was beginning to get dark – or at least as dark as it ever did get at that time of the year. We went in and started to tear off bits of bark and chips of wood to make a fire.

'We did manage to get some sort of blaze going, and I suppose we must have been there about fifteen or twenty minutes when we heard a whistle outside. Somewhat startled because we thought there was no one else within miles of us we rushed to the door, Birdy leading. To our amazement we saw five or six Huns [there were in fact only three including the wounded observer Uffz Auchtor] dressed in flying clothes coming up the last few hundred yards of the hill towards our hut. The first one, who had just blown his whistle, was carrying a revolver, and as far as we could see all the rest had some sort of weapon. We, on the contrary, possessed between us one pocket-knife. Something had to be done and Birdy did it. After only a few moments' hesitation he stepped out of the doorway and shouted, "Do any of you speak English?" I think the Huns must have been just about as surprised as we were ourselves; at any rate, after a slight pause, the leader shouted back that he could speak English. By this time they were all collected in a bunch about 20 yards away and all had drawn their revolvers. This did not seem to deter Birdy in the least. He simply shouted, "Come here! You are my prisoners. There was a most painful silence, which seemed to last for years. Then they all stepped forward and held their hands up! It had worked. And now, having got our prisoners, we had to decide what to do with them. After a number of questions and answers in broken English, we discovered that the Huns were the crew of our Heinkel. They had crashed on the other side of the hill, and having burned their aircraft had seen the hut and had made for it with the same idea as ourselves. It was an awkward situation, to say the least, and we thought it better to say we were the crew of a Wellington reconnaissance aircraft. This seemed to satisfy them, although the nearest they could get to Wellington was "Welling-bomb."

'One thing they all flatly refused to do was to part with their guns, and for a time things looked awkward. However, while we were outside the hut and Birdy was arguing with them, I noticed that there was some sort of large building halfway down the hill on the other side, and eventually we told the Huns that they could stay in the hut for the night, and that we were going down the slope to the other place. They were to report to us there next morning. When we got to this house we found that it was a chalet or hotel, quite empty. Having forced our way inside via a window we found that not only were there beds and sheets – but provisions as well. We decided that a packet of 'Quaker Oats' seemed about the safest item, and after a meal of this and biscuits we turned in and had what was really, under the circumstances, a most comfortable night.

'Next morning we were both up early, and I started to make some more porridge for breakfast, while Birdy went outside to see what the weather was like. He had not been gone more than a minute or two when he came running back with the news that our Teutonic "friends" were on their way down the hill towards us. Of course, we had naturally hoped that they would run away during the night: the last thing we wanted was to have fully armed Germans in our company, in what amounted to enemy territory. However, when they did arrive outside our hotel the leader greeted us quite submissively with, 'You told us to report in the morning, and here we are.' He and one of the NCOs spoke very indifferent English. The latter, to our great surprise, was a Jew. There did not seem to be much love lost between him and the rest of the crew.' [103]

The German-Jewish airman was 25-year-old Fw Karlheinz Strunk. Lt Bostock continued:

'After Birdy and I had talked the matter over, we decided that he should go off and try to get help while I stayed behind in charge of our "prisoners." The Jew didn't like the idea of remaining with his friends and requested most earnestly that he be allowed to go with Birdy. So they went off while I took the Huns inside and started to make some porridge for them.

'It must have been about three or four minutes after Birdy and the Jew had left when I heard a shot, and immediately jumping to the conclusion that the Jew had shot my pilot I seized the only available weapon – a bread knife – and went outside to see what I could do about it. Sure enough, when I got outside there was Birdy lying in the snow, but to my surprise the German was standing with both his hands in the air. I then saw that a Norwegian ski patrol had arrived on the scene – we afterwards learned that they had seen our aircraft burning the night before and had been sent to investigate. There were only four Norwegians and they had divided themselves into two pairs, one in front of the house and the other going round behind. When they saw me they motioned me forward, and indicated that my hands should go up as well. At the same time, to my great joy, Birdy stood up. The Norwegians had fired a warning shot when they saw him, and being a sensible man he had decided that the closer he got to mother earth the better.' [104]

Of this latest twist Capt Partridge wrote:

'Off we set, an ill-assorted couple [he and Fw Strunk]. I wasn't doing very well on my skis as I kept on losing one, but my German companion really was floundering and after I had gone some 200 yards or so I was beginning to outdistance him by 20 or 30 yards and thought that at this rate I was likely to arrive at the farmhouse well ahead of him. This comforting thought was rudely shattered by the vicious crack of two rifle shots, a cry from the German and a spurt of snow between my legs. I looked back to see the German collapsed motionless in the snow with an ominous spreading red stain, then looked up and around to see that we were surrounded by a ski patrol dressed all in white and that I was covered by five steadily-held rifles. There was another shot and the snow spurted up just alongside me. It must have been a warning because if they wanted to kill or hit me they could hardly miss at that range. I stood still with my hands up and as they approached me I heard Robin come storming out of the hotel having heard the shots. I let out a great shout to him to stand still and put his hands up, which thank God, he immediately did. You would have thought that my situation was just about as dire as it could get, but fate had even one more trick to play. There was suddenly the roar of an approaching aircraft and a Heinkel 111 appeared fast at about 3,000 feet and proceeded to machine-gun the lot of us. We all hit the snow regardless of nationality and remained motionless until the sound of the aircraft faded into the far distance. Then we all got up except for the huddled grey figure in the snow with an ever increasing crimson mark spreading around him. The fact that a German aircraft was attacking this area confirmed what I had thought, that we were in Norwegian-held territory, and that the ski patrol was Norwegian.' [105]

Lt Bostock takes over again:

'While two of the patrol held us up, the other two routed out the rest of the Heinkel crew, and we were all paraded in a line with our hands up. Birdy and I did our best to tell the Norwegians that we were British, but although they could speak a sort of English, they were not prepared to accept our word without proof. The situation was rather tricky. They seemed to have an idea that we might have guns or weapons stuck in the tops of our flying boots, and the fellow in front of me said, "Take off your boots." I lowered my hands to comply when a loud voice from behind me said, "Put up your hands." As he accompanied this last order with a jab in the back from his rifle, I thought he deserved more attention, and so put my hands up again. This was greeted by a shout from the front to the effect that my boots must come off, and so in desperation I started to put my hands down again. The man at the back seemed quite infuriated by this and threatened that unless my hands did stay up he would shoot me. I think I might say that the situation had now grown rather more than tricky. I know I didn't like it a bit.

'Then Birdy had an idea, and between us we tried every dialect and language known to us both, from "Look 'ere, 'old cock" to "Bai Jove, old man" including schoolboy French and Spanish. But all to no effect. Then I had a brilliant idea. I quickly dropped my left hand, turned my breast pocket inside out, showing the tailor's label, and shouted, 'Look – Gieves – London,' and it worked like a charm. Birdy clinched the matter by producing a half-crown coin displaying the King's head. They were still a little suspicious, but we two were allowed to put our hands down and were treated in a rather more friendly manner. Very soon afterwards the officer in charge of the patrol arrived, and he could speak English. We got on very well from then on, and it was an amazing coincidence when he discovered that his sister was married to a very great personal friend of Birdy and I – a lieutenant commander in the Fleet Air Arm. To meet his brother-in-law in the middle of Norway under those circumstances, and at that time, seemed like a miracle.

'The ski patrol officer then told us that as the snow was rather deep and the nearest town, Aalsund, was three miles away, he would send a man to collect some skis for us, and in the meantime he would lend us his to practise with. Eventually the messenger returned – not with skis – he had been unable to find any – but with two Norwegian nurses who had come up to see the British "heroes." As it was only three miles and the snow was fairly hard, we decided we would walk, and at about 8 o' clock that night we set off. It was not until we had been walking for about an hour that one of the nurses casually remarked to me that a Norwegian mile was equal to seven British. We did it, although I don't know how. We eventually staggered into Aalsund, for myself, more dead than alive, and there our Norwegian friends left us in, the care of a marine major [probably Major Lumley RM].

'We tried to get transport on to Aandalsnes, but Aalsund was by now reduced to a pile of rubble, and we were being bombed round the clock. After spending several days trying to find some means of getting across to Aandelnes, we eventually managed to commandeer an old motor car and some petrol, and after tinkering with the engine we started on the last part of our journey. What with bombs and bomb craters, falling masonry, and similar hazards, the journey was not uneventfu. But we arrived safely at the fjord separating the two towns, and eventually found the so-called car ferry. It consisted of an open barge propelled by oars, and the sole man in charge, an elderly Norwegian, flatly refused to venture either himself or his contraption across the fjord. By this time we were getting desperate, because we had heard that the evacuation of the British Expeditionary Force had commenced.

'At the point of our borrowed pistols we forced the old man to take our car on board, and· we cast off. The water was fairly calm, and we got about half-way across without untoward incident when we heard a sudden increase in the gunfire, which of course was going on the whole time, and an even greater increase in the bomb explosions. The noise appeared to be coming from farther up the fjord, and thinking that we were in a conspicuous position, we redoubled our efforts at the sweeps. After a few minutes, we saw a British cruiser coming down the fjord very fast, zigzagging all over the place, and being pursued by what seemed to be every German aircraft in the area. Her guns were blazing, but during the time she was in sight I did not see her hit – although to us in our small boat it appeared to be raining bombs. Somehow, and I cannot explain why, we were not hit either by bombs or the cruiser, although we thought some of the near misses were much too close. This was pretty well the end of our journey. We reached the other side safely and drove into what was left of Aandalsnes, where we found that the rumour was true, and our troops were being evacuated.' [106]

Meanwhile, four more Skuas from 803 Squadron were also up, having taken off from *Glorious*, but as this carrier was now ordered to withdraw to refuel, the pilots were advised to land on *Ark Royal* on termination of their patrol. It was a successful patrol for Yellow Section (Lt Skeet Harris RM in L2910 and Sub-Lt(A) Guy Brokensha in L2905/A8K) who intercepted a Heinkel, which was also attacking *Flamingo* – and forced it down on a hillside at Bjorli near Romsdalsfjord, before coming aboard *Ark* at 14:35. Harris recorded:

> 'With Sub-Lt Brokensha carried out a patrol over Aandalsnes. Encountered one He111 and attacked after Brokensha. Both engines stopped. Crashed on mountainside. Certainly No.1. Landed on the *Ark*.'

Guy Brokensha added:

> 'Skeet and I worked in a grand combination: I go in, burst at the rear gunner, fix starboard engine. Skeet in, rear gunner short burst, fix port motor, fairly knocked 'em down.'

Two of the German crew from the downed Heinkel – 1H+JP of 7/KG26 – were wounded/injured. Fw Hans Giezen and Gfr Kurt Sipps and were taken to the local hospital at Aandalsnes, from where they were later liberated, while the aircraft commander, Oblt Hans-Ludwig Steinbach, and observer Uffz Willi Liermann attempted to reach German-held territory only to be captured by British troops and taken to England.

At 15:15, five Skuas – three of 800 Squadron and two from 801 – were off on patrol as a large bombing force approached. Six Heinkels of II/KG26 and twenty-six Ju88s from KG30, were followed by thirteen more Heinkels of KGr.100. The Skuas intercepted two Ju88s, which were dive-bombing a convoy entering Aandalsnes harbour an hour later; both made off to the south with engines apparently on fire (but probably pouring black exhaust smoke). Two aircraft identified as Do17s [*sic*] were then driven off, before a formation of He111s were seen approaching (the KGr.100 aircraft). All five Skuas attacked, and one Heinkel turned for home with an engine on fire. By now all ammunition had been expended and the Skuas returned, one crew reporting that during the fight they had been attacked by a Ju88. The Heinkel initially credited as a probable to the 800 Squadron men – Lt Ned Finch-Noyes (L3000), PO(A) Eric Monk and Mid(A) Len Gallagher – was an aircraft of 2/KGr100, which had been badly damaged before lack of fuel had caused the Skua pilots to break away. Obfw Richard Hansel attempted to get his bomber back to Stavanger, but the damage was too severe, and he subsequently forced-landed near Hoyanger on Sognefjord. Here the crew set fire to the aircraft before becoming prisoners but were liberated a few days later. During the German raids, the Norwegian MV *Nyhaus* was sunk in Moldefjord, while the British tanker *Delius* and the sloop HMS *Black Swan* were both damaged. Aboard Obfw Paul Wiersbitzki's 2/KGr.100 Heinkel 6N+FK was observer Fw Hilmar Schmidt, who recorded in his diary:

> 'Our orders were to attack warships and transports, with the railway line to Dombaas an alternative target. We found the warships all right – the defensive flak was truly frightful and my two SC 250 bombs missed their intended target. On our second bombing run I tried with my 50kg bombs. The flak was worse than ever – below, above, in front, behind and beside us the shells exploded, producing a veritable cloud of black smoke. It was hell. 'Bombs away!' I called, and switched off my bombsight. Paul (Wiersbitzki) dropped the right wing and we dived away at more than 400kph

> (250 mph). I was willing to have another go, but none of the others wanted to join me! In any case we only had 50kg bombs left, so we set off for the railway line near Lesjaskog. Here we found an auxiliary airfield, but only managed one hit.'[107]

With all this action going on, Lt Bob Everett of 810 Squadron was given the task of flying off in his Swordfish to search for HMS *Black Swan*, to which he was to drop a message bag:

> 'One the way up to the fjord we met up with some British destroyers. They had been bombed all day and were in a mood to let loose at anything that came too close. Digger Gerrett in the back seat fired what he thought was going to be a Very light signal, which would establish our friendly intentions. Unfortunately, the pistol produced instead a brown smoke puff. The destroyers saw it and thought it was flak and let fly at the Swordfish. I hurried down to the sea and put him right.'

While the fighting over Aandalsnes was still in progress, *Ark Royal* launched a further trio of 801 Squadron aircraft, and at 17:35 these attacked a single He111 of 2/KGr.100. Return fire from the gunners struck L2931/A7L flown by Lt(A) Bill Church, which burst into flames; the engine broke completely off the aircraft and it dived vertically into the sea, Church and his observer Sub-Lt(A) David Willis being killed. The other two Skua pilots, Lt Ronnie Hay RM and PO(A) Henry Kimber (L2912/A7G), then shot down the Heinkel, which fell into the sea near Aalesund, as recorded by Hay:

> 'We ran into a He111. Bill attacked from astern and the bomber dived to sea level. They exchanged fire, and when Bill pulled upwards to break off the attack, his aircraft was struck in the belly and crashed into the sea without survivors. I had learned my first lesson in air fighting with a vengeance – never break away upwards. I therefore sat on the tail of the bomber and fired short bursts until it crashed into the sea.'

Uffz Kurt Rippke and his crew (Uffz Heinz Thieme, Uffz Joachim Förster and Gfr Gerhard Hunger) were picked up by a British destroyer. Fw Schmidt noted:

> 'Of the seven aircraft of our Staffel two did not return. The Hansel crew (Hansel, Harbel, Hansen and Böhne) turned up in Bergen eight days later after being captured. [Fw Ernst] Hansen had lost a leg. This was the crew I liked best of all; they were all great chaps. Anyway, thank God they are all back again. Soon I will be able to speak to them. What happened to Rippke and his crew nobody knows. It was their first flight against the enemy. Among them was Uffz Thieme who had been married for only one week. Petermann managed to bring his aircraft back on one engine, in spite of icing and attacks by fighters (as did the Boss, [Oblt Gerd] Korthals).'

A section of Skuas from 801 Squadron flown by Lt Robert Strange (A7F), Sub-Lt (A) Jack Marsh (ex-RAFVR in L2912/A7G) and Mid(A) George Baldwin (A7H) engaged a raid by ten Heinkels of II/LG1, two aircraft from 4 Staffel being intercepted over Lesjaskog, the rear most aircraft of the pair coming under attack. With smoke pouring from the port engine, it went down into a forest, Fw Werner Schulz and his crew being captured by the Norwegians and shipped to Britain. Of his first engagement, Mid(A) Baldwin recalled:

'We had launched to cover the first evacuation from Norway, and it was one of my first operational patrols. Over the very rugged and snow covered coast, we spotted several aircraft that the formation leader identified as Heinkels and he ordered us into a line astern to make an attack on one of them. I dived in turn, and through my inexperience probably opened fire at far too great a range, although I did at least see some hits on its seemingly enormous wings.'[108]

To reduce interference with the evacuation from Namsos and Aandalsnes, *Ark Royal* launched her air group on another dawn raid on Vaernes airfield next day (**28th April**). At 03:05, six Swordfish each from 810 (led by Lt Bob Everett in P4137/A4K) and 820 (led by Capt Nigel Skene RM in L2721/A2A) took off with four 250lb, four 20lb and four 25lb incendiary bombs apiece. 820 attacked at 04:32, obtaining hits on huts and barrack blocks, while 810 came in ten minutes later, Lt David Godfrey-Faussett (L2826/A2P) destroying the last hangar – he had been responsible for the destruction of another during the previous attack. Intense flak was encountered and several aircraft were hit, but all returned safely.

Meanwhile six escorting Skuas, drawn equally from 800 (Lt Ken Spurway in A6K, Lt James Rooper in A6L and Mid(A) Len Gallagher in A6M) and 801 Squadron (Lt Robert Strange in A7F, Sub-Lt Jock Marsh in A7H and PO(A) Henry Kimber in A7G), attacked the slipway and floatplanes at Trondheim. Merchant ships were seen at anchor and dive-bombed. Hits were observed and the floatplanes strafed. The attack destroyed five He115Bs of I/KüFlGr.506, two of 1 Staffel and three of 2 Staffel, the second occasion in three days that Skuas had wreaked havoc upon the floatplanes. All Skuas survived the attack but Mid(A) Len Gallagher's A6M became separated and, low on fuel, landed at the airstrip at Setnesmoen near Aandalsnes (from where the RAF's 263 Squadron had been operating). Despite the confusion there due to the evacuation, he nonetheless managed to get his aircraft refuelled from the tanks of a damaged RAF Gladiator. Having spent an uncomfortable night sleeping under the wing of their Skua, Gallagher and his TAG, N/Air George Halifax, decided to fly directly to Hatston. Taking off in the early morning with only a borrowed Norwegian school atlas to guide them and with the airstrip under attack by He111s, the intrepid crew safely reached Hatston using their navigation skills only – plus a goodly slice of luck.

During the morning Ju87s of StG1, Heinkels of KG26 and LG1, and Ju88s of KG30 attacked shipping in the fjord at Aalesund and Aandalsnes, and the harbour at the latter town. A RN anti-submarine trawler was sunk by the Stukas, while KG30 sank the small Norwegian coaster *Brand IV*. Meanwhile however, another pair of Heinkels from 2/LG1 on reconnaissance over the coastal zone spotted *Ark Royal* and reported its presence. With *Glorious* and her Sea Gladiators withdrawn, the Rocs aboard *Ark Royal* were required to provide fleet defence. The Heinkels were intercepted by three Rocs of 801 Squadron that were scrambled after them – Lt Ronnie Hay RM, N/Air Syd Bass in A7P, Sub-Lt(A) John Myers, N/Air Pat Bolton in A7Q, and Mid(A) George Baldwin, L/Air Steve Smailes in A7R – but could only drive them off, the crews reporting that they had seen one of the bombers shot down by AA fire. On receipt of the sighting report ten more Heinkels of II/KG26 were sent off to attack. Lt Hay RM reported:

'Soon, we spotted a Ju88 [*sic*] reporting the fleet's position. Diving down at maximum speed, we got to within 200 yards of the bomber – but I had no front guns, so I attempted to slew my aircraft to enable the turret to bear. Shouting 'Fire!' to the gunner, I heard one bang – and silence. All the guns had jammed. The German flew off with a startled puff of brown smoke from his engines.'

Mid(A) George Baldwin had similar recollections of the encounter:

'Even in a dive with my throttle fully open, I had real difficulty in getting ahead or even abeam of the bombers to allow my gunner to open fire. It was so frustrating!'

At 11:05, three 803 Squadron Skuas were flown off, followed by three more from 800 Squadron, which were to provide escort for convoy *TM.1*. At 12:18 the first trio saw a Ju88 bombing a sloop (HMS *Flamingo*) and Lt Bill Lucy (L2925) at once attacked with a short burst, followed by Sub-Lt(A) Guy Brokensha (L2905/8K), whose fire missed the German aircraft. PO(A) Johnno Johnson then got in an attack, and the bomber was reported to have crashed; it was credited to Lucy and Johnson jointly. This was possibly 4D+EH of 1/KG30 flown by Ltn Kretschmer that came down at Bekkvaselv; the crew survived. Half an hour later these same pilots saw eight Heinkels of 4/KG26 approaching, and three of these were attacked, Lucy and Brokensha shooting down two including the Staffelkapitän's aircraft (Hptm Eberhard Schnoor von Carolsfeld). The bomber put down in the sea near Molde and Hptm von Carolsfeld and crew (Fw Karl Babkuhl, Obfw Walter Cramer and Obfw Heinz Vogel) got out into their dinghy, save one man who had been killed during the fighters' attack; they were picked up and made prisoners. Fw Karl Pflüger's aircraft fell into the sea south of Digerhalsen (Kjørsvika) in flames; there were no survivors. Lost with Pflüger were Uffz Hans Träumner, Uffz Gerold Simdorn and Obfw Jakob Best. The three Skuas then chased the other seven Heinkels out to sea, breaking up their formation. Several jettisoned their bombs and two were seen with engines on fire, one being credited to Brokensha as a probable, the other to Johnson's gunner (L/Air Frank Costan) also as a probable. In a graphic letter to his parents, Guy Brokensha described the action:

'After recovering from the first shock of seeing a black cloud of Heinkels, I whistled in and shot up old arse-end Charlie. My observer [PO(A) Stan Andrews] got fearfully excited when he broke away and then burst into flame, crashing into the sea, kept on saying "That's one for you, sir. Oh well done, sir." I felt good. One values praise from Andrews – in the air and when we are chatting on the ground I call him Andy and he uses my familiar Brock. The CO (Lucy) produced his usual one out of the bag. Give him an aeroplane and he's an ace, he's more – there's no other word – he's a genius. Many times he has shown it. While I was fixing the last one, he climbed up over them and just after I'd seen mine go down I followed him and then he just dived vertically on the remaining six. I was about 100 yards behind him coming down and those bastards just dropped every bomb they had and scattered all ways. He's terrific. I attacked one who was a bit slow in nipping into a cloud and managed to put his gunner and starboard motor u/s before my ammunition ran out. Lucy did the same to another. Johnson had a probable, too. Six between us! We heard that Johnson had used up his own ammunition but was chasing the sods away from their targets with his rear-seat single Lewis gun! Not bad! The Admiral sent for us and gave us gin, dirty and filthy, as we were, having no kit. He was pleased, too!'

By now the KG30 and LG1 bombers were in the area, attacking the shipping in the Molde region, and close behind came a third wave of thirteen more Heinkels of III/KG26. These were met by the 800 Squadron trio. All three pilots – Lt Ned Finch-Noyes (L3000), Lt Teddy Taylour (L2934) and PO(A) Eric Monk – shooting down an 8 Staffel aircraft, which Uffz Hans Liesske managed to force-land in a valley near Sunndalsfjord, with two of the crew dead. Liesske and the observer then set fire to their aircraft before being captured by Norwegian troops. Finch-Noyes and Taylour then each claimed one of the bombers damaged in head-on attacks, while Finch-Noyes' gunner, PO(A) Cuts Cunningham, claimed damage to a Heinkel. Monk also claimed that he had set one engine of another bomber alight. With all ammunition gone, 800 Squadron crews then made five dummy attacks on incoming bombers, which broke up their attacks. In all these latter engagements the German aircraft escaped serious damage, and one Skua was claimed shot down by KG30 gunners. One LG1 Heinkel was slightly damaged, apparently by AA fire.

Later, in the afternoon, the original pair of 2/LG1 snoopers returned. The three Rocs, having been refuelled, took off after them but again returned empty-handed two hours later. At this stage *Ark Royal* retired out to sea for two days to rest her tired aircrews and allow maintenance to be carried out to her depleted stock of aircraft. Meanwhile at Aalesund, Lt Kik Filmer, who had been rescued by Norwegians the previous day following his ditching in L2991, reported:

'The aircraft was later salvaged through the kindness of the Norwegians and with the help of Major Lumley RM and Lt Copeland-Griffiths RN. It was hoisted on a pontoon, the engine was removed, and the wings were folded in order to deceive the enemy. Norwegian engineers had only partly examined the engine when I left for Molde, but the carburettor induction pipe had been shot away, one cylinder had seized up, and one bullet had passed through twelve fins without entering the cylinder. The fuselage was fairly well preserved except for approximately sixty bullet holes, one group of which tore a large hole in the starboard petrol tank. The forward tank was pierced, the remainder of the bullet holes being scattered from below the pilots seat to the after end of the cabin. All important gear in the aircraft was removed, the five guns being added to the defences of the British forces in Aalesund.

'I placed myself under the orders of Major Lumley. I was occupied in salvaging my aircraft on Saturday 27th April and in the evening Petty Officer Gardner and his Air Gunner, Todd, arrived in Aalesund with important information from Bergen. On Sunday 28th I was sent with this information to the SNO [Senior Naval Officer], Molde. I travelled by car with an interpreter and an official of the Norwegian Secret Service to Vestnes, where we embarked aboard a small motorboat for Molde. This journey by boat was very hazardous as numerous enemy aircraft were flying overhead, some attacking us and others attacking a sloop [HMS *Flamingo*] in the vicinity. I arrived at Molde in the middle of an air raid, but reached the Headquarters safely and reported to the SNO, Captain Denny, who placed me under his orders to help in the operations. We were bombed continuously in Molde.'

Although Allied forces were withdrawing from Central Norway, a landing was made on **29th April** in Northern Norway at Bodø, well to the south of Harstad, where it was hoped that an advanced airfield could be set up to act as a fighter base for operations against Luftwaffe aircraft heading towards the main battle area from Trondheim. Tromsø was now the seat of the Norwegian government, the King and his ministers having been transferred there from Molde on the cruiser HMS *Glasgow* on this date.

5. NARVIK AND THE NORTH

May 1940

The Gladiator had insufficient performance to chase and hold the aircraft employed by the enemy … can be complied with by giving us Spitfires … can be complied with by giving us practically any US Navy fighter.

Lt-Cdr John Cockburn 804 Squadron

By the first day of the new month, the evacuation from Namsos and Aandalsnes was reaching its final stages. The carriers returned to provide cover for the departing convoys, *Glorious* having taken on board nine Sea Gladiators of 802 Squadron (Lt John Marmont), and a further ten of 804 (Lt-Cdr John Cockburn), plus a dozen Swordfish of 823 Squadron (Lt-Cdr C J T Stephens). She had also taken on board three replacement Skuas for 803 Squadron, and one additional Roc. On arrival at her station, *Glorious* received the surviving 803 Squadron Skuas (four in total) from *Ark Royal*.

Early in the morning of **1st May**, four Do17Ps of 1(F)/120 left Trondheim, one of these reporting two aircraft carriers, one heavy and two light cruisers, at about 07:00. The aircraft was at once intercepted by two of 804 Squadron's Sea Gladiators, and was damaged. The alarm had been given however, and He111s of II/LG1 set out from Stavanger during the afternoon. They launched a bombing attack but failed to gain any successes. The Sea Gladiators next engagement occurred at 15:40, as reported by Lt Richard Smeeton (N2275/F) leading Blue Section of 804 Squadron:

> 'At 15:20, we observed AA fire over the fleet, and we climbed to 12,000 feet, the height of the bursts, but did not sight enemy aircraft. The Section remained at 12,000 feet and, at 15:40, AA fire was again observed. A Heinkel 111 was sighted well above this fire, and the Section climbed to intercept. The enemy aircraft had released its bombs and was retiring on a course 120, at 16,000 feet. Blue 2 and 3, who were stepped up on Blue 1, managed to get in some short bursts from an almost stalled position under the enemy aircraft. Section then chased on a course 120, but were unable to close, due to the enemy's superior speed, and the chase was broken off.
>
> 'At 16:00, I observed a Heinkel 111 approaching the fleet some 2,000-3,000 feet above the Section. I altered course to intercept. The enemy released his bombs at 17,000 feet; I was then about 800 yards astern and saw the bombs released. Blue 2, again being stepped up, managed to get in some bursts from about 450 yards. It was immediately after this that the enemy released his bombs and, opening out his en-

gines, went into a shallow dive; his speed was then too great for the Gladiators to attempt a chase.'

Red Section of 804 Squadron took off at 16:30 to relieve Blue Section, Lt Rodney Carver (N2276/K) leading the trio of fighters after a single raider, which was spotted at low altitude. Having chased this away, they climbed to 18,000 feet and at 17:50 were ordered to intercept another intruder at sea level. This time a He115 was seen about 20 feet above the waves, and during a long, fruitless chase, all ammunition was expended. This floatplane was believed to have been an aircraft of 2/KüFlGr.506, which had just led six Ju87Rs of I/StG1 to the area, and at this stage the Sea Gladiators were called back to the ship to try and aid in heading off the incoming raid by the Stukas, which had only arrived at Drontheim the previous day, as recalled by Hptm Paul-Werner Hozzel, the Gruppenkommandeur:

'Hardly had we landed when [Major Martin] Harlinghausen [Chief of Operations X Flgkps] issued the first operation order. The British had gained a footing in Namsos, north of Drontheim. They were supplied by transport ships passing through the deep cut and long Namsosfjord with Namsos port located at its end. There the transports were discharged under the guard of warships. The I/StG1 was then the only available operational unit to be put into action against the British base and its supply vessels. The following day we fully concentrated on those targets. With the exception of the first Staffel the mass of our pilots were not experienced in dive-bombing attacks against moving marine targets. During our first sorties many a bomb missed its target but soon we learned.'

Six Ju87s attacked *Glorious* unsuccessfully. Mid(A) Roy Hinton, of 823 Squadron was standing on the quarterdeck:

'This was the first action that any of us had been involved in. It was a tremendous spectacle. The Gladiators were up and everybody was opening up on the enemy bombers. We were standing watching when they decided to open up with the 4.7in. There was one on either side of the quarterdeck. We weren't given any warning that the guns were going to fire. One moment we were standing there watching the aircraft having a dogfight up topsides and the next a great flash of flame, an enormous great noise! We all thought, God, a bomb on the ship, and we all went flat on the deck!'

The second group of seven Ju87s were driven off by sections of Sea Gladiators, 802 Squadron's Blue Section of two Sea Gladiators flown by the CO Lt Jack Marmont (6A) and it is believed by Lt(A) Reg Miles (6B), having been scrambled at 1800, followed at 18:15 by another three 804 Squadron machines led by Lt-Cdr Cockburn (N2265/), who reported:

'At 18:23, six Junkers 87 dive-bombers were sighted three miles ahead, on an opposite course, in open V formation. The order to open fire was given and the Section half-rolled individually on to the tails of the enemy aircraft, each pilot attacking one enemy. Fire was maintained in short bursts, as the enemy twisted and turned, until the final bombing dive was commenced. The attack was broken off at this point as I imagined, quite erroneously, that the pom-pom fire would take effect below this.'

Lt-Cdr Cockburn claimed a Ju87 damaged. Marmont's section had gone off initially to chase another shadower – a He115, which once again escaped. The three 804 Squadron aircraft were by then engaged with the incoming Ju87s, and seeing them so involved, Marmont and his wingman hurled themselves into the fray and shot down one dive-bomber at 16,000 feet over the fleet at 18:25. This 2 Staffel aircraft crashed into the sea west of Namsos, Obfw Erich Stahl and Uffz Friedrich Gott being picked up by a British destroyer. The 804 pilots had first seen six Ju87s approaching at 18:23, in an open V formation, and had rolled onto their tails, each pilot attacking one of the Stukas until it went into its bombing dive. At this point they broke off, leaving them to the ships' pom-poms. One pilot then engaged another Ju87 at low level, but no decisive damage could be inflicted.

During the raid one bomb missed *Ark Royal* by only 30 feet but no serious damage was inflicted. Oblt Heinz Böhne of 2/StG1 claimed this as a hit on *Glorious*. Two hours later another Do17P of 1(F)/120 appeared overhead when the group was west of Namsos, and this too was slightly damaged by intercepting Sea Gladiators. The ships put up a very heavy volume of gunfire and in the mêlée the Sea Gladiators were lucky not to be hit and seriously damaged or even shot down; some were certainly peppered. On breaking away after their dives, some of the Stukas attacked destroyers in the screen. Two or three attacked HMS *Fury* with machine-guns and small bombs. One of the Swordfish on anti-submarine patrol was also attacked with front and rear guns by a Stuka and the surprised pilot, Capt Nigel Skene RM, had to extricate himself with a steep climbing turn, but A2A suffered two hits.

There were lessons to be learned. On returning to the carrier, Lt-Cdr Cockburn wrote in his report: 'High-angle fire from *Glorious* and *Valiant* was concentrated chiefly on our own Gladiators. Fortunately, it was grossly inaccurate.'

Lt Jack Marmont reported that his section 'was subjected to heavy pom-pom fire which fortunately had no effect, although on landing one of my section was found to have been hit by a fragment, presumably from an HAA shell.'

While Lt Rodney Carver of 804's Red Section said they were 'fired at continuously by all ships' pom-poms and 4in from HMS *Berwick*'.

Lt-Cdr Cockburn recorded that his squadron were heavily handicapped operationally because they had to fly at dangerously low revolutions in order to make their petrol last throughout their patrols. Even then, the times on patrol were often half an hour longer than the safe endurance recommended. In Cockburn's view, combat had shown:

1. That the Sea Gladiator had insufficient performance to chase and hold the aircraft employed by the enemy.
2. The time between sighting the enemy by our own pilots and the time the enemy drops his bomb is very short; therefore a high concentration of gunfire is required and Fleet Air Arm fighters should have at least eight front guns.
3. To save the fleet turning into wind frequently the Fleet Air Arm fighter should have a reasonable endurance, e.g. five hours.

Lt-Cdr Cockburn concluded: '(1) and (2) above can be complied with by giving us Spitfires; (1), (2) and (3) can be complied with by giving us practically any US Navy fighter.'[109]

During the afternoon of 1st of May, searching Heinkels from 1(F)/I22 had found one

British group west of Namsos, and another group further south, near the coast. The former group, reportedly comprising two heavy and one light cruiser, five destroyers and three other vessels, was attacked by a dozen He111s of II/KG 26, but suffered no damage. The bombers were intercepted by patrolling Skuas, but these were not able to gain any success on this occasion. Four Skuas of 803 Squadron had taken off from *Ark Royal* to patrol over HMS *Devonshire*, which had signalled that enemy aircraft were in the area. Two of the fighters encountered fog and on emerging found they were directly over the convoy escorted by *Devonshire*. Despite Sub-Lt Brokensha's observer (PO(A) Stan Andrews)[110] signalling frantically with his Aldis lamp, their aircraft (L2905/A8K) came under intense short-range AA fire, forcing them to ditch in the sea. Fortunately, their plight was seen and they were promptly rescued from the sea by attendant destroyer HMS *Nubian*. The other Skua, flown by PO(A) Johnson, returned safely to the carrier. In a letter to his parents, Guy Brokensha recounted:

> 'Coming back in the fog we got shot down and picked up by a destroyer. Andy and I both quite OK except for a few bumps and bruises – it's quite hard to do a gentle arrival in the drink! But ours wasn't too bad.
>
> Then 'we' [meaning *Nubian*] went back and evacuated Namsos. What a shame and how I wished I had my faithful old 'K' [his Skua]. The scene at Namsos was incredible, we all stayed up all night. It never really got dark and the scene on the jetty was lit up by the remains of burning coal. Lorries and troops poured in and at last we got away soon after 4am when the sun was just coming up. We had a nasty moment at the entrance of the fjord when one of the transports flashed a panic signal to us: 'Stay with me, engines broken down'. An anxious half hour followed with everybody scanning the skies for the first of the bombers. At last she fixed it and we got away.'

Both carriers were now ordered to return to Scapa Flow. On arrival, the five Rocs aboard *Ark Royal* and one Roc on *Glorious* were flown off to Donibristle and the six remaining Skuas in *Glorious* were flown off to *Ark Royal*. Immediate preparations were put in hand to restock, refuel, and rearm the *Ark* for operations off North Norway, in support of the impending landings at Narvik.

As the evacuation from Namsos and Aandalsnes reached its final stages, the Royal Norwegian Naval Air Service began evacuating its surviving aircraft, three seaplanes flying northwards to Tromsø, while a He115A (F-52) and another MF-11 (F-328) headed for Scotland during the early morning hours of **2nd May**. The Heinkel, flown by Lt Haakon Offerdal and carrying two Fleet Air Arm officers who had been shot down, safely reached Invergordon in the Shetlands, but the MF-11 configuration was again misidentified and the biplane was shot down by British AA in error as it approached Invergordon. All four occupants – Fänrik (Sub-Lt) Knut Oscar, Fänrik Johan Daniel Stub Ravn, Kvartermester Odd Braenne and Harald Svend Døsen – were lost; only the body of Ravn was recovered and interned in Knab Cemetery in the Shetlands. Three more RN or NAS He115As would follow this route to Scotland, including one carrying an American pilot, Don Willis,[111] who had been flying for the Finns against the Russians before he escaped via Sweden to Norway.[112]

A further landing by Allied forces at nearby Mosjoen followed, intended as a diversion for the main landing at Narvik, while two days later a small force landed at Mo. Air support for this distant area could not be provided from the United Kingdom direct, hence in the Narvik area the main support would again be provided by *Ark Royal*, which departed Scapa Flow on 4th May to support continued operations in the area, carrying 23 Skuas of 800, 801 and 803 Squadrons and 21 Swordfish of 810 Squadron (Capt Nigel Skene RM) and 820 Squadron (Lt-Cdr Guy Hodgkinson). Included in the 800 Squadron group were Mid(A) Chris Treen and N/Air Doc Goble, who had escaped from Norway following their ditching on 24th April. After being landed in the Shetlands by a destroyer they were flown to Inverness in a Sunderland flying boat, and collected a replacement Skua, L3055, which they flew, via Hatston, back aboard the *Ark Royal*, as recalled by Doc Goble:

> 'Eventually, we were landed in the Shetlands and taken to Invergordon in a Short Sunderland flying boat, where I was kitted out in natty silk underwear and a grey pin-stripe suit. Then on to Inverness, to pick up another Skua, and back to the ship. The Skua did not have a very good reputation, and I am reliably informed that the Commander Flying had to be restrained from throwing me overboard, and only relented when he was told that I was not the representative of the manufacturers. In spite of the Commander's opinion, I rather liked the Skua. It was comfortable to fly in and, with a more powerful engine, it would have made a good aircraft, the more so as it was originally designed as a dive-bomber. We were headed once more for Norway.'

Meanwhile, the Germans were also preparing for further action in the far north, and as Trondheim became a more secure base, more units moved to Vaernes and also Sola at the start of May, fighter cover for the area now including 4/JG77 (Bf109Es), 11(N)/JG2 (Bf109Ds), 1 and 3/ZG76 (Bf110Cs) and the Z/KG30 (Ju88Cs). A further 20 Bf109Es of 5 and 6/JG77 were available on call at Kristiansand-Kjevik. And there were at least 70 serviceable He111s from Stab, I and III/KG26, and KGr.100, plus 27 Ju87s of I/StG1, supplemented by He115s, He111s, Do17Ps and Do215s for reconnaissance duties. The bombers of KG4, KG30 and LG1 had been withdrawn from Scandinavia pending operations against the Low Countries. Even so, there remained a considerable force to confront the Skuas.

The returning fleet was spotted by Do17s of 1(F)/120 and a FW200 of I/KG40, and again next day (**6th May**) as the task force arrived off Narvik, where it was joined by *Ark Royal*. Included with the fleet was the cruiser HMS *Curlew* equipped with Type 79Z radar, which could detect raiders up to a distance of 90 miles and to a height of 20,000 feet. It was anticipated that this aid would assist the fighters as well as the defence of the fleet. A number of Heinkels from KG26 and KGr.100 attempted attacks on the ships during the day, albeit without success and for the loss of one of their number to ships' AA fire.

Ark Royal's Skuas first engaged German aircraft over the new area of operations during the afternoon of **7th May**, when five Heinkels from 5/KG26 arrived to attack following an earlier reconnaissance by four aircraft from the Geschwader's III Gruppe. Two 801 Squadron aircraft had taken off at 13:30 – Lt(A) Tom Gray in L3030/A7K and Mid(A)

Derek Martin in L2878/A7L – followed at 14:50 by three from 803 Squadron – Lt Bill Lucy (L2925/A8F), Lt Godfrey Russell (L2918/A8G), and PO(A) Harry Glover (L3046/A8H) At 16:30 four Heinkels (apparently the III Gruppe aircraft) were sighted over Ofotfjord, two of which had just completed their bombing. The other pair jettisoned, and the bombers pulled close together, their formation-keeping and return fire being reported as much better than with those aircraft previously encountered over the Trondheim area. Lt Russell's aircraft was hit, and he lost the tip of one finger to a bullet and suffered splinter wounds to his face, force-landing in Ofotfjord where he and his gunner (N/Air Harry Pickering) were picked up by a destroyer. Meanwhile, the 801 Squadron pair reported seeing one Heinkel go down in a vertical dive south of Ofotfjord. This 8/KG26 aircraft in fact managed to limp back to Trondheim and crash-land on Vaernes airfield, where some 100 bullet holes were counted. A second bomber returned to claim one Skua shot down – obviously Russell's aircraft. Lt(A) Gray of 801 Squadron reported:

> 'Approaching Narvik from the west when rear gunner [Lt Webb] opened fire on two He111s approaching from astern. Sub-flight formed into line astern and turning sharply came up behind the enemy aircraft. These were engaged by 803 Skuas. The 801 sub-flight attacked in turn and observed one Heinkel diving and out of control. We resumed attack on remaining aircraft with one aircraft of 803 Squadron [Lt Lucy]. This aircraft made off east and finally crossed the Swedish border and was observed to jettison large quantities of what are presumed stores. On turning away from the attack, two more enemy aircraft were observed attempting to reach Narvik. The sub-flight carried out two good attacks and drove the enemy machines far south.'

803 Squadron's CO Lt Lucy added:

> 'Enemy remained in formation carrying out medium turns. Both aircraft of first attack seen to jettison bombs. After one enemy of the first formation had been forced down, second aircraft made off at speed, and after one attack was not overtaken. All own aircraft attacked by diving from astern. I disengaged as other enemy aircraft had been seen. Aircraft 8F and 8G hit several times.'

On returning from another fighter patrol over Narvik, PO(A) Henry Kimber crashed L2912 on the deck of the *Ark*. The aircraft was written off but neither Kimber nor his TAG N/Air Lionel Miles was injured. Whilst off Narvik the carrier recovered a Walrus – P5662 flown by Lt Phil Francklin – from Harstad at 06:10. Later, when the day's activity had ended, the Walrus (presumably having been serviced) was despatched to Harstad to be transferred to HMS *Effingham*.

Next day (**8th May**), the Luftwaffe was out in force looking for the carrier, but was unable to find her in clouds and mist. Four He111s of I/KG26 were first to arrive early in the morning. Further attacks by thirteen Heinkels of KG26 and six escorting Z/KG30 Ju88Cs, making their first bomber support sorties over Narvik, gained no success at all.

In an attempt to reinforce the German garrison at Rombaksfjord, two Do24s and five Do26s of KrzbV.108 departed Trondheim with 103 troops on board but ran into bad weather, forcing the two Do24s and two of the Do26s to return to Trondheim. One of the remaining Do26s landed safely at Rombaksfjord, one landed at Beisfjord, but the fifth

– P5+BH – had the misfortune to encounter a patrol of Skuas of 803 Squadron as it approached the Narvik area alone; the Skuas formed one of two flights which had taken off on patrol, and were flown by Lt Skeet Harris RM (L2910/A8K), Sub-Lt Freddy Charlton (L2916/A8M) and PO(A) Johnno Johnson (L2992/A8L). The flying boat was intercepted at 16:15, engaged and was last seen diving away south of Ofotfjord, the Skua pilots believing that they had disabled it. The official report stated:

'Section carried out successive astern attacks. Leader and No.2 each carried out one beam attack. Enemy was firing single cannon. Many bullets seen to enter fuselage and engines of enemy aircraft. Enemy last seen diving from 7,000 feet through 10/10th cloud immediately above mountains 5,000 feet high. Cloud base 4,000 feet. Yellow 3 was hit by bullets in the oil system. He carried out a successful forced landing at Tovik.'

Sub-Lt Charlton's Skua was obliged to ditch in Ofotfjord, he and his gunner (L/Air Fred Culliford) being rescued by a destroyer:

'Following the attacks on the flying boat, my Skua's engine gradually failed from return damage and I ditched in a fjord near Narvik. Rescued from the village of Tovik by the Polish destroyer *Blyskawika* and commenced return journey from Harstad in Polish liner *Chrobri* only to be bombed and abandoned in Narvikfjord. Rescued by the sloop *Stork* and taken to hospital in Scotland via *Ulster Prince*.'

Lt Harris and PO(A) Johnson circled overhead while Charlton carried out his ditching, reported the location to HMS *Curlew* and then returned to the carrier. Harris simply noted in his logbook:

'Encountered a large flying boat Do26. Enemy disappeared through 10/10th cloud and forced-landed near Narvik.'

The flying boat had indeed been hard hit, and with three of its four engines out of action it escaped in bad visibility and forced-landed by the east bank of the entrance to Vestfjord. Here Oblt d.Res Siegfried Schack and his crew destroyed the aircraft. They, Hptm Joachim Fehling who was acting as observer, and the 17 men of 3/GJR.138 who had been their passengers, became prisoners eight days later. Surprisingly, none had become casualties during the fighter attack.

Meanwhile at 16:30, Mid(A) Stephen Griffith (L3961), one of the pilots of the other sub-flight of Skuas led by Lt Bill Lucy, attacked and claimed damage to both a He111 and a Ju88 – the latter in a surprise head-on attack – but the other two crews were unable to spot the bombers due to thick cloud. Of the attack on the Heinkel, Griffith reported:

'Own aircraft carried out diving attack from astern. Enemy aircraft dived steeply towards clouds. Many accurate bursts were fired. Rear air gunner believed killed, tail and fuselage believed badly damaged.' Ten minutes later another twin-engine aircraft was sighted, believed to have been a Ju88, and was engaged at 300 yards: 'One short head-on attack and enemy was lost in the clouds, own ammunition being expended.'

Other activity during the day saw an 820 Squadron Swordfish – P4127/A4F piloted by Lt Hugh Hunter – fly a photo-reconnaissance mission over Bogen at the request of Flag

Officer Narvik; the mission was interrupted by the appearance of three Ju88s, which chased the Swordfish until it was able to escape by diving steeply into a narrow fjord. Hunter flew back to the *Ark* at a height of ten feet to avoid being seen, his observer tapping out the laconic message 'Delayed by three Junkers'. An afternoon anti-submarine patrol around the task force by two 810 Squadron machines concluded with the loss of A2R, which crashed over the side while landing aboard, seriously injuring the pilot, although all three members of the crew – Sub-Lt(A) Woodrow Adams,[113] Sub-Lt Howard 'Pancho' Pain, and L/Air Harry Edwards – were rescued by HMS *Maori*. Flying for the day ceased at 21:30 when the last fighter patrol was recovered. Maintaining standing fighter patrols over the Harstad area, per the request of Flag Officer Narvik, *Ark Royal* planned a strike on German positions at Nordalsbroen, Hunddalen and Sildvik.

Thus, at 08:00 on **9th May**, three 800 Squadron Skuas led by Lt Ken Spurway took off to escort a bombing mission by Swordfish against a bridge at Nordalen and the Hunddalen area. At 08:05, Capt Nigel Skene RM led off nine Swordfish of 810 Squadron, each armed with 4x250lb and 8x20lb bombs. Almost immediately things started going wrong; three aircraft had to abort, one of which, L2723/A2B, could not make it back to the ship and forced-landed, the crew, Lt Alex Stewart, Mid(A) George Shaddick and L/Air Harry Burt, being rescued by an escorting destroyer. Weather conditions were less than spectacular, though the other Swordfish were able to push on and bomb the targets assigned. Both Capt Skene (L2824/A2A) and Sub-Lt(A) Ralph Eborn (L2760/A2C) claimed direct hits on their designated targets, while Capt Norrie Martin RM led his section in an attack on the railway east of Narvik. This involved a two-hour flight to reach the target. Martin's section found a train at Hunddalen station and he scored a direct hit with a 250lb bomb, leaving the train on fire and the front half overturned. Several of the Swordfish sustained damage but all returned to the carrier including Sub-Lt(A) Randy Pearson's L9722/A2Q and Sub-Lt(A) Tony Dixon's A2H, which was found to have about 40 shrapnel and bullet holes.

Finding no enemy aircraft in the air, the Skuas strafed the abandoned Ju52/3ms on Lake Hartvigvann that had already been disabled during the attacks in mid-April. The crews were not to know that Norwegian forces had chased away German aircrew and troops in the area and were in the process of flying some of the least damaged machines to Bardufoss. Following the latest attack, none of the aircraft remained airworthy.

One Skua crew – Mid(A) Chris Treen and N/Air Doc Goble in L3055/6H – suffered engine failure and had to make a force-landing. As soon as the remaining aircraft had landed back aboard, *Ark Royal* withdrew from the area out to sea due to the very adverse weather conditions then prevailing. The missing crew, Treen and Goble, having already survived one landing in Norway, were again lucky, as the latter recalled:

> 'Apart from being engaged by friendly anti-aircraft fire at intervals, nothing much occurred to inconvenience the section. However, our engine suddenly went silent on us. There was no opportunity to reach the fjord for another water landing. Instead, we made a glide approach to an upward snow-clad slope, the useless engine breaking away as the bolts sheared on impact, with the rest of the aircraft slithering to an undignified halt about 100 yards further along. In the Skua rear cockpit you sat on a covered crossbeam with no back to it and to use the gun you stood up and used a

thick strap, known as the fighting strap, across your back and pulled the gun up with its arc mounting. This was the position I was in when the crash came, and, in consequence, my back took all the impact while I held on to the gun. This caused severe damage to the muscles so that my head dropped and I couldn't straighten up. My pilot, Midshipman Treen, appeared to be OK but you don't crash like this without some damage.

'After getting ourselves clear of the wreck, we attempted to set fire to it before the Germans, who were all around in the nearby mountains overlooking Narvik, arrived on the scene. We tried burning Very lights at the front, but this had little effect. Treen bravely went back to the rear cockpit and used the onboard axe to split open the fuel tanks. Once done, another Very cartridge was fired directly into the aperture, which did the trick, igniting the aircraft satisfactorily and igniting Treen's clothing with equal vigour. He had to roll in the snow to put the flames out and did not appreciate my reaction – laughter – which we later attributed to shock. Soon the ammunition began exploding so we beat a hasty retreat.

'I had only the vaguest of idea of where we were. All I really knew was that it was in a cold climate and there were some Germans around who were unlikely to be friendly! The pilot thought we were within about three miles of the Swedish border, and I expected to head that way, but he decided that we should make for the coast, and so we headed in what we hoped was that direction. Now, this was not my idea of an enjoyable stroll. Flying boots were never meant for long distance walking in deep snow, but after about three hours we reached the top of a glacier, without any apparent way of getting down.

'In the distance, we could see Narvik and, as this was a well-patrolled area, we expected that, at any moment, ski troops would swoop down upon us, whether Norwegian or German was anybody's guess. In the end, we decided to chance it and started down, ending up glissading for about 500 feet down the steep slope. At the bottom, we faced another hazard, a panorama of sheet ice with a stream running down the middle. Having managed to cross this, we turned more to the south and reached Rhombaks Fjord about a quarter of a mile from its head. Keeping just inside the tree line, we made our way further west until we came upon a house at the water's edge.

'Careful approach told us that there were children about, and there being no signs of uniforms, we made ourselves known and were taken inside. Their hospitality was marvellous; we were given coffee and sandwiches in front of a roaring fire, and our host spoke excellent English. We were told that a British destroyer [HMS *Bedouin*] patrolled the fjord and when she showed up, with the aid of a cycle lamp, I was able to signal our name and tell them that we were part of *Ark Royal*'s aircrew. She answered, but was understandably reluctant to lower a boat, so one of the Norwegians rowed us out, and was given 1,000 cigarettes for his trouble.

'All this time we were expecting trouble from the other side of the fjord, but all stayed quiet until late in the evening, when hostile aircraft showed up and did their evil best to sink us. They were out of luck and the destroyer shot down at least one of them. This destroyer carried a Sick Berth Attendant, who was very helpful to both of us until we landed in Orkney and were transferred to a hospital ship. My back was X-rayed and bound up with miles of sticky tape, and they wanted me to go to hospital, but I persuaded them that I knew of a more effective treatment, so it was off to Mum and home cooking!' [114]

At 16:30, eight Skuas of 806 Squadron, each armed with a single 500lb SAP bomb and led by Lt-Cdr Evans, together with six Blenheim IVFs of 254 Squadron RAF led by Sqn Ldr Geoffrey Fairtlough, departed Hatston to attack Bergen, where the German gunnery training ship *Bremse* was reported at Doksjeir Jetty. This was not, in fact, the case. One section was led by Lt Colin Campbell-Horsfall, who had returned to 806 on recovery from his ditching on 24 April while commanding 801 Squadron. The Skua crews were:

	Blue Section		**Red Section**
L301	Lt-Cdr C L G Evans	L3013	Lt O J R Nicholls
	Lt D Vincent-Jones		PO(A)G A Muskett
L2935	Sub-Lt(A) I L F Lowe	L2878	Lt W L LeC Barnes
	L/Air N E Tallack		N/Air S H Gould
L2939	Sub-Lt(A) S G Orr	L3014	PO(A) A Jopling
	N/Air C H Thomson		N/Air K Jones

	White Section
L3016	Lt C P Campbell-Horsfall
	PO(A) L G Clare
L3018	Mid(A) G A Hogg
	N/Air D Pulsford

The defences at Bergen were taken by complete surprise and when the Skuas emerged from cloud, two ships were seen alongside the jetty. The pilots all later reported that on coming down through the clouds they were already practically in a dive and had insufficient time to select the best target. Between three and five hits were claimed on the ships. Two other Skuas attacked a merchant/auxiliary vessel alongside Skoltegrund Mole, gaining a near miss. An escort vessel in Byfjord was machine-gunned as were five or six MTBs and their depot ship at the entrance to Puddefjord. To complete this successful sortie, Lt-Cdr Evans strafed fuel tanks at Breivikin but without visible effect. As a result of this attack the 500-ton minesweeper *M.534* (ex-*M.134*) was sunk, with three dead and eight wounded, although the latter was later salved and restored to service as patrol boat *Jungingen*. Mid(A) Gus Hogg, on his first operational sortie (and flying with N/Air Doug Pulsford), later wrote in his journal:

'At 4 o'clock we received our orders and instructions and were airborne by 4.30. It was a lovely evening with light, wispy clouds and 200 miles of North Sea stretching in front of us. What lay on the other side? As I flew, I looked at my body – my hands on the control column and my legs and feet on the rudder bar. Would they be slashed and torn by flying steel? Could I stand the awful agony?

'For just under two hours we flew over the grey menacing North Sea, with anxious eyes on our engine gauges. A line loomed up on the horizon – the coast of Norway. Crossing over it a few minutes later, we went into line astern. My heart was thudding like a steam hammer and I had a funny feeling in the pit of my stomach. We swept round the back of Bergen and came in at 5,000 feet, through a thick black cloud. The bay lay below us; it was filled with shipping. I picked my target, two large ships anchored alongside one another, and dived down with my diving brakes lowered. At 2,000 feet I released my bomb and pulled up my flaps, continuing in a shallower dive to keep up a good speed. As I screamed down the fiord I espied a German sloop escorted by three MTBs. I immediately made towards them and machine-gunned the decks of the largest ship. To get away I had to cross over the MTBs, and climb to avoid a hill. Slowly! Oh, so slowly, I left them behind. Tracers were flying past my right wing. Would I never get over that hill? That mass of earth became indelibly printed on my mind – I can see it now.

'At last I was over and, finding some more of our aircraft, flew back with them to Sumburgh, in the Shetlands, where I successfully landed. I saw Stanley [Orr] make a doubtful touch-down and noticed that his aircraft was covered in oil. As soon as I could get hold of him, I asked him how he had fared. "Well", he said, "when we went through that cloud over Bergen, instead of flying by my instruments I tried to follow the man in front. I lost sight of him and while peering round, the aircraft stalled and I fell 4,000 feet on my back. I turned the right way up at 1,000 feet to find myself a few miles from Bergen. I climbed up slowly and dived from no great height. Ack-Ack was bursting all round and I heard one or two nasty clangs. Crossing the enemy coast on the way back I was somewhat disturbed to find that the engine would only run with the throttle in the take-off position – imagine the amount of petrol it was using! I was practically growing grey hairs all the way across the North Sea. As I was circling the aerodrome here the engine coughed and stopped. I put the nose down to land in the sea and the motion must have pumped the last drop of petrol into the carburettor. The engine lasted long enough for me to land – my prop stopped as I finished my landing run. There seems to be a hole in the air intake and a few other places." We flew back to Hatston in the failing light and landed in semidarkness, using lights. I landed and was very proud to discover that the man before me had pranged. I had not. The whole squadron was waiting to welcome us and I am sorry to say that some of the officers had become inebriated to celebrate our safe return or mourn our loss. I went to bed a thankful man.'

L3014 flown by PO(A) Arthur Jopling, crash-landed on arriving back at Sumburgh, but there were no injuries. He annotated his logbook thus:

'Direct hit on German light cruiser *Bremse* (believed sunk). Attacked and machine-gunned destroyer and six MTBs (damage unknown). Received shrapnel in undercarriage. Night landing.'

A second Skua, L2939 flown by Sub-Lt (A) Stan Orr, was also damaged by shrapnel to the engine induction pipe, engine cowling and starboard side of the centre section, but after repair at Sumburgh, returned to Hatston. The other six landed at Hatston, where one tipped on to its nose and was considerably damaged though the crew was unhurt. Meanwhile, the Blenheims attacked various targets with 20lb bombs, also machine-gunning as they swept over. One – L9482 flown by Flt Lt Alick Heath – was hit by AA fire and crashed into the harbour at Bergen, in which the crew were lost including FAA observer Lt(A) Robin Nuthall.

Captain Howe, OC Hatston RNAS sent a message to Vice-Admiral Commanding, Orkneys and Shetlands, praising 806 Squadron's effort:

'No.806 Squadron had not attacked before and was composed largely of young and inexperienced pilots. The difficulty of selecting a target without previous reconnaissance and the choice of targets given, resulted in insufficient bombs being retained for [attacking] the fuel tanks [at Breivikin]. These will, however, be the target for our next attack. Lt-Cdr Charles Evans led his squadron in a most able manner and achieved complete surprise. In this he was assisted by Lt Desmond Vincent-Jones whose navigation was excellent. PO(A) George Muskett and PO(A) Leslie Clare deserve mention for the part they played in the operation.'

During the morning of **10th May**, Narvik was heavily bombed by two-dozen Heinkels from I and III/KG26, escorted by Ju88Cs from Z/KG30. Early in the afternoon, three Skuas from 801 Squadron led by Lt(A) Moose Martyn on a patrol over the fleet, chased a He115 over Harstad, losing it in cloud. An hour later they were relieved by Lt Bill Lucy's 803 Squadron section, and these chased a He111 into clouds. PO(A) Harry Glover (L3046/A8H) was the only one to make contact:

'At 7,000 feet over Aandelnes. Cloud height decreased towards Narvik and leader decided to separate section and search independently. Sighted one He111 over Harstad. Enemy was proceeding below cloud layer and own aircraft carried out attack from astern, but was unable to close. Enemy escaped into cloud due to superior speed.'

Glover fired 1,800 rounds at the fleeing aircraft but admitted with 'unknown result'. However, his quarry may have been a Ju88C – 4D+FH of Z/KG30 flown by Uffz Alfred Weimann – that forced-landed on the mountainside at Storfjellet, west of Namskogan, due to engine failure apparently following combat. Weimann, Fw Krebs and one other were taken prisoner and sent to England. Deteriorating weather conditions then brought operations to a halt.

Early next day (**11th May**), six Skuas of 806 Squadron led by Lt-Cdr Evans departed Hatston escorted by three Blenheims of 254 Squadron to repeat the attack on fuel dumps at Asko Island near Bergen. Cloud covered the target, but the Skuas managed to dive-bomb seven oil tanks at Florvaag on the island of Strusshamn from 8,000 feet, claiming to have set two of these on fire. The Blenheims then added their incendiaries to the conflagration, and strafed the area generally. In fact all seven tanks were destroyed, burning for nearly a week. It proved impossible to extinguish the blaze and 19,000 litres of oil and petrol was lost. Mid(A) Gus Hogg later wrote in his journal:

'Strangely enough, I slept like a top but did not feel so good creeping around in the half-light at 4 o'clock in the morning. We repeated the same manoeuvres as before and successfully fired some oil tanks without damage to any of us. It was a goodly blaze. I certainly enjoyed my breakfast at 9 o'clock.'

He added:

'Photographs that came in that morning showed that in our first raid (9th May) we had sunk a training cruiser [*sic*]. She had received three direct hits – one forward, one amidships and one astern. My bomb looked uncommonly like the splash plume in the middle of the harbour. Two Norwegians, who had just rowed across from Bergen, said that the last bomb in the first raid had been an unqualified success. It must have been Stanley's. German Officers of occupation had been entertaining some local Quislings to a big party in a hotel on the dockside. Just as the President rose to propose a toast, a large and beautiful bomb spoilt the whole proceedings by landing smack in the middle of the room. The majority of the revellers are now, undoubtedly, toasting in Hell.

'I take the opportunity, here, of noting how one feels before any action. Prior to take-off, I, personally, have a horrid sensation in the pit of my stomach, which soon goes away until the lead starts to fly. Then it comes back again but I am like a man possessed and completely ignore it. To my knowledge, very few people are unfrightened [*sic*] in action but the majority hide or overcome it extremely well. I know one or two pilots who are impervious to fear but I consider that they are the exceptions.'

During the day *Ark Royal*'s fighters provided cover for two troop convoys heading for Narvik, and also protection for the battleship *Resolution* and cruiser *Penelope*. Continuous patrols were flown by both 800 and 803 Squadrons but no enemy aircraft were encountered.

Captain Howe (OC Hatston) was keen to send his Skuas to Bergen once again on **12th May**, but this time for them to attack an enemy transport, escorted by torpedo boats, reported operating in the fjord. Eight Skuas with Blenheim escort duly carried out an attack but no successes were gained. All returned safely. Mid(A) Hogg commented:

'We set off to attack shipping in the mouth of the fiord and discovered a medium-sized merchant ship steaming towards Bergen, escorted by two MTBs. Taking full advantage of a suitable cloud formation, we swept down one after the other. As soon as they saw us coming, the two MTBs scuttled off as fast as they could go and away from the steamer. I was the last to dive and, to my alarm, saw that all the other bombs had dropped about 50 yards astern. It was all up to me. I dived down, taking extremely careful aim and released the bomb at 1,500 feet. I would like to be able to say that the ship heeled over, blew up and sank; she did no such thing. I missed by a good 100 yards and the enemy vessel carried on to Bergen! If we had met any enemy aircraft on the way home I should have felt sorry for them. There were eight extremely annoyed and vicious Fleet Air Arm pilots flying in the North Sea air. We felt sorry for ourselves when we reported in the Operations Room.'

Meanwhile, *Ark Royal* was experiencing bad weather but endeavoured to maintain fighter patrols. Three 800 Squadron aircraft led by Lt James Rooper (L3001), with Mid(A) Bob Kearsley (L3024) and PO(A) Les Burston (L2938), on patrol from 0405, chased a He111 and a Do17. No claims were made but a Heinkel, F6+DH of 1(F)/122, flown by the Staffelkapitän Hptm Edgar Caesar on a dawn reconnaissance flew into a mountain shrouded in fog on the island of Vanna; pilot and crew (Uffz Otto Karnapp,

Uffz Hans-Joachim Müller and Uffz Georg Ableitner) were later found dead by German troops. This may have been the aircraft pursued by the Skuas. Mid(A) Kearsley (with L/Air Charlie Eccleshall) noted in his logbook:

> 'Patrol Ran Fjord. Spotted He111 which disappeared into cloud (much low cloud). Then spotted Dornier 17 or Do215. Got to about 400 yards before he saw me. Then he opened his throttle (black smoke) and I could not get closer than about 400 yards. Emptied my guns at him from that range, chased him through clouds and then at sea level for over 20 minutes. Received one bullet in port wingtip. Time airborne: 4 hrs 15 mins.'

Lt Skeet Harris RM of 803 Squadron led one of the later patrols:

> 'Convoy alert. Took-off in bad weather and eventually found convoy in fjord. Clouds at 400 feet. On return could not find *Ark Royal*. Carried out search in very bad weather. Visibility half-mile in patches. Found ship after five-and-a-half hours, with one wheel down!'

At 17:25, Green Section of 803 Squadron led by Lt Christian took-off from *Ark Royal*, tasked to bomb the railway line at Romsbakfjord. After flying through low cloud and heavy rain, the section entered the fjord an hour later and attempted to reach their objective, but were unable to owing to low cloud and heavy snow. Christian (L2963/A8A) decided to turn back but not before he and Green 3 (Mid(A) Stephen Griffith in L2961/A8C) released their bombs elsewhere along the railway line, with unknown results. All three returned safely to the carrier, landing on at 20:40.

13th May was to prove relatively quiet for air operations, but a bad one for aircraft losses. Both 800 and 803 Squadron continued patrols over the task force, the first being flown by 800 Squadron departing *Ark Royal* at 02:15, led by Lt Ken Spurway. The next patrol, at 04:25, under Lt James Rooper, ran into difficulties, both L2938 piloted by PO(A) Les Burston and L3001 flown by Rooper, were forced to make emergency landings, Burston's aircraft coming down in the sea south of Harstad. He and his TAG, N/Air George Halifax, were picked up by the destroyer HMS *Brazen*. Meanwhile, Lt Rooper forced-landed at Sandsoy, north of Harstad, he and PO(A) Wallace Crawford also being rescued. Fog curtailed a third patrol mounted by three aircraft from 801 Squadron.

Six Swordfish of 820 Squadron were tasked to carry out a diversionary and support attack on railways while the French Foreign Legion were making a landing at Bjerkvik. Led by Capt Newson RM, they flew off at 04:20 in two flights, setting course to make landfall at Maaneset.

A4A	Capt A C Newson RM	Lt-Cdr G B Hodgkinson	L/Air R H McColl
A4F	Lt B E Boulding	Lt A W N Dayrell	N/Air R Finney
A4G	Lt H de G Hunter	L/Air D D Smith	
A4K	Lt R N Everett	Lt H B Gerrett RAN	N/Air A L Johnson
A4B	Lt R S Hankey	L/Air C Pendleton	
A4M	Sub-Lt(A) A Owensmith	Lt C C Ennever	N/Air C Sanders

Visibility was so poor that some 20 minutes later it was decided to abandon the operation. However, on climbing above the cloud layer, the crews could clearly see the coast and the aircraft again headed towards their objectives. At 06:15 the sub-flights separated and the first group successfully bombed the end of a railway tunnel west of Sudvik. On reforming over Herjangsfjord they investigated a submarine in Sulberg Fjord, which turned out be Norwegian. However, A4A and A4G, after turning on an easterly course, disappeared in dense fog and it was later learned they had both forced-landed near Harstad. Lt Bob Everett's sub-flight managed to find the target and bombed a tunnel at Hunddalen. Both missing crews were able to return to the carrier.

810 Squadron also reported two Swordfish missing from patrols, although Lt Nigel Corbet-Milward and his crew of A2K (Capt Keith Ford RM and L/Air Joe Black) were able to return following a landing at Skaanland. The second Swordfish, A2H flown by Sub-Lt Tony Dixon landed on a frozen lake near Reisenvaan. He and his crew Mid(A) Hector Dangerfield and N/Air Vince Labross, were safely recovered unhurt and the Swordfish was removed to Harstad and later returned to the UK aboard the French steamer *Albert Lebougne*.

In the early hours of **14th May**, British and French troops began an opposed landing near Narvik, soon linking with Norwegian and Polish forces approaching from the north. The assault was supported by Skuas and Swordfish from *Ark Royal*. Luftwaffe reconnaissance aircraft were quick to locate British warships in Ofotfjord, Vestfjord and off Harstad, launching two-dozen He111s of KG26 to carry out an attack, but all that could be found by the bomber crews was a single Norwegian fishing vessel.

Later in the day the Skuas began a new series of attacks on Lake Hartvigvann, three 801 Squadron aircraft taking off at 11:00 to strafe the derelict Ju52/3ms there. An hour-and-a-half later three bomb-carrying 803 Squadron Skuas headed for the same area to break up the ice on the lake by dive-bombing. Having completed this task, they then saw several He111s of KG26 at 17,000 feet and chased these for some time. Lt Bill Lucy in L2925/A8F and Lt Tom Gray in L2918/A8G inflicted damage on one and then chased another down to low level and saw their fire hitting it; an aircraft of the Stabskette II/KG26 was hit and later crash-landed at Vaernes, its hydraulics shot up, suffering 30% damage. As the Skuas attacked the second bomber, Lucy's aircraft became the target for crossfire from this and another Heinkel, and suddenly exploded at only 50 feet above the sea off Tranby. Gray at once flew off to seek aid, leading the destroyer HMS *Whirlwind* to the area. Here Lucy's body was found (and committed to the sea) but of his observer, Lt Michael Hanson, there was no trace. By now, low on fuel, Gray forced-landed at Andlilya from where he and L/Air Clayton were rescued by the destroyer HMS *Encounter*. In his official report, Lt Gray wrote:

> 'Observed almost direct hit by leader. Patrolled Narvik area for approximately one hour. Received enemy bombing report – climbed west to *Resolution*. At 17,000 feet observed He111 above *Resolution*. Chased this south for approximately ten minutes. Abandoned chase and returned to Narvik and found No.3 in Section [PO(A) Glover in L3046/8H] had become detached. On return received further enemy report from *Resolution*. Returned to west and observed heavy AA fire at one bomber. This turned towards Narvik and dropped two bombs on destroyer, which missed by two lengths. This machine climbed steadily out of range. Observed almost immediately two twos and one single Heinkels approaching from east at 18,000 feet.

'We broke formation and did head-on attack at leading two to split formation, while leader did stern attack. We did one astern attack after leader (port engine appeared to be on fire), who then dived after other two Heinkels, who had dropped to water level. Leader went very close and fired burst – then swung away. Machine appeared to flash as we passed. Fired good burst and observed port engine smoking in one machine. I then broke off attack and searched for leader. Found wreckage consisting of tail unit floating and dinghy off Trandy. Observed no signs of personnel – but proceeded to pick up destroyer at Ramsundet. Having shown spot to destroyer, proceeded to Ramsundet where I forced-landed at approximately 18:00, due to petrol shortage.

'Lt Lucy's machine appeared to explode at about 50 feet and dived astern of me. I did not see him crash as I was engaging enemy at time.'

Salvaged from the sea by the destroyer *Whirlwind* were: one beacon set; two Very pistols, two parachutes and harness, W/T coils, one transmitter and receiver, one generator, one Lewis gun and pans of ammunition. Lt Lucy was a sad loss; the most successful of the Skua pilots to date, he had been credited with taking part in the shooting down of at least six Luftwaffe bombers, and had also led the successful strike that sank *Königsberg*, for which he was awarded the DSO. Of the loss of his friend Capt Birdy Partridge recalled:

'This triumph [the attack on the *Königsberg* at Bergen] was not enough for Bill, and he organised long and hazardous reconnaissance flights over to Norway searching for further worthwhile targets. He revelled in those trips and I hated them; the longest I did lasted 4 hours 35 minutes – so much for the official endurance of 4 hours 20, but it was stretching things and I had only just enough fuel left to taxi in after landing. Meanwhile, Bill's luck (or skill?) was holding and be had managed to pounce on another Heinkel. Before taking off, I looked round for Bill to say goodbye and found him as usual in the Ops Room champing to find some worthwhile target, the more hazardous and unexpected the better! That was the last time I saw him. He had been seen doing one of his attacks on an enemy aircraft and just as he was about to collide with the enemy's rear turret he had broken away in a steep dive with smoke pouring from the Skua – the rear gunner had got him first.'[115]

Two more 803 Squadron Skuas returned to Lake Hartvigvann at 15:35, again bombing the ice, which was now reported to be melting. Seven more II/KG26 He111s also arrived over the Harstad and Narvik area to attack shipping at this time, and two of these were encountered by Lt Skeet Harris RM (L2910/A8K) – promoted to lead 803 Squadron following Lucy's loss – and PO(A) Johnno Johnson (L2992/A8L), who identified them as a Heinkel and a Ju88. Harris claimed damage to the latter, the undercarriage of which dropped down, while Johnson fired at the former. Harris' report revealed:

'Carried out astern and quarter attacks. Enemy aircraft used all available cloud as cover. After first burst, the undercarriage of the enemy aircraft fell down. Six more attacks were then carried out before the enemy disappeared in thick cloud. (Second action) I carried out an astern attack, closing to 100 yards, but fire was inaccurate, as the reflector sight was not working. No.2 carried out one good astern attack. Enemy disappeared in a cloud.'

Two 5 Staffel Heinkels were damaged in this combat, one suffering 30% damage while the other (1H+DN/2501) forced-landed on a frozen lake near Fauske on the Norwegian border by Uffz Siegfried Blume after his crew [116] had baled out. They endeavoured to walk back to German lines but were captured by Norwegian forces at Skjomen, from where they were shipped to the UK.

Bad weather next day (**15th May**) prevented much action, although a few bombing attacks were undertaken by *Ark Royal*'s air group, which now mustered a dozen serviceable Swordfish and 18 Skuas. The new CO Lt Harris RM (L2910) and PO(A) Johnson (L2992) were up at 07:00 and again sighted an intruder:

> 'On sighting enemy aircraft, I climbed towards it. No.2, who was in formation above me, went ahead and managed to get in an astern attack before the enemy retired into a thick cloud. I was unable to close enemy aircraft owing to superior speed. The pilot of No.2 aircraft received a bullet wound in the right shoulder and returned to *Ark Royal*. I continued patrol over Narvik but no more enemy aircraft were encountered.'

PO(A) Johnson was able to land safely aboard the carrier. His TAG, L/Air Frank Costan received some splinters in his face. It seems their victim may have been Ju88C 4D+RH (0154) of Z/KG30, which was reported to have crashed at Narvik with the loss of two of the crew.[117]

A Swordfish of 816 Squadron ditched in Ofotfjord after receiving damage during an attack on German aircraft at Lake Hartvigvaan. Sub-Lt Nigel Ball, Lt Anthony Marshall and N/Air R. Pike were picked up by the destroyer *Zulu*. Nine Skuas of 806 Squadron and three Blenheims set out from Hatston to raid Bergen, but were forced to return owing to fog. Meanwhile, the Allied desire to take Narvik finally gained some momentum, with the British pushing up from Harstad and the French establishing a force ashore at Bjerkuick, north of the objective.

Improved conditions off the Norwegian coast on **16th May** saw a more active day in the air as *Ark Royal*'s seemingly tireless Skua crews were up again maintaining their regular patrols. At 07:10, eight He111s of KGr.100, followed at 09:10 by eleven more from II/KG26, set out for Narvik. At 11:30, the battleship *Resolution*, anchored at Tjeldsundet, was struck by a bomb that pierced the starboard side of the quarterdeck and exploded in the Royal Marines' mess deck. One rating was killed and another died of wounds; 22 Marines and four ratings were wounded.[118]

The bombers were escorted to the Narvik area by two Bf110s of I/ZG76, and two Z/KG30 Ju88Cs. The Messerschmitt pilots reported an inconclusive fight with four (*sic*) Skuas, whilst Oblt Herbert Bönsch of Z/KG30 claimed an aircraft which he identified as a 'Blackburn Roc' to the south-east of Narvik at 13:00, and it seems that his wingman, Uffz Peter Lauffs, claimed another. They had in fact engaged two 803 Squadron Skuas flown by Lt Skeet Harris RM and PO(A) Harry Glover, who had taken off from *Ark* at 11:50 and had spotted two aircraft near Narvik which they identified as Do17s, but were probably the two Bf110s. These were bounced by the Skuas, which were in turn attacked by two more German aircraft, identified as being of the same type, but almost certainly the two Ju88Cs. Lt Harris (L2910/8K) later recalled:

'Fighter Patrol Narvik. With PO(A) Glover attacked five Ju88s. One shot down. A bullet splattered through my windscreen and into my left shoulder after several head-on attacks and I parked in a fjord off Narvik. The Skua, sedate to the end, waddled to the seabed. Luckily, the Royal Navy had had a ringside seat and after a remarkably short but very cold bath they picked up my observer [Lt Medlicott-Vereker] and myself.'

The crew was rescued by the destroyer *Matabele* from which Lt Harris was transferred to hospital at Harstad. His tenure as CO of 803 Squadron was thus very brief. PO(A) Glover returned safely to the *Ark* and reported that he had tried to draw the aggressive twin-engined machines over the British warships, where it was thought that one had been hit by both the ships' pom-poms and fire from Glover's gunner (N/Air Wright), and had been shot down. The action lasted a full 30 minutes. Glover commented:

'Two aircraft were seen, and on engaging them, two more dived to assist them. Our aircraft were hopelessly outclassed in speed and manoeuvrability, and a dogfight ensued. Yellow Leader was forced down and enemy attacked me from all angles. Astern and quarter attacks were carried out.'

Three Skuas of 801 Squadron were also up and engaged the Ju88s (or He111s), as Lt-Cdr Peter Bramwell (L2907) reported:

'This section had orders to locate and bomb the derelict Polish transport *Chawvry* which was reported as lying stranded and a danger to navigation at the southernmost entrance to the Vestfjord, and afterwards to carry out a fighter patrol in the vicinity of Narvik and the Fleet Anchorage. There was no sign of the Polish transport, and after searching for 45 minutes, the section released their bombs into the sea and proceeded on fighter patrol, climbing to 12,000 feet.

'At 13:05, three Ju88s were seen approaching the Fleet Anchorage from the direction of Narvik, flying in Vic formation, the Skua section promptly formed line astern and turned to intercept and attack the enemy. Unfortunately, the enemy aircraft were some 2,500 feet above the Skuas so the rate of approach to attack was very slow. The Skuas were seen by the enemy fairly soon and the Junkers formed very tight Vic formation. Eventually the Skuas carried out attacks separately on one wing aircraft at long-range, 600 yards, closing to 300 yards. The enemy brought good crossfire to bear and took avoiding action, with the result that no bombing attack was made. The Junkers then made off in a southerly direction and then turned round in a large circle to make further bombing attack on HM ships. The Skua section waited over the anchorage ready to intercept the enemy.

'An interception was made and attacks were carried out and the enemy once again made off at full speed, taking avoiding action. The Junkers were last seen heading eastwards; Skuas meanwhile had run out of ammunition and so returned to the carrier. It is thought that the enemy must have been severely 'peppered' but no engines were put on fire. Throughout the engagement the enemy maintained close formation, bringing good crossfire to bear. No bombs were dropped.'

The other Skuas of the section were flown by Sub-Lt(A) Wigginton (L2921) and

Mid(A) Dick Martin (L3005). As the Germans withdrew, the crew of one of the Heinkels spotted the aircraft carrier, a battleship and two heavy cruisers, and at once all available bombers were sent off to attack, the force despatched comprising 18 He111s from KG26 and eight Ju88s from 6/KG 30.

Three more 803 Squadron Skuas – Green Secton led by Lt Christian (L2963/8A) – were off at 13:30, and at 14:15 reported engaging six Ju88s over Ofotfjord. A tremendous dogfight followed, during which the German aircraft dived, steep-climbed, turned, and in one case spun to 1,000 feet. Sub-Lt Ian Easton (L3010/8B) claimed one Ju88, which he saw crash into Ofotfjord, while Mid(A) Stephen Griffith (L2961/8C) claimed a second, which he reported crashed on a mountainside south of the fjord. His TAG, N/Air Fred Dooley also fired at the Ju88, noting: 'a possible claimed with rear gun.' In his report, Lt Christian wrote:

> 'After initial sectional astern attack, the action developed into a dogfight. Enemy had superior speed, but were willing to fight. When attacked from astern they dived away, but went into steep climbing turns if unimpaired. One enemy machine was seen to spin as a method of avoiding attack, recovering at about 1,000 feet. When diving away they endeavoured to lead our aircraft over Narvik within range of their flak. One enemy was brought down in Narvikfjord, and the second was seen to crash on mountainside on south side of Ofotfjord.'

6 Staffel did indeed lose an aircraft to fighters, probably the aircraft flown by Ltn Heinrich Diermeyer that forced-landed south of Ofotfjord. It would seem that both Skua pilots had attacked the same aircraft. All four members of the crew were taken prisoner and Ltn Diermeyer was despatched to the UK; however, the remaining three – Uffz Anton Schlosser, Gfr Georg Schultz and Gfr Heinrich Koch – were later liberated and returned to their unit.

Four 800 Squadron Skuas led by Lt Rooper began a patrol at 16:50. After attacking a He111 that escaped them, the two sections became split up and one pair returned to Harstad where they saw a single bomber identified as a Ju88. Sub-Lt(A) Bas Hurle-Hobbs (L3049) and Mid(A) Bob Kearsley (L3024) both attacked. Hurle-Hobbs (with N/Air Northfield) reported:

> 'I sighted the Ju88 flying at about 500 feet above me while over the Fleet anchorage. The enemy did a vertical dive down to about 4,000 feet and dropped one bomb very close to the port of the cruiser *Aurora*. I dived down after her and got in a quarter attack at about 350 yards. Mid Kearsley cut off the turn to my right and gave a burst from full astern and the enemy's port engine was seen to be hit. I then carried out another quarter attack on the enemy's port engine, Kearsley remaining on his tail. At 2,000 feet I broke away and observed the Ju88 landing in the fjord. A crew of five got out and swam ashore.'

Mid(A) Kearsley, flying with L/Air Charlie Eccleshall, noted in his logbook:

> 'To patrol Narvik and protect anchorage from bombers. Put myself on the tail of a Ju88 and fired a short burst, which stopped its port engine. Remained 300 yards astern, firing short bursts into fuselage and starboard engine. Flew alongside twice and my AG fired some rounds until the Ju88 hit the water. Crew swam ashore.

Landed (the Ju88) in Bogenfjord. Received one bullet in my airscrew spinner. Time airborne: 4 hrs 30 mins.'

Their victim was 4D+AP of 6/KG30 that ditched in the sea at Forra in Bogen. The crewmembers swam ashore where, according to locals, Fw Ernst Kubler was killed by the strafing Skua as he reached the shore. The survivors, Hptm and Staffelkapitän Günter Noll and Fw Willi Schell attempted to make a run for it but were soon captured and handed over to the authorities, two being sent to England while Schell, who was injured, was able later to return to his unit. Another section from 800 Squadron encountered two He111s, which were attacked without success, as Lt Ken Spurway (L2909) reported:

'18:15: Enemy aircraft was sighted on starboard bow and 500 feet above. Enemy steering south. Turned towards enemy and fired two bursts using full deflection. I believe first burst hit. No fire from hostile aircraft. He later escaped by superior climb. Second Heinkel sighted [at 19:00] on same level at 13,000 feet steering south. Closed and fired from astern. Enemy returned fire and dived away. I endeavoured to close, firing short bursts. Pursued enemy out to sea and down to 300 feet. In both cases enemy escaped by superior performance. No definite result was obtained.'

Further down the coast nine Skuas of 806 Squadron from Hatston again bombed Bergen during the midday period, claiming six oil tanks bombed and destroyed at Kaarven, Florgasaaspynt and Strudshavn. All aircraft returned safely. PO(A) Jopling flying L3004: 'Attacked oil tanks – several left burning (own bomb unobserved).'

On **17th May**, as the *Ark* departed for Tromsø to refuel, *Glorious* and *Furious* arrived, carrying two RAF fighter squadrons (263 Squadron with Gladiators and 46 Squadron with Hurricanes) while the former carried six 802 Squadron Sea Gladiators (including N5521, N5525-5527 and N5530) for defence, a detachment of six Swordfish from 823 Squadron (P3998/G4C, L9762/G4F, K8867/G4G, P4035/G4H, K5937/G4Q and L9766/G4R) and six Walrus amphibians of 701 Squadron, the latter for transfer to Harstad. The RAF Gladiator unit, having been decimated a few weeks earlier, had received new aircraft though most of the pilots were survivors of the first expedition bolstered by half-a-dozen replacements. It had been intended for the RAFVR/FAA contingent to fly the Gladiators aboard *Furious* as Sgt Jim Pickering recalled:

'On 4th May, all were posted back to the FAA in great haste, joining 759(T) Squadron at Eastleigh. After an intensive two-week refresher course they were posted to Hatston in the Orkneys, being intended to fly Gladiators of 263 Squadron and Hurricanes of 46 Squadron onto HMS *Furious* (sic) for transfer to Norway, since the pilots of these units had not undertaken carrier landings. Their arrival was too late, however, for the Hurricanes had been hoisted aboard from lighters, while the Gladiators had been flown aboard by FAA pilots. Consequently, the group was posted to 804 Squadron which had been formed at Hatston, to fly Sea Gladiators on land-based defensive duties. There, Sgt Sturges was killed in a landing accident.'

One of the returning 263 Squadron pilots had earlier suffered shrapnel wounds, and it was agreed that his place be taken by FAA volunteer Lt Anthony Lydekker. He was a qualified fighter pilot and had been serving as the Armament Officer on the Air Staff of *Furious* since the recommissioning of the ship in 1939.

To date, Hurricanes had not been flown operationally from the deck of a carrier but the pilots were fairly confident. The two carriers joined the Home Fleet west of the Lofoten Islands. Initially however the airfields ashore were not quite ready to receive the RAF aircraft, and for the time being these stayed aboard although *Glorious* was ordered back to Scapa Flow with her charges intact. However, the ground parties were now arriving, that of 46 Squadron reaching Harstad on the 17th, moving on to Skaanland next day.

That night (**17/18th May**), six Swordfish of 823 Squadron, (those not required aboard *Glorious,*) arrived at Hatston and carried out the unit's first airborne minelaying operation (named Operation Bottle) in the Haugesund area. The force took-off at 21:30, each aircraft fitted with an internal auxiliary fuel tank. The mines were to be dropped in level flight and at a height not exceeding 500 feet. Land was sighted at 00:45 and the two sections led by Lt Robert Furlong and Lt John Reed commenced the operation. The leading Swordfish dropped in the correct position at 01:00 but the following sub-flight, finding itself in a bad position to drop, was led overland and manoeuvred from south to north. The mines were then dropped in the correct position at 01:05. On the return flight, Sub-Lt(A) Harry Mourilyan signalled that his engine was giving trouble and immediately afterwards his reduction gear flew off. The Swordfish was last seen gliding down towards the sea. Hatston was informed, but Mourilyan and his TAG N/Air Roy Parkinson were not found. Mourilyan's friend Roy Hinton recalled:

> 'The aircraft were lined up on the airfield. We were going off that night. We were checking our aircraft to see everything was all right. I still remember walking past Mourilyan and I said, "How are you doing?" He said, "I'll never get back; this wretched aircraft, the engine is losing oil." I said, "For God's sake tell them and don't go!" He said, "No, I can't do that, I must go." We were flying in Vic formation coming back. Mourilyan was on our port side. All we saw was a ball of flame and the whole of the aircraft began to sink into the sea. I didn't actually see it go in. When we got back I tried to pinpoint the position. He went straight in, never seen or heard of again. He was the first of my close friends to be lost in the war.'

Meanwhile, Sub-Lt(A) Alastair Easton of the second sub-flight forced-landed on the Isle of May and two other machines forced-landed on return to Hatston. In both cases oil leaks appear to have been the cause. As a result, a report was submitted suggesting that an extra oil tank was desirable in long-range Swordfish.

During the early morning hours of **18th May** (01:30-03:15), three 800 Squadron Skuas (led Finch-Noyes and probably included Mid(A)s Kearsley and Gallagher) again intercepted a He111 which was believed to have been damaged; this may have been an aircraft from 3/KG26 that returned from a sortie over Narvik with a wounded crewman on board. The Skuas led by Lt Finch-Noyes experienced the frustration of being out-performed by the Heinkel. Finch-Noyes (L3000) wrote:

> 'The fight developed into a chase and the Skuas could just hold the enemy but could not close to effective range. It was very noticeable that the Heinkel was firing with two guns from the top gun position and the bullets were being sprayed as opposed to being aimed at our machines.'

At noon, two Bv138 flying boats serving with KGrzbV.108 left Trondheim to convey 15 troops of 2/GJR.138 to Beisfjord. They were spotted by British troops as they landed, and were subsequently strafed by four Skuas of 800 Squadron led by Lts Ken Spurway and James Rooper. Both flying boats were so badly damaged that they had to be abandoned.

The day also saw the arrival at Harstad of the six Walruses of 701 Squadron (P5656, P5697, P5702, P5705, P5707 and P5711) that had been flown from the deck of *Glorious* before she was recalled for reconnaissance and ferrying/transportation duties, and was to be known as 'Bishop Force' under the command of Lt Hugo Bracken. An advance party had already arrived at Harstad to set up a headquarters and maintenance facility for the flying boat unit. Additionally they were also to be responsible for the maintenance of Walruses from the cruisers HMS *Effingham* (P5662 flown by Lt Phil Francklin) following the cruiser's grounding in Vestfjord; *Glasgow*'s P5649, and later *Southampton*'s P5651. It was intended that nine Swordfish floatplanes of 816 Squadron would follow as soon as possible, although this order was later rescinded. The Walruses were moored to existing buoys in the harbour. During the ensuing weeks the crews would fly in all weathers on ferrying duties in addition to carrying out anti-submarine patrols in all the fjords within range of Harstad. Aircraft were sent on numerous occasions to investigate intelligence reports received from Norwegian sources. These were often received too late to be acted upon, and were sometimes inaccurate. Instructions were given to all pilots that they were to keep as close to the side of fjords as possible and not to exceed 500 feet unless absolutely necessary. The aircraft wore a dark green camouflage as used by the Norwegian Air Force, which proved very effective against the mountain background.

Southampton's Walrus P5651 came close to becoming a victim of friendly fire when it overflew the little town of Liland near Narvik, while conveying Admiral Lord Cork to a meeting aboard the cruiser *Aurora*. Based around the town were 1/Irish Guards, who had been pestered by German aircraft and whose light AA gunners were, understandably, somewhat trigger-happy. On this occasion, the Walrus suddenly appeared out of cloud, to be met by a burst of Bren-gun fire. The pilot, Lt(A) Paul Woods, climbed steeply and then came down again for recognition, only to be greeted by another burst of fire. The unfortunate gunner, a lance corporal, was marched into the CO's office charged with being 'idle in the recognition of aircraft.' Sympathetic friends were waiting outside the office for when the gunner reappeared. 'What did you get?', they enquired. 'A reprimand' was the reply. 'What for?' 'For missing a low-flying admiral' was the response! The Admiral no doubt took his narrow escape with a pinch of salt, since before the Walrus had taken off on this flight, he had requested that a 20lb bomb be delivered to him, which he carried on his lap:

> 'The opportunity seldom occurs in modern war for a Commander-in-Chief to lead a personal attack on the enemy – I am not going to miss this chance.'

While flying over a single-track railway that fed Narvik, he leaned out of the starboard window and dropped his bomb on the line. The result was not observed.

The day Bishop Force landed at Harstad, HMS *Devonshire* was taking part in operations farther north near Tromsø; and at the late but still day-lit-hour of 23:30, Lt Ronald

Benson-Dare was launched in Walrus P5647 to investigate a U-boat report in Melangenfjord. While flying up the fjord the Walrus suddenly encountered a He111 – a machine from Stabskette X Fliegerkorps piloted by Hptm Robert Kowalewski. Also on board as observer was Major Martin Harlinghausen.

Benson-Dare dived to sea level while his observer Mid(A) Tony Corkhill and L/Air Bill Hill struggled quickly to their respective gun positions. Instead of attacking them head on, the Heinkel's chief tactic was to make passing runs so that he could bring all his guns to bear, to which the Walrus responded by violent alterations towards each approach. An early hit carried away Corkhill's foresight, so that he was reduced to hose-piping, using his tracer rounds to get on target; expensive in ammunition, it was the only hope he had of hitting it. The fight raged inside the fjord for fifteen minutes or more. About three-quarters of the way through, Hill was hit in the head. Corkhill was also cut about the face and legs by flying splinters, but in one of his hose-piping efforts before he expended the last of his six pans of ammunition, he had the satisfaction of noting that the enemy's upper rear gunner was failing to take any further interest in the action. One of the Walrus's fuel tanks had been holed and petrol was streaming aft. Corkhill, hit in the head at about the 17th or 18th attack, was sitting partially dazed on the step in the bow when another burst of fire came from the Heinkel. There was an explosion as the petrol ignited; at the same time the Walrus nosed into a dive as if the pilot had been hit and fallen on to the stick. P5647 went straight in.

The biting cold water must have wrenched Corkhill back to full consciousness, for he found himself doubled under the instrument panel. A disc of pale daylight glowed from the direction of the Scarff-ring and he immediately struggled through it to the surface. Debris floated everywhere, so he clung in the lee of a wing-tip float until the Heinkel, after making a final passing run, disappeared down the fjord. Neither of Corkhill's companions was in sight, so he struck out for the shore; he must have been swimming for two painful minutes when, looking back, he saw Hill come to the surface. The TAG appeared semi-conscious and unable to swim, so Corkhill went back to support him on a piece of wreckage. He then saw two men ashore, who must obviously have heard the fight. They were running towards the crest of a hill. He shouted and waved and shouted. Time passed, and he was at the limits of endurance when a rowing boat, with presumably the same two men in it arrived and picked them up, Hill unconscious, Corkhill nearly so.

They were transferred to a small motor fishing boat and taken up the fjord, being transferred again to a Norwegian auxiliary trawler. Corkhill was told later, when he had recovered more fully, that the trawler skipper, when alongside, had shouted down, 'Are they German or English? If they're German, throw them back.' When one of the seamen had asked Corkhill in English how he felt he had replied, 'I'm fucking cold!' At which the other had shouted back to the skipper, 'They're English all right.' Lt Benson-Dare's body was never recovered and L/Air Bill Hill died shortly thereafter.[119]

Hptm Kowalewski and his Heinkel crew rounded off their successful mission when they attacked and sank the small Norwegian coastal cargo vessel *Sirius* in Solbergfjorden, between Finnlandsnes and Solbergnakken, while on the return leg to their airfield Vaernes. Eight of the crew lost their lives.

On **20th May**, another He111 of 1(F)/122 appeared over Narvik and only just escaped interception by three fighters – believed by the crew to have been Sea Gladiators – by diving into cloud. The crew reported two transport vessels in Beisfjord, and later reconnaissances also noted other shipping here, so 14 Heinkels from KG26 and KGr.100, and six KG30 Ju88s were sent off, escorted this time by eight Bf110s of I/ZG76 and four Ju88Cs of Z/KG30. The Heinkels of III/KG26 bombed the freighter *Pembroke Coast* in Harstad harbour and the vessel, carrying petrol, provisions and military supplies, was set on fire; she had to be sunk by British warships next day, after her crew had been taken off safely. A second ship, the Norwegian freighter *Deneb*, was also set ablaze, and two of her crew were killed. As she was also carrying petrol, she was towed out to sea by a destroyer and sunk with gunfire. One of 701 Squadron's Walrus amphibians (P5702) was sunk at its moorings but later raised by lashing 18 empty oil drums under the wings, lowering the landing wheels at high tide, and hauling her higher up the shore. Her hull was temporarily repaired at low tide, and equipment and fittings removed. Since, by then, engine and aircraft had been submerged for over three days it was subsequently decided to sink her in deep water. On the same day, a patrol from 803 Squadron failed to meet enemy aircraft but were subjected to AA fire, as noted by Lt Tom Gray (L2878): 'Fired at by French, British and Germans!'

A refuelled and replenished *Ark Royal* rejoined the Fleet on **21st May**, ready to provide cover for the belated despatch of the 18 RAF Gladiators from *Furious* to Bardufoss, Flt Lt Stuart Mills describing the take-off from *Furious*:

> 'The weather was very bad, visibility was poor and it was snowing hard with intermittent blizzards. Baldy [Sqn Ldr Donaldson] asked me to take Plt Offs Richards and Francis with me and try to get through. A Swordfish from *Furious* would lead us in. Baldy then took off with fifteen Gladiators and two Skuas to navigate, but after a short while decided it was too bad to continue and landed back on the carrier without incident. The carrier, which had not obtained a sighting of land all the days it had been at sea, was, in fact, 60 to 70 miles out of position. Instead of being opposite Bardufoss it was nearer Torsking Island and we were confronted by mountains rising to some 4,000 feet.
>
> 'We pressed on, climbed to 1,500 feet and, then, in the appalling conditions, there were three crashes almost simultaneously. The Swordfish hit a mountainside, but the crew escaped. Richards flew into the face of a mountain and was killed. My Gladiator hit 2,000 feet up a mountain and at once burst into flames; I was able to get out. Francis, alone, got away with it and, with a remarkable piece of navigation, eventually made Bardufoss. I was taken, with Richards, whose body was a terrible sight, in a motorboat to Harstad where he was buried. I was then moved, under medical escort, to Tromsø, and was later evacuated in the cruiser *Devonshire*, with the King of Norway, members of the Norwegian Royal Family and Parliament and a consignment of gold.'

One of the RAF pilots later added:

> 'The other lot got off at 03:10. This batch came to grief. It was a saddening affair. By probably the most meagre error of navigation this lot was led by its Swordfish slap into a mist-covered mountain, a peak of 3,300 feet on Senga Island north of

Soreisa. It seems that they were bang up against the mountain wall before they saw it. The Swordfish piled in, but its crew escaped.'

The crew of the 818 Squadron Swordfish (P4216), Sub-Lt(A) Jack Welply and L/Air Harry Simpson survived the impact, as the latter recalled:

'We finished up on top of a mountain near a place called Torsken, which just happened to be on the track from *Furious* to Bardufoss. One of the Glad pilots must have had second sight and pulled up and got away, but one hit just before our arrival and the other hit with us in tight formation.'

Later in the day conditions improved and all the remaining RAF Gladiators were flown off during the next two days, landing at Bardufoss under an umbrella provided by sections of Skuas from 800 and 803 Squadrons. Her task completed, *Furious* returned to Scapa Flow.

At 13:00 on **26th May**, three Gladiators of 263 Squadron including one flown by Lt Tony Lydekker were detached to Bodø to provide cover for troops retreating northwards in the face of the German advance. En route they were engaged in an inconclusive combat with one of the KGr.100 Heinkels on its way to Bardufoss. When they landed on their new airfield their aircraft all stuck fast in the mud. They managed to get the Gladiators to drier ground, where they began refuelling from four-gallon tins. This arduous task was by no means complete when a He111 of 1(F)/122 was seen overhead, and all three pilots leapt into their cockpits to take off. Lydekker got off safely, but the mud clung to the wheels of the two following Gladiators, and one crashed. Lydekker's aircraft had not been refuelled however, and he had little petrol left and he was ordered to land again. The Heinkel was shot down by Flt Lt Caesar Hull, who went on to shoot down three Ju52/3m transports before his ammunition ran out.

Both Gladiators were airborne later during the evening covering ships leaving Bodø as the evacuation continued, all three pilots participating. Lt Lydekker flew the first patrol, taking off at 23:30, and was followed at midnight by the second Gladiator. There would be an overlapping of half-an-hour in their patrols. Flt Lt Hull recorded in his diary:

'At 24:00 off and met Tony over Salte valley. It was a beautiful morning, but at Rognum the troops were blowing up ammunition and pushing off in larger puffers, as the flat-bottomed boats were called. One had a feeling of impending disaster as the evacuation looked so vulnerable, and we were a puny force to protect it against vigorous onslaught. Tony and I did some formation, and then he went off to refuel. I amused myself by 'shooting up' the boats – and how those chaps waved. It did one good to see their pathetic confidence.'

It was decided that take-off and landing conditions would sooner or later cause problems and that one of the Gladiators was likely to sustain damage; therefore these patrols were soon suspended. *Glorious* arrived off the coast that evening, flying off the first six Hurricanes of 46 Squadron, all got into the air without difficulty. The first batch landed at Skaanland at 21:30, a second batch arriving soon afterwards. Two of the Hurricanes nosed over on a patch of soft ground so the final six landed at Bardufoss instead.

The following morning (**27th May**) at 08:00, things started heating up when 11 Ju87Rs from I/StG1, escorted by three Bf110s from I/ZG76, appeared over Bodø and began dive-bombing radio masts at Bodøsjøen, only 800 yards from the landing ground. Lt Lydekker took off at once, followed by Flt Lt Hull, the latter immediately disposing of one of the Stukas before being shot down by a Bf110. Lydekker meanwhile was being attacked by most of the remaining Luftwaffe aircraft, his aircraft being badly shot up and himself wounded in the face and shoulder. Unable to land at Bodø as three Stukas were circling overhead, he set course for Bardufoss at low level, where he eventually landed with his Gladiator (N5705) a complete write-off. A second claim for a Gladiator was put in by Oblt Hans Jäger, and was obviously Lydekker's aircraft. Watchers on the ground at Bodø reported that the Gladiators had shot down at least two aircraft, Hull and Lydekker being credited with one apiece. This was not in fact the case, for only one Ju87 had been lost, both possibly having attacked the same Stuka, that flown by Fw Kurt Zube. Both crewmembers survived and were rescued by German troops. Of his combat with the Ju87, Lt Lydekker reported:

> 'At 08:00 two aircraft were at readiness on aerodrome Bodø when air raid warning was received, and town and W/T station was dive-bombed. F/Lt Hull's aircraft failed to start and I took off to engage enemy. 5,500 feet was reached and beam attack made on third e/a of leading section. E/a were in four sections of three a/c. Target e/a turned away losing height and remainder attacked me simultaneously. Evasive tactics were employed firing when opportunity presented itself. The chase led all e/a south of Bodø across the fjord and one by one e/a turned and headed south. Last three e/a were evaded south of Bodø. These patrolled over Bodø and as F/Lt Hull had not taken off I returned to Bardufoss.'

One of the RAF pilots at Bardufoss added:

> 'Later that day our Fleet Air Arm pilot, Tony, arrived back in Bardufoss with blood all over his face from a bullet-grazed nose, and with a wounded shoulder. His machine was well shot up, its windscreen coated, and ailerons rocky, and so on. He had been chased practically all the 200 miles from Bodø by a score of Ju87s. He said he had been scared absolutely fartless!' [120]

While the RAF Gladiators and Hurricanes were constantly in action during the closing days of the month, scoring many successes, *Glorious* and her escorts were left unmolested. Early in the morning on 27th May, *Glorious* received a signal from Flag Officer Narvik 'inviting consideration of the possibilities of attacking enemy troops and transport on the Mosjoen-Jamo road and at Mosjoen aerodrome.' [121] Hurried consultation of maps failed to locate 'Jamo', which seems likely to have been an error of encryption, for the location should have been Mosjoen-Mo. Commander Heath opined 'that troops and transports on roads were not targets for which FAA flying personnel had any training in recognition or attack, and that the aerodrome was the only suitable target, provided its position was known within reasonable limits.' [122] He added: 'We held the view that an air operation without an objective clearly defined and accurately located is fundamentally unsound for low-performance aircraft.' At this stage, Captain D'Oyly-Hughes was said to have agreed with the opinion.

However, in the morning, D'Oyly-Hughes had a change of mind and was in favour of a Sea Gladiator-escorted strike by the Swordfish. He told his officers that he would take the carrier to within 40 miles of the target.

Furthermore, he had made out a flight plan which was provocative: the Swordfish were to go to Hemnes first, on the coast, and then fly 40 miles south to Mosjoen. Heath pointed out that if Hemnes was attacked first, Mosjoen would be forewarned and ready. D'Oyly-Hughes overruled the objection.[123]

He stated that the force of five Swordfish and three Sea Gladiators should depart the carrier at 20:00 that evening. At this point, Lt-Cdr Charles Stephens, CO of 823 Squadron, approached Commander Heath to request an interview with the Captain. Permission was granted:

> 'Stephens said that he was fully prepared to carry out whatsoever operation was ordered, but he wanted to point out that this operation was, in his opinion, a bad one, on account of the smallness and poor performance of the forces available and the indeterminate objectives. D'Oyly-Hughes then said, "Will you make out your operation orders, Stephens?" Stephens replied with what Heath called "some diffidence" that he would try. Finally D'Oyly-Hughes said, "Go away with the Wing Commander, Stephens, and make them out." Heath was not asked any question or addressed during this interview.'[124]

Shortly before 14:00, Captain D'Oyly-Hughes sent for Heath and the other senior officers. He addressed Heath in some anger and said:

> 'You have been reluctant all day to produce a plan. Heath replied, "Not reluctant, but I found great difficulty in producing a satisfactory one due to lack of intelligence and the inadequate force available." D'Oyly-Hughes exultantly exclaimed, "That's what I want!" and ordered Heath to put that statement on paper.'[125]

Which he did, and was promptly relieved of his duties and sent to his cabin although not placed under arrest. D'Oyly-Hughes made it clear that he intended to make this state of affairs on board known to the highest possible authority on return to the Clyde.

Next morning (**28th May**), as *Glorious* headed back to Scapa Flow, she was spotted by a He115 of 2/KüFlGr.506, as reported by Commander Heath:

> 'Shadowing aircraft was first observed by Able Seaman Herbert Jones, one of the ADO's crew. A section of 802 Squadron was ranged immediately and flown off. A corrected bearing was subsequently passed by R/T and they attacked about 20 minutes after flying off. The Heinkel 115 was shot down almost at once, each of the three Sea Gladiators having fired two bursts in the attack. The Heinkel appeared to have been taken by surprise. The rear-gunner did not start firing until the attack had developed, and got no hits. The Heinkel broke up at once on hitting the water. Two of its crew were seen swimming strongly, and later, clinging to the wings, which were then sticking out of the water. HMS *Wren* however, which was despatched to pick up survivors, could only find one body, which was shot through the head. She also picked up the rubber dinghy and reported there was some blood on this, but no other sign that it had been used. By the time *Wren* reached it, the aircraft had sunk.'

The Sea Gladiator pilots reported on their success. The section leader, Lt David Ogilvy

(N5527/6G) reported:

> 'Head on and line astern attacks. E/a zigzagging. First attack from 300-30 yards, second attack down to 80 yards. Crashed into sea. Rear part of fuselage broke off just aft of rear gun [position].'

Lt Guy Lyver (N5530/6H) added:

> 'Astern attacks – two runs from 300-100 yards. Two bursts of six seconds each.'

While Lt(A) George Feeny (N5526/6F) wrote:

> 'Combat height 50-100 feet. One stern attack, one beam attack from 200-80 yards. E/a zigzagged after first burst then dived into sea and broke up.'

The doomed He115 was S4+K? (2763) flown by Fw Fritz Stahl, who had just radioed that a carrier had been sighted 520km off Vestfjord, but this message was followed by silence. Lost with Fw Stahl was observer Ltn.z.See Hans-Joachim Urban and gunner Obgfr Franz Fohmann.

At about 03:00 on **29th May**, three He111s of 2/KG26 were intercepted in the Narvik area by Hurricanes of 46 Squadron and two were shot down. A little later six more Heinkels from I/KG26 arrived in the same area to attack British warships. One of these was also shot down by a 46 Squadron Hurricane, the 1 Staffel machine flown by Uffz Paul Richter carrying out a crash landing near Ankenes, as recalled by crewmember Fw Alfred Kull:

> 'On our second mission, on 29th May, we were briefed to attack ships in Narvik harbour but before we could reach our target we were attacked by a British fighter [a Hurricane of 46 Squadron flown by Sgt George Milligan]. Despite our defensive fire of three machine-guns, our aircraft was hit in the course of several attacks and eventually both engines seized up. We were lucky that there were clouds beneath us where we were able to hide. After the combat we landed our aircraft on swampy ground.
>
> 'I was the last one to leave the He111 and set fire to our plane using two incendiary bombs. At some distance and armed with a machine-gun, I followed my crew who were hurrying on ahead, carrying with them a dinghy and two containers with food. Suddenly about ten Norwegians in civilian clothes, wearing white armbands, appeared and fired some shots into the air. One of my comrades shouted that we should not give up but I replied that it was senseless because they had the greater strength. Then I threw my machine-gun, the pistol and my paperwork into a small pond. When the Norwegians approached we opened our food containers and handed out chocolate and cigarettes.
>
> 'After about half an hour a lorry came and took us to a village at a fjord where we were brought into a school building. A doctor came and dressed the wounds of one of my comrades who had been hit by a bullet. The same night we were taken to Narvik on a British destroyer. There we spent the next five or six days in a prison cell until the English troops left Narvik ...' [126]

What Fw Kull failed to relate was the arrival of Walrus 5C flown by Sub-Lt(A) John Hoath and Lt Hugo Bracken (the CO) who were ordered to investigate 'a large German seaplane' that had landed at Dvyberg, 30 miles north-north-west of Harstad. On approaching the town they observed a large fire about seven miles inland, but no seaplane. They investigated the fire, which proved to be Uffz Richter's Heinkel. Four men were seen to run away from the wreck, one opening fire with a rifle. Lt Bracken, manning the machine-gun, returned fire. The Walrus then returned to the coast and alighted. Lt Bracken proceeded ashore to determine whether the crew had been taken prisoner. This proved to be the case, and he found the German crew and their Norwegian captors fraternising over glasses of beer in a local schoolhouse! After searching the prisoners he telephoned FAA HQ at Harstad, and suggested bringing the prisoners back in the Walrus. This was not permitted, and it was arranged that they should be transferred by destroyer

While waiting for the destroyer to arrive, Lt Bracken discovered that his machine-gun fire from the Walrus had wounded a Norwegian in the hand. After expressing regret, the affair was settled amicably over several glasses of beer. After seeing the prisoners transferred to the destroyer, the Walrus returned to base. The report on the incident ended by stating that the interrogation of the prisoners by Bracken was facilitated through the medium of a Norwegian girl who was tri-lingual.

Narvik was captured on **28th May**, and the following day Lt(A) Bob MacWhirter was up in *Suffolk*'s Walrus L2284 carrying a number of French Foreign Legion officers to survey the scene. Their flight was interrupted by the arrival of seven He111s that commenced bombing the French positions. Two days later (31st May) – on this occasion carrying Admiral Lord Cork – MacWhirter avoided an attempted interception by a Ju88, one of a number bombing Narvik harbour.

Glorious reached Scapa Flow on 30th May. Feeling over the Commander Heath affair was divided among the aircrews. Some considered that the Swordfish should have carried out the strike; others felt sympathy for Heath and considered his decision to have been the correct one. Gladiator pilot PO(A) Dick Leggott of 802 Squadron did not agree:

> '[Lt-Cdr] Stephens came into the ready room and said, "I want all the aviators to go down to the quarterdeck and cheer off J.B. Heath." Half the aviators said no. Not to Stephens, but after he had gone. They said, "We will not. We don't agree that those Swordfish should not have gone." My own Squadron CO said to us, "You do as you please." Half went. Half didn't. I did not go.' [127]

One young officer, Lt Nick Ward also of 802 Squadron, took such an entirely opposite view that he sent a letter to Commander Heath before his departure from *Glorious*:

> 'Dear Commander Heath, I hope you will not mind my writing this purely personal note to you; but I know if I was to try and say anything to you, I would not be able to do so and would probably make us both extremely uncomfortable.
>
> 'I have only just heard that you are leaving, though nothing of the circumstances. However, from what I do know, and from the fact that you are apparently leaving under a most unjustifiable cloud, I can see that a gross injustice is being done. Of one thing you can be quite certain – every single officer and man in the ship will know before long who is to blame. A man who can boast that he will ruthlessly

sweep from his path anyone who looks like threatening his own 'success' may be able to fool the Admiralty (and possibly a lot of officers) but he will never get past the troops.

'For your own sake, and even more for the sake of the Navy as a whole and the FAA in particular, I do implore you to fight to clear your name; and if no charge is brought against you to demand an explanation.

'I don't know what you will think of this, coming from a young lieutenant, but I hope you will realize (from my normal inability to say what I feel) that it comes from a very deep feeling, and an equally strong desire to see you vindicated. The FAA needs you, and people like you, badly, and I only hope that I may serve under you again in the future under more favourable conditions.

'P.S. I can't think how I had the nerve to offer advice to you; but I know you will take it as from a friend and not as from an impertinent junior officer.'[128]

With this vote of confidence, Heath left the ship:

'I realized that the wardroom were boiling. I had to pack up quick. I didn't dare go into the wardroom. I knew there would be trouble. The ship was near mutiny. I didn't say goodbye to D'Oyly-Hughes. Once I'd left the bridge after that showdown, I never saw him again. The trouble was that the Captain's cabin in harbour was right by the quarterdeck and the gangway came down past it. I dreaded an awful hurrah hurrah as I went over the side. I managed to escape. There were a number of chaps there. I pleaded with them not to make a noise. I was smuggled out. It was the nearest thing I've been to tears.'[129]

Commander Heath was put ashore but not placed under arrest although he was sent to the depot ship *Dunluce Castle* 'until further orders.'

Sub-Lt Guy Brokensha of 803 Squadron, who had been shot down in error by ships' gunfire on the first day of the month, had been given two weeks' leave on his return to Scotland on 4th May aboard the destroyer *Nubian*, and wrote to his parents:

'I finally reported back to Hatston and found to my great joy that all the laddies we'd almost given up on had come straggling back in much the same way as I had. Many, in fact, with a much more interesting story than mine. They had all come down over land – in fjords, in the snow or on lakes. The Norwegians had been most helpful to all of them and had helped them back to some British ship or post. We have been given a fortnight's survivors leave. Actually, I didn't want any but wanted to get back to Skeet and the CO. Still, reinforcements had just been sent the day before I reported. Poor old Skeet, still battling on. God, I hope he's all right.'

He obviously did not know that Bill Lucy had been killed and Skeet Harris wounded.

'One thing this business has made me realise (and Skeet, too) is to grab every moment of the present with both hands and try to live instead of just sitting back and taking it as it comes. We have kept well away from any form of morbidness – no letters marked 'Post only if ......' and all that. You do see, don't you, so don't worry, please.

Skeet says he is absolutely sure we will both get through OK. It's sort of tragic-funny if we don't go up together – a shy smile, a mutter "Give my love to the folks" and then by the door or from the flight deck "Don't drink all the gin before I'm back!" It's the way it should be – he's a great guy, our Skeet.

'So, my dears, I had better bring this tome to a graceful, if overdue, termination. Hope I haven't bored you. Aw shucks! I hope to see Margaret for a day or two before going back but expect I shall be recalled any minute.'

---

805 Squadron was formed at Donibristle in early May with the intention that it should become an all-Roc squadron to operate in the floatplane role against the Germans in Norway. Lt Ronnie Hay RM was appointed CO but the plan was quickly scrapped and the squadron was disbanded only a few weeks later.

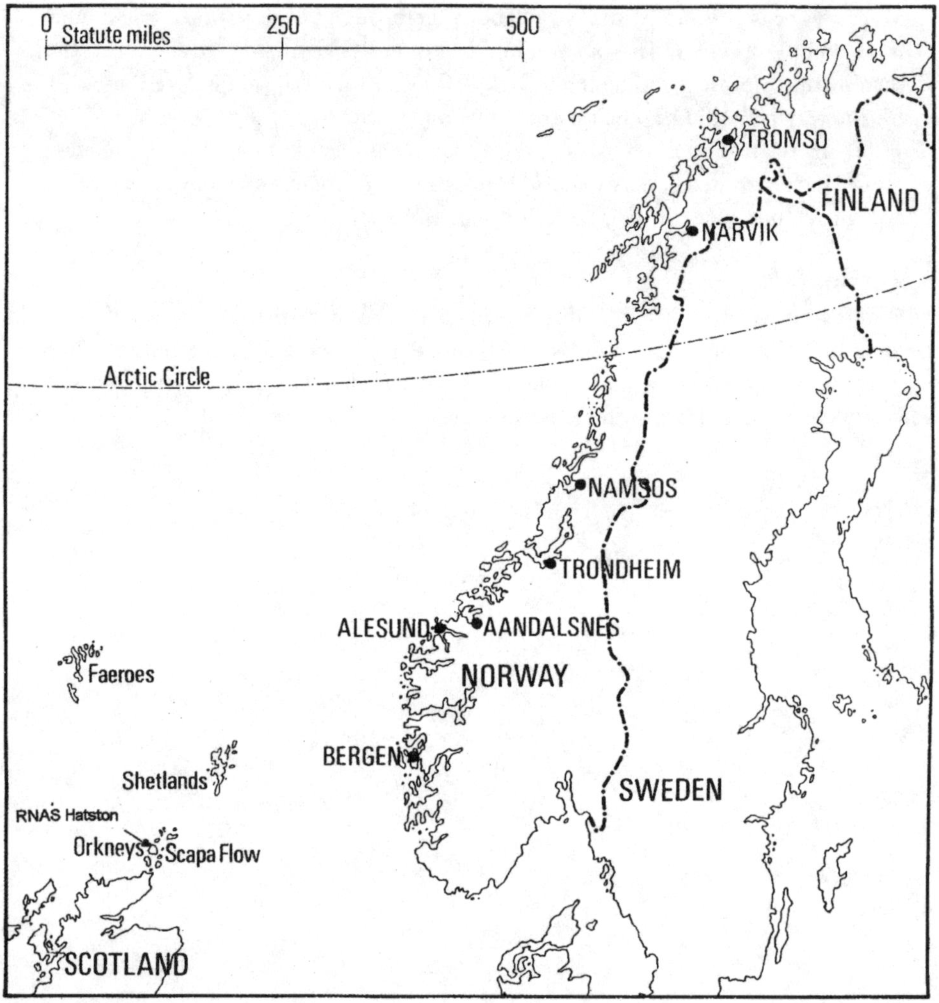

Norwegian coastline.

6. BLACK SUNDAY – 8th JUNE 1940

The loss of HMS *Glorious*

*'*Glorious *appears to have been caught unprepared for action and to have been unsuspecting of enemy forces in her vicinity and no evidence has been obtained as to why this state of affairs existed.'*

Comment by C-in-C Rosyth

By mid-May the German Naval High Command had prepared an operation against the supply lines of the British army still fighting in northern Norway. Primary areas of operations was to be Harstad, Andfjord, Vaagsfjord and possibly Ofotfjord, while secondary targets were to be convoys directed to Trondheim, Saltdal, Bodø and Mo. The codename for this operation was *Juno* and the force comprised the battleships *Gneisenau* (flagship) and *Scharnhorst*, the heavy cruiser *Admiral Hipper*, four destroyers and five support/repair ships. The operation commenced 4th June at 09:00, when the German squadron sailed from Kiel and by the afternoon of the next day the escort ships were detached to Wilhelmshaven.

Meanwhile, *Ark Royal* and *Glorious* had returned to the fray, arriving off the coast of Norway on 2nd June. 803 Squadron's new CO was Lt-Cdr John Casson[130] and among the new pilots was Canadian Sub-Lt(A) Dick Bartlett, who later recalled:

> 'Some of the pilots in the Fleet Air Arm were a surprise to me. Their hair was long, they smelled of cologne, and carried handkerchiefs that hung out of their sleeves. But they would come back from a rough operation saying things like "Wasn't that fun! Let's go for a drink." Meanwhile I was trying to regain my composure thinking to myself, "Gee, I better go change my underwear before I go for any drink." '[131]

The tasks of the two carriers were quite different – the *Ark* was to continue in an offensive role, while *Glorious* was to re-embark the RAF Gladiators. She had on board just six Sea Gladiators (from 802 Squadron) and six Swordfish (823 Squadron) for her own protection.

Ark Royal with 800, 803, 810 and 820 Squadrons on board, began her fighter patrols at 23:30 on **3rd June**, launching two Skuas (and two Swordfish) and continued patrols throughout the night, the following morning and forenoon and into the afternoon. Six 810 Squadron Swordfish, in two sub-flights led by Lt Godfrey-Faussett (A2K) and Lt Corbet-Milward (A2F), set out to bomb the railway stations at Hunddalen and Sijdvik, respectively. All returned safely from what the crew believed to have been successful attacks, with just A2M flown by Sub-Lt(A) Ian Richardson returning with damage sustained by ground fire. Cloud conditions throughout the remainder of the day were unsuitable for further bombing, but at 11:15 next day (**4th June**), two Skuas flown by Capt Partridge and Lt Ken Spurway were sent to reconnoitre the road between Sorfold and Drag, and one of them managed to bomb the jetty at Sorfold. Fighter patrols began again at 23:45 led by Lt-Cdr John Casson:

> 'We saw a couple of tanks and some lorries moving slowly northwards. We radioed the position to the *Ark* and then in line astern we dived down on them and opened up with our front guns and dropped a few 20lb bombs.'

But flying had to be called off early in the morning because of rain and low cloud. Mid(A) Derek Martin remembered:

> 'We were mainly supporting naval activities and any army activities, so we were flying CAPs above wherever the fleet happened to be. We were flying those every day, and sometimes twice a day. Occasionally we would see a German Heinkel, a floatplane, and do a bit of chasing. I was never attacked by a German fighter – none of us were [*sic*]. On one occasion, when I was chasing after a German floatplane I suddenly found myself surrounded by flak – which turned out to be from an RN destroyer! Fortunately on this occasion the flak was inaccurate.'

Bad weather on 5th June, with patches of fog, which thickened later, prevented much flying. *Glorious* rejoined *Ark Royal* at 14:20. At dawn next morning, the German task force passed Bergen Strait in rain and poor visibility and by 22:15, the ships were moving towards the Harstad area. Both *Scharnhorst*'s and *Hipper*'s Arados were airborne. Two British ships, the *Oil Pioneer* and anti-submarine trawler *Juniper* were intercepted and sunk, quickly followed by the 19,000-ton troopship *Orama*. Some 275 survivors were picked up by the escorting destroyers. *Hipper*'s Arado was recalled when it transpired that the crew had possibly been reporting the movement of their own ships.

In the early hours of 6th June, Captain D'Oyly-Hughes was able to mount a bombing raid very similar to that opposed by his former Commander Flying, Commander Heath. At 02:00, four Swordfish of 823 Squadron, led by Lt-Cdr Stephens, took off to bomb General Dietl's HQ at Hunddalen. They were led by a Swordfish from *Ark Royal* and escorted by three of *Ark Royal*'s Skuas. But this final effort by *Glorious*' aircraft turned to anti-climax. Low clouds prevented them reaching their target, whereupon they jettisoned their bombs into the sea and landed on again at 05:30.

This day also witnessed a unique event in the annals of the FAA, when five Walruses carried out a formation bombing raid on a concentration of German troops reported at Solfolla. The attack was ordered by Rear Admiral, Narvik. All available aircraft of 701 Squadron, with attached aircraft from HMS *Southampton* (P5651) and *Effingham* (P5662), took off at 14:15. Each aircraft was armed with eight 20lb bombs. The formation was led by Lt(A) Frank Temple-West who, in addition to having the CO Lt Hugo Bracken as his observer, carried Cmdr Sir Geoffrey Congreve from HMS *Raven* (formerly the Norwegian steamship *Ranan*), whose vessel had bombarded Solfolla the previous day. His advice and local knowledge was deemed invaluable.

P5656	Lt(A) F E O Temple-West Cmdr G C Congreve RN	Lt H H Bracken	L/Air T A Woolmer
P5711	Lt(A) W R J MacWhirter	PO(A) F Creagh	N/Air R P Stanesby
P5707	PO(A) V Redgrave W O Marshall RAF	Sub-Lt(A) B J Furlong	L/Air H T Goddard
P5651	Lt(A) P R E Woods	Lt J S Manning	Sgt Luck RAF
P5662	Lt M B P Francklin	Mid(A) P C Brooker	N/Air J Camp

Prior to take off it had been decided to approach Solfolla from seaward and to attack from over the hill to the west in order to have a concealed approach.

The formation proceeded down Tjelsundet and thence to a position three miles to the west of Tranoy. The weather during this part of the journey was overcast with cloud at 2,000 feet. It became obvious that due to the strong headwind encountered that, unless a short cut was taken, the attack could not take place at the time ordered (15:15). The weather cleared with a blue sky. The CO therefore led the Walruses down Sagfjordan and then over the mountains into Solfolla. Just as the turn was made, two Hurricanes from 46 Squadron rendezvoused. The weather now became overcast again with cloud at 3,000 feet. The hill to the west of Solfolla was identified but the town could not be seen due to heavy rain in that direction.

Undaunted the formation split up for the attack, with Lt(A) Temple-West in the centre and two aircraft on each wing in line abreast. Temple-West was first to attack, in a north-easterly direction from over the hill. The point of aim was just to the south of the church where Cdr Congreve had reported a howitzer. A stick of bombs was released in four pairs. The last pair fell about 30 yards short of the church. Machine-gun fire was opened on a large red warehouse with the rear gun manned by L/Air Tom Woolmer. It was considered that if the howitzer was still in the same position, the bombs fell within 20 yards of the objective.

Next to attack was Lt(A) Bob MacWhirter in 5G. On his first run two bombs were dropped but these fell into the sea off the pier. A second run was made and two more bombs dropped, one of which fell between the road and the warehouse, the other at the junction of the warehouse and the pier. A final run was made and one bomb hit the pier, the other falling into the sea. N/Air Stanesby fired a burst at the red warehouse.

A stick of bombs was dropped by Lt(A) Paul Woods' aircraft, and hits were observed on the road and a small warehouse, while Sgt Luck machine-gunned the large warehouse. Next to attack was Lt Phil Francklin (5A), two sticks of four bombs being dropped. The first was observed to fall alongside a large black motor car parked near the red warehouse, the second stick falling on the large warehouse. N/Air Camp fired at German troops firing from the hillside. Finally, PO(A) Vic Redgrave made his run, his first stick of bombs falling wide, but the second were seen to explode near the red warehouse. L/Air Goddard machine-gunned the warehouse and also fired at two army lorries seen leaving the town at high speed.

All five Walruses returned safely. Following debriefing, it was considered that the crews' reports of damage inflicted tended to be optimistic, although they argued that bombing from about 700 feet could not have been very inaccurate.

Unaware of the drama elsewhere, *Ark Royal* undertook a full day's flying. Besides maintaining fighter and anti-submarine patrols and long-range Swordfish searches, she launched two Skuas to bomb Sorfold and Drag shortly after midnight, including one flown by Sub-Lt Bartlett and N/Air Lloyd Richards:

> 'It didn't work out too well, the weather was very bad. I saw what looked like wisps of straw going past which I realised were tracer bullets. I was rather in disgust that someone was shooting at me! I tried to shoot back but couldn't align the gun.'

At 17:15, Red and Yellow Sections of 803 Squadron left *Ark Royal* to attack a German HQ at Fauske. Each Skua carried one 250lb, four 20lb and four incendiary bombs.

	Yellow Section	
L2909	Lt C W R Peever	Lt C C Ennever
L2992	Sub-Lt(A) J A Harris	N/Air S R D Stevenson
L2891	PO(A) J A Gardner	N/Air H Pickering
	Red Section	
L2984	Lt D C E F Gibson	Sub-Lt M P Gordon-Smith
L2955	Sub-Lt(A) R E Bartlett	N/Air L G Richards
L2956	PO(A) A W Theobald	N/Air F J L de Frias

The sections were to attack independently selected targets in the town. Yellow Section was first to attack, and Lt Charles Peever later reported:

> 'We proceeded to our objective and an extensive reconnaissance of all roads was made at 1,000 feet for troop movements. The weather deteriorated towards the south and at Fauske. Fire was opened by the enemy as we approached and no troops were visible at any point of the town. From this it can be assumed that warning of our approach had been given to the enemy sometime before our arrival there. The first objective was a hotel, believed to be the enemy headquarters, near a large warehouse at the south-east of the town. The attack was made at 18:45. However, owing to the low ceiling accurate dive-bombing was impossible and no hits were observed on the hotel. An attack was then made on the warehouse with incendiary bombs dropped in sticks of four. One fire was observed but lasted only a short time.'

Lt Peever then attacked a row of houses to the right of the main pier from which intensive flak and machine-gun fire was coming. A stick of four 20lb bombs was dropped and direct hits were observed. It was estimated that three or four machine-gun and flak posts were destroyed. Next to attack was Sub-Lt(A) John Harris, who bombed the main pier. His stick of bombs fell just north of the pier, damaging houses were troops had been previously reported. PO(A) Jimmy Gardner followed Harris into the attack, scoring one direct hit on the pier. On completion of the attack, Red Section then carried out theirs, Lt Donald Gibson reporting:

> 'Owing to extremely bad visibility and clouds at 1,200 feet accurate bombing was difficult. Red 1 and Red 2 were hit in several places by small calibre anti-aircraft fire. This appeared to come from the shrubbery of the wireless station. The unit was made to stop firing, and probably put out of action by the 20lb bombs and extensive low

altitude front gun attack. On completion of the attacks, Red Section left the target and proceeded up the road leading north from Fauske. Military lorries on this road were attacked closely with the remainder of our front gun ammunition. They were obviously hit. The lorries had drawn under the trees and the personnel had taken shelter in a wood.'

All six aircraft returned safely to the *Ark*, though four had bullet holes in the fuselages. Next into the attack at 22:10 were six Swordfish of 810 Squadron, one sub-flight led by Lt Godfrey-Faussett to bomb Hunddalen; the other led by Lt. Corbet-Milward with Sijdvik as its target:

A2K	Lt D F Godfrey-Faussett	Lt R D Wall	PO(A) T E Wibrow
A2M	Sub-Lt(A) I H B England	Mid(A) D G Richardson	N/Air F C Moore
A2L	Sub-Lt(A) G M M C Wheeler	Mid(A) L A Royall	N/Air G Dawson
A2F	Lt N R Corbet-Milward	Lt H Westacott	PO(A) J Clarke
A2Q	Sub-Lt(A) R B Pearson	Lt J H Lang	N/Air J G Ellis
A2G	Sub-Lt(A) J R C Callander	Capt K L Ford RM	N/Air R Thompson

Lt David Godfrey-Faussett in 2K reported:

'The objective was sighted at 22:10 and approached from a height of 4,500 feet. A group of four Bofors [*sic*] guns immediately opened fire. These guns were well concealed in some scrub, about 400 yards north of the village of Hunddalen, and could only be located by the gun flashes. Flak was observed coming from positions on the hillside. The target was buildings at Hunddalen. The approach was in line astern on a southerly course. Continuous fire was experienced. A2K dropped a number of bombs on a group of small buildings and a large fire was started, which appeared to be spreading satisfactorily when the sub-flight returned. A2M [England] scored a direct hit on a large white building several stories high, with a number of windows and was possibly a residential building of some nature. Further bombs were dropped amongst smaller buildings. A2M was hard hit astern, causing considerable damage to the tail unit and severing one control wire, but the aircraft remained airworthy. Two of the bombs hung up on A2L [Wheeler] but near misses were obtained with the remaining bombs on the tunnel mouth and on some corrugated-iron roofing over the railway lines.'

The strike on Sijdvik led by Lt Neville Corbet-Milward did not experience any ground fire:

Sijdvik was approached from the north-east in line astern at 6,500 feet, then A2F made an approach dive from 4,000 feet to 2,500 feet and released; the second attack by A2G [Callander] was made from eastward along the railway line. As no fire was experienced, it was carried low and a hit was made. A2Q [Pearson] followed after one minute, making one attack from the north-east and thereafter machine-gunning huts in the vicinity.

The last strike aircraft had only just landed on when, at 02:00 (on 7th June), *Ark Royal* began fighter patrols over the transports embarking troops from destroyers at Risoy, and continued the patrols throughout that morning, afternoon and evening. Three Swordfish of 820 Squadron meanwhile carried out a repeat attack on Hunddalen, the strike being led by Capt Alan Newson RM, the CO, in A4A:

A4A	Capt A C Newson RM	Lt-Cdr G B Hodgkinson	PO(A) R H McColl
A4B	Lt(A) G R Humphreys	Lt D. Williams	L/Air C Pendleton
A4C	Lt(A) D J Gudgeon	Sub-Lt(A) H G Mays	L/Air J Watson

Lt-Cdr Guy Hodgkinson reported:

'The section took-off at 04:45 with orders to attack enemy position at Hunddalen, paying particular attention to flak positions which had been noted in the previous raid by a section of 810 Squadron. On approaching the land the section climbed to 7,000 feet above a scattered layer of cloud and conditions appeared ideal for bombing. However, the cloud layer became more dense and more extensive as the objective was approached, and when within 20 miles the section was forced to come below the clouds.

'Rombaksfjord was entered in the base of the clouds at 1,500 feet with clouds down on the hills either side. Breaks in the cloud were observed at the head of the fjord and it was decided to press on in the hopes of getting through to Hunddalen. Fire was encountered from a Bofors gun when passing Sijdvik. On reaching the head of Rombaksfjord it was found that Hunddalen could not be reached and it was decided to attack enemy positions at Sijdvik.

'Direct hits were obtained on two buildings and a fire started. Four bombs fell on the railway lines. A machine gun was silenced. Fire was encountered by what was probably a Bofors gun which appeared to be located in the mouth of the tunnel, also from machine-guns. No hits were obtained by the enemy.'

By now 263 Squadron at Bardufoss was down to ten serviceable Gladiators whilst 46 Squadron also had only ten flyable Hurricanes. Evacuation was clearly very close. Plans had been made to fly the Gladiators, but not the Hurricanes, out to *Glorious*. It had never been intended that the Hurricanes should fly back to the carrier, but the CO Sqn Ldr 'Bing' Cross disliked the alternatives suggested – flying to Skaanland and destroying the Hurricanes there, or flying to some airfield far in the north and dismantling the Hurricanes – 'a ridiculous idea' Cross called it. Somebody even suggested flying out to sea and ditching alongside destroyers.

Cross himself flew out to the carrier in Lt John Iever's Walrus to confer with D'Oyly-Hughes, who thought Cross' proposal feasible and promised that his ship would once again work up to full speed for the occasion. Cross then flew to *Ark Royal*, whose flight deck was some hundred feet longer than *Glorious* but whose lifts were smaller. The Hurricanes' wings would have to be removed before they could be struck down in the hangar. It was decided that the Hurricanes would try *Glorious* first and then, if that failed, go to *Ark Royal*.

At 14:30, *Glorious* flew off four Swordfish to Bardufoss to guide the fighter aircraft back to the carriers. *Ark Royal* flew off one Swordfish to Bardufoss at 16:15, with orders for the fighters to embark. Three Hurricanes (piloted by Flt Lt Pat Jameson, Flg Off Bert

Knight and Sgt Bernard Taylor) took off at about 18:00 and were over the carriers just after an hour later. Jameson reported:

> 'The Captain of the *Glorious* kept his word. When we saw the *Glorious* it was going flat out, with steam pouring out of every rivet-hole. While we were waiting for the signal to land on, Sergeant Taylor went down and made a perfect landing on the carrier. When I tackled him about it later, he said he had engine trouble, but I suspect he really wanted to be the first chap to land a Hurricane on a carrier.
>
> 'When I looked at *Glorious* again, her deck reminded me of the back of an elephant – grey, and the flight deck had a round-down at the stern which was moving up and down like a cantering elephant's backside! We had to touch down as near the top of the heaving rump as possible to minimize the chance of over-shooting. There was quite a swell on and *Glorious* was at full tilt (about 30 knots), which meant that the landing spot was moving up and down at an alarming rate! Before taking off from Bardufoss I had decided that the only way to find out if it was possible to land on *Glorious* was to commit myself completely to the landing. If one got three-quarters of the way along the deck and then realised that one was not going to stop in time, it would be too late to take off again anyway!
>
> 'I came in on the approach just above stalling speed, feeling my way because of the sandbag away down in the tail affecting the flying characteristics, when suddenly, as I was getting near the touchdown point, the Hurricane dropped rapidly and it seemed she was trying to land on the quarterdeck. I slammed on full throttle and that beautiful Rolls Royce Merlin engine never faltered. It dragged us up onto the flight deck and the Hurricane and I stopped about a quarter of the way along. All three of us managed to get down OK, none using more than three-quarters of the deck.' [132]

While *Ark Royal* was landing on the five remaining Walruses of 701 Squadron from Harstad, *Glorious* flew off a Swordfish to Bardufoss with orders for landing on the rest of the RAF fighters. 263 Squadron's Gladiators and the remainder of 46 Squadron's Hurricanes took off about midnight, having kept up fighter patrols over Narvik and Harstad all day. Sqn Ldr Cross wrote:

> 'We left at 00:45 hours, dead beat; and as we left we were pleased to see the Skuas of the Fleet Air Arm coming in to cover the embarkation of our troops who had a destroyer standing by for them at a little fishing village seventeen miles away. We were navigated out to sea by a Swordfish at 100 knots and the old Hurricanes had to do some fairly hearty zigzagging to keep behind. It wasn't a nice feeling knowing that if we couldn't get on the deck there was no way out.' [133]

Glorious began to receive the fighters, the ten Gladiators first, followed by the seven Hurricanes. Cross continued:

> 'We had taken the precaution of having a sandbag weighing 14lbs put in the tail so we could use our brakes pretty coarsely. I was level with the deck, then hoisted the Hurricane over the round-down, cut the engine and came down bonk! I broke a strut in the tailwheel. Otherwise a piece of cake. I didn't use more than two-thirds of the deck. There was a hell of a wind over the deck this time. The last one landed at 03:00.

Most of the boys were pretty tired and after some welcome eggs, bacon and cocoa we all turned in ...'[134]

Following the Hurricanes came Lt Ievers' Walrus 5F with Grp Capt M. Moore, OC the RAF's Air Component on board and, last of all, the Swordfish guide. Having offloaded his passenger, Ievers was told to transfer to *Ark Royal*, there being no room for his aircraft. Grp Capt Moore accompanied him, the Walrus landing on at 02:07.

'I objected strongly because I wanted to stay with the squadron but I was overruled and given a course for *Ark Royal*, where I landed-on some 40 minutes later.'

He added:

'Some 36 hours afterwards the news came through to *Ark Royal* that *Glorious* had been sunk. I suspect that I was the last person to land on and fly off from her deck. A lucky escape.'[135]

But all this activity did not escape the prying eyes of Luftwaffe reconnaissance crews. At 07:00, one such crew sighted four ships and three escorts on a southerly course, about 360 miles north-west of Trondheim, later reconnaissance flights confirming their presence, as noted in the German War Staff Diary:

'Air reconnaissance in the area Harstad-Narvik spotted three groups of vessels between 12:35 and 13:55, about eighty miles north-west of And Fjord. They consisted of one light cruiser, two destroyers, two large ships on a westerly course, two destroyers to the north-west of these, and further to the north *Ark Royal*, *Glorious* and one destroyer stopped. In the evening three patrol boats were sighted by air reconnaissance, 240 miles north-west of Trondheim, steering south-west. The only British heavy ship in the Narvik area was identified by 'Y' [radio listening service] as *Valiant*. Radio traffic between Narvik and England shows nothing unusual. The German battleship formation has not so far been spotted. Thus the prospects for our operation are good.'

Operation Alphabet, the evacuation of all British and Allied forces from Norway, was well under way. Two troop convoys were formed, the first sailing on 7th June and the second sailing next day. Both convoys reached the UK safely. During the night of 7-8th June, *Ark Royal* and *Glorious* were operating in company north of Andenes Point, Lofoten Islands. Both carriers were to have formed part of the escort of the second convoy, but in the early hours (03:00) of **8th June**, *Glorious* made a signal to Vice-Admiral Wells in *Ark Royal*, asking for permission to proceed independently to Scapa Flow, via a route which would take her some 300 miles to the west of the German-occupied airfield at Trondheim and then south-west to pass between the Faeroe Islands and the Shetlands. The request was approved and *Glorious* and her two destroyer escort *Ardent* and *Acasta* parted company with *Ark Royal* at 03:53. Incredibly, *Glorious* had been permitted to return to Scapa Flow not for the sole reason that Scapa was the closest refuelling base, but because the Commander-in-Chief Home Fleet's staff wished to process the outstanding court-martial of Commander Heath![136] On board *Glorious* all seemed well, as recorded by PO(A) Dick Leggott of 802 Squadron:

'We were to report at our aircraft in the hangar at 09:00. Our CO and the CO of

823 appeared some twenty minutes later, having conferred with the Captain. One of our pilots noticed that warheads were being removed from torpedoes and other armaments that were normally in 'ready-use' stowages when we were in the war zone were being struck down or stowed away. The chief torpedo instructor, in reply to one of our squadron, said with a happy smile that they were getting a 'lap ahead' to get ready for giving leave. This seemed very wrong to some of us.

'It was a nice warm day, not much wind blowing over the flight deck, and we pilots of the fighter squadron left the hangar, climbed the ladders to the flight deck, enjoyed the sunshine and watched the wake making a trail to the horizon astern of us in a fairly calm sea. We relaxed and laughed about this and that. Not a care in the world. Other people may have had their problems, but not us. These were the golden days of our lives. Court-martial? Not us. Our fighter squadron was 'fireproof'. Half the squadron at a time was stood down for forty-five minutes to go to lunch and similarly for tea. Otherwise we remained on the flight deck or in the aircrew ready room in the island.'[137]

With Commander Heath[138] contemplating his future back at Scapa Flow, Captain D'Oyly-Hughes was effectively in charge of flying operations aboard *Glorious*, and he apparently deemed it unnecessary to have his Swordfish patrols airborne. Therefore, when the third salvo fired by the *Scharnhorst* at 16:48 pounded the flight deck and entered the upper hangar, exploding and wrecking Hurricanes, starting fires and setting off lots of .303 ammunition, it came as a complete surprise even though two 'strange ships' had been sighted on the horizon at 16:00. The escorting destroyer *Ardent* had been sent to investigate. PO(A) Leggott recalled:

'I was in the aircrew mess, enjoying tea, toast with strawberry jam and a thick slice of Madeira cake when sharply and suddenly *Glorious* heeled over to port as she turned hard to starboard and through the glass of a closed porthole I saw Splash! Splash! Splash! And heard the sharp crack of explosions. Over the Tannoy system came a pipe and the boatswain's mate's voice: 'Range one Swordfish'. It sounded mighty odd to me ... when the pipe came again: 'Range two Swordfish' and within seconds: 'Range all Swordfish aircraft'. I had finished my cup of tea, also my toast and the remnants of the Madeira cake, when the alarm [came]. My most beauteous and indulgent Guardian Angel had just laid a gently restraining hand on my shoulder. For then I heard the pipe: "All aircrew muster at their aircraft!" '[139]

Another aircrew member, N/Air Bob McBride of 823 Squadron, later wrote:

'I was flat on my back trying to decide what to get for tea from the NAAFI when 'Stand by Aircraft' was piped to be ranged, and "Crews to the Ops Room". Two Swordfish, mine and another, were ranged and in the Ops Room I learned we were to carry out an "identification flight" to find out about two unknown ships, hull down, but closing. At this stage everything seemed normal. I manned the aircraft and carried out my checks but when I looked out of the office I saw water spouts from salvoes which had dropped short. The flight deck was completely clear of personnel. I appeared to be entirely alone, with no signs of the pilot or observer, whom I presumed to be still in the Ops Room. I left the aircraft and headed for the Island to find our what was happening. I reached the starboard nets and heard shells coming, so I dropped into the nets. There was a loud explosion, and both aircraft were gone.' [140]

With Hurricanes stowed in the hangar on fire and .303 ammunition ricocheting off aircraft and bulkheads, creating terror and confusion. 802 Squadron's CO, Lt Ginger Marmont, requested permission to despatch one of his Sea Gladiators to find the *Ark*. However according to PO(A) Leggott, Captain D'Oyly-Hughes' only comment was: 'Surely you don't wish your pilots to behave like rats leaving a sinking ship.' Leggott added:

'We had been so engrossed in our discussion that the first shock of exploding shells barely registered until, in my case, I saw my fitter had been hit in the chest with a largish heavy fragment of black smoking shell. He fell flat on his back on the hangar deck, He exclaimed, 'Oh my wife and children' and was dead before a move to assist him could be made.' [141]

The next salvo demolished the bridge, killing D'Oyly-Hughes and many of his staff. Following one rescinded order to abandon ship, the final order to do so came at 17:40. N/Air Bob McBride was still on the flight deck:

'Men were lying around dead, resembling bundles of rubbish more than people. By this time I had reached the starboard forward gun sponson and an officer called for a volunteer to go the bridge for information. Somebody in the crowd behind me yelled, "I'll go!" and moved me up the ladder! Around this area chaos reigned. Various people whose Action Stations positions had been knocked out were wandering around looking for something useful to do. At this point I met the Senior Pilot, who told me that the hangar was an inferno. I turned to go forward and Lieutenant-Commander Stephens, the CO of my squadron, told me that the order to 'Abandon' had been given. His words were "Pass it on and jump". At this point men who appeared to be mostly stokers began to pop up from all sorts of places, through hatches and holes, escaping the searing heat below.' [142]

For every man there was the personal decision of whether, when and where to jump. Sqn Ldr Cross was on the quarterdeck:

'I said to Marmont [802's CO], who was standing beside me, 'What's the form on this?' We were still doing a fair speed. There was a stream of Carley floats going past. He said, 'Wait until they drop one of those, and then go. Otherwise you'll have a long way to swim.' So that's what I did.

'I swam to a raft and a few minutes later young Jameson came swimming along. We eventually had 29 aboard, but after three nights and two days, when we were picked up, we had but seven left of whom two died later ... The boats that got away [after the sinking] were sunk by heavy seas, but in most cases they had been so badly holed by gunfire that they sank as they launched. When we were in the raft the Germans came up, had a look and then went straight away.' [143]

The *Glorious* finally went down at about 18:10. Both escorting destroyers *Ardent* and *Acasta* were also sunk, but not before the latter had inflicted severe damage to the *Scharnhorst*, caused by a 21in torpedo which struck her starboard side close by the after turret.

Admiral Wells in *Ark Royal* received a signal at 20:14, advising that enemy surface forces were at sea, following which she closed the main convoy at about midnight and began flying patrols to cover herself and the convoy. At 04:00 on the **9th June**, four Swordfish took-off to carry out a search, to a depth of eighty miles, in a broad sector from which were considered the most probable directions of any possible enemy surface craft's approach to the convoy. At about 07:00, two Swordfish were flown off to search for a vessel that was missing from the convoy but neither the Swordfish nor a destroyer sent to search could find her. But German aircraft did and sank her off Andenes Point.

Admiral Wells received another signal at 10:31, giving details of *Glorious*' last message. *Ark Royal* flew off three Swordfish to search to a depth of 80 miles, and at 13:00 another six Swordfish and two Walrus to search for 100 miles. Three Skuas patrolled 20 miles from the convoy but nothing was sighted on any bearing. However, the Walruses were sighted by some of the desperate men in the sea. PO(A) Dick Leggott and a colleague saw one Walrus and possibly the second fly close to their float. They stood up like oily scarecrows, clasping each other for support, and waved and shouted and screeched through parched, cracked lips but neither aircraft saw them.

During the afternoon, the crew of a He115 of 1/KüFlGr.506 reported sighting a flotilla of warships some 360 miles west of the southern entrance of Saltfjord, but the floatplane was spotted by a section of patrolling 800 Squadron Skuas from the *Ark*. The Skuas, flown by Lt George Callingham (A6P), Sub-Lt Bob Kearsley (A6Q) and PO(A) Bill Heard (A6R)) pursued it for about 100 miles eastwards, firing as they came into range, eventually causing Fw Augustat, who was wounded during the attacks, to ditch. The crew were rescued by another He115 but their aircraft was lost.[144]

Obviously as a result of the German crew's report, six Ju88s from 6/KG30 followed later by 13 He111 of II/KG26 set out to attack the carrier, but only three of the former located their target and dive-bombed without effect. When the Heinkels arrived they encountered six Skuas, three each from 800 and 803 Squadrons. The latter section – Lt Don Gibson (A7P), Sub-Lt Dick Bartlett, (L2995/A7Q), and PO(A) Bill Theobald (A7R) – engaged and shot down a 5 Staffel aircraft flown by Oblt Kurt Böcking[145] – although Bartlett believed that he and his gunner were responsible for its demise:

> 'A He111 came at us three Skuas, flying in vic formation, head-on and our section leader apparently did not see it. I was on the right-hand side so I gave it a burst as it went by, and I swung in behind, firing at him with my four .303 wing guns. I ran out of ammunition and then pulled up alongside to let Lloyd shoot at the damaged bomber with his Lewis gun. I saw four of the crew get out of the bomber after it hit the water. I put in a claim, but my gunner was the only person to witness it crashing. They said after I told them where it hit the water: "Well, that must be the one that the section leader claimed." With the rank of leading seaman, the Skua gunners were not included in briefings prior to operational flights and their opinions were of little consequence. It seemed unlikely they would credit me just on my own say-so.'[146]

The 800 Squadron section (Callingham/Kearsley/Heard) claimed damage to a second Heinkel. Half an hour later, the relief sections chased another He115 but this managed to escape with minor damage inflicted by Lt Finch-Noyes' section.

Next day (**10th June**), one of six He115s of 2/KüFlGr.606 that had been sent out from Trondheim to re-locate the convoy and her escorts, found itself confronted by a Sunderland flying boat and two sections of Skuas from 803 Squadron. Led by the new CO, Lt-Cdr John Casson (L2992/A7A), Sub-Lt Guy Brokensha (A7B) and PO(A) Tommy Riddler (A7C) attacked the floatplane and claimed some damage before it escaped. In fact, the Heinkel had suffered 40-50 hits, killing Ltn z.see Prikker and wounding a second member of the crew. The pilot ditched the aircraft near Trondheim on return and the survivors managed to evacuate just before the aircraft sank, and were later rescued from the sea. Meanwhile, Lt Ned Finch-Noyes section had intercepted the Sunderland, which had been mistaken for a German reconnaissance aircraft. No damage was done – only to pride. One of the *Ark*'s Swordfish (L2731/A2C) flown by Sub-Lt(A) Ralph Eborn of 810 Squadron failed to return from a search for the *Scharnhorst*. Fortunately for Eborn and his crew (Mid(A) George Shaddick and L/Air Percy Clitheroe) the Norwegian armed fishing vessel *St Syrian* saw their plight, picked them up and took them to Iceland.

Two days after the sinking of *Glorious*, *Arden*t and *Acasta*, Carley floats with dead and dying were spread over a wide area. Many of those who had escaped death aboard the ships had by then already succumbed to the elements, most perishing during the first few hours from hypothermia, shock or injury. But help arrived for a lucky few. The 350-ton Norwegian motor vessel *Borgund* on her way to the Faeroes Islands fortuitously came across a cluster of Carley floats and picked up a total of 38 survivors (of whom three died within a few days) from about 21 rafts located, most of whose occupants were dead. The lucky few included PO(A) Dick Leggott of 802 Squadron, Sub-Lt(A) Ian MacLachlin, Mid(A) Eric Baldwin and N/Air Bob McBride of 823 Squadron, Sqn Ldr Bing Cross and Flt Lt Pat Jameson of 46 Squadron. The *Borgund* then continued her journey to the Faeroes, en route being circled by a He115, which fortunately did not attack. A second Norwegian vessel followed, her skipper relating how a German aircraft, probably another He115, had overflown his ship before dropping a bomb and firing its guns to indicate the location of other Carley floats. Sadly, no survivors were found aboard these. Four survivors were, however, picked up by another Norwegian vessel and taken to Norway.

These were the only survivors. The total number killed or missing in *Glorious* was approximately 1,207, including 18 RAF pilots of 46 and 263 Squadrons. A further 312 were lost from the two destroyers. Among FAA personnel lost were the following aircrew:

802 Squadron Sea Gladiator pilots:
Lt J F Marmont (Squadron CO), Lt D N H Ogilvy, Lt N E Ward, Lt G D D'E Lyver, Captain R J W Nott RM, Captain J R Owens RM, Lt(A) G H J Feeny, Lt(A) R J B Miles.

823 Squadron Swordfish aircrew:
Lt-Cdr C J T Stephens (Squadron CO), Lt J L Hallewell, Lt S F W Hebblethwaite, Lt G Starkey, Lt B J C Wise, Sub-Lt(A) J H Radclift, Sub-Lt(A) G P Ritchie, Sub-Lt (A) J M Franklin, Sub-Lt(A) J F Shillitoe, PO(A) E H Puntis, L/Air B Brett, L/Air A W Crichton, L/Air J Heath, L/Air W H Hill, L/Air J Houldsworth, L/Air P McN McLennan, N/Air W H Burns and N/Air D C Morton.

The report of the subsequent Board of Inquiry into the loss of *Glorious* concluded:

(a) There were no aircraft in the air for 12 hours prior to or during the action.[147]

(b) An enemy sighting report was originated in *Glorious* and transmitted on low power. A report that *Glorious* was sinking was originated, but there is insufficient evidence to show if this report was transmitted.

(c) That the consequence of the action could not have been avoided in the situation in which the ships found themselves, which arose from the circumstances beyond the scope of this inquiry, which has been confirmed by taking evidence of survivors.

The Board reports the following facts, arising out of evidence, to which they considered attention should be drawn:

(1) The length of the boat's falls of No.2 boat out of *Glorious* were insufficient to enable the boat to be lowered into the wake whilst the ship had a heavy list.

(2) Provisions and water were not attached to the Carley floats in *Glorious*.

(3) HA shells and HE fuse only were provided at the guns before the action commenced.

(4) No lookout in the crow's nest in conditions of extreme visibility.

Comment by C-in-C Rosyth:

> 'I concur with the finding of the Board. *Glorious* appears to have been caught unprepared for action and to have been unsuspecting of enemy forces in her vicinity and no evidence has been obtained as to why this state of affairs existed.'

Among those lost was Able Seaman Alfred Davey, a 36-year-old from Bristol, whose son Bryan remembered:

> 'My father served on HMS *Glorious*. My mother was having a cup of coffee when she noticed a man opposite reading a newspaper, the headline stated: 'HMS *Glorious* sunk in Norway – Narvik". My mother [Dorothy] thought he was in Scotland! When she applied for a widow's pension, the man in charge stated that 'he could be missing and not dead'. Very Distressing, I was only nine years-old.
>
> Many families with loved-ones aboard *Glorious* and her escorts would have been similarly shocked. They would seldom have known where the ships were operating.'

7. BLACK THURSDAY – UNLUCKY 13th

13th June 1940

"Well, Sir, the bloody fool who laid this trip on ought to have his head tested."

PO(A) Eric Monk 800 Squadron

Following its successful sortie against *Glorious* and her escorts, the German task force returned to Trondheim were the ships triumphantly arrived at noon on **9th June**. During the afternoon divers ascertained the extent of the damage to *Scharnhorst*, and found a hole 12 metres by 4 metres. Emergency repairs were carried out by the repair ship *Huascaran* and the salvage ship *Parat*, the damage being temporarily patched over. Ammunition was replenished from the supply ship *Alstertor*. Next day, the spying eyes of the RAF made a sighting of the *Scharnhorst* and two cruisers in harbour, a Coastal Command Hudson returning to base with the news, although the *Gneisenau* had already departed with an escort of four destroyers. A raid by a dozen Hudsons from 269 Squadron followed in the early afternoon of **11th June**, but all bombs missed their mark despite two hits being claimed on the cruisers. Four Bf109s and a Bf110 engaged the Hudsons, four being claimed including one by Flak gunners, while two were in fact lost.

Having failed to inflict further damage on the stationary prize target, *Ark Royal*, escorted by the battleship *Nelson* and a covey of destroyers, was despatched next day to finish the job. A plan had been conceived to attack the ships using Skuas of 800 and 803 Squadrons in their dive-bomber role. When Capt Dicky Partridge (800's CO) learned of the proposed strike, he suspected what the planners had in mind was a repeat of the successful attack on the *Königsberg* in April, and pointed out there were now clear skies and good weather, and thus no cloud cover. In addition, Bf109s and Bf110s were installed at Vaernes airfield near Trondheim. But the strike was to go ahead. Lt Don Gibson wrote:

> 'At the briefing we realised that we were in for a nasty job. We were, by this time, used to danger and were not unnecessarily apprehensive but it was not an easy time for us between teatime and midnight. We were exceptionally intelligent young men with imagination and one or two wrote letters for others to post in case of dire events. I believe that John Casson did some conjuring tricks in the wardroom anteroom, but he did not come back, being captured and made a prisoner of war.' [149]

Fifteen Skuas – nine from 803 and six from 800 – were to take part. They were to depart the *Ark* at midnight and commence the attack at 02:00, to coincide with a diversionary raid on Vaernes airfield by seven Beauforts from 22 Squadron. It was intended that the Beauforts should bomb Vaernes just ahead of the arrival of the Skuas, thereby keeping the German fighters on the ground. Unfortunately, the bombers lost formation in bad visibility, three returning to base while only four attacked at about 01:50. On the ground five men were killed and 27 wounded, but material damage was slight, and the Bf109Es of 4/JG77 and Bf110s of 3/ZG76 were scrambled after them. The Beauforts could not be caught, but the result was that when the unescorted Skuas arrived over Trondheimsfjord at 02:00, it was to find a considerable force of fighters already in the air and waiting for them. In addition, six Blenheims of 254 Squadron were to provide cover for the Skuas as they flew in and out again. However, one of the latter was shot down by a Bf110 before the Skua strike even got under way. The crews selected for the strike were:

803 Squadron		
L2881/A7A	Lt-Cdr J Casson	Lt P E Fanshawe
L2997/A7B	Sub-Lt(A) G W Brokensha	L/Air F Coston
L2915/A7C	PO(A) T F Riddler	N/Air H T Chatterley
L2963/A7F	Lt C H Filmer	Mid(A) T A McKee
L2961/A7G	Mid(A) A S Griffith	N/Air F P Dooley
L2992/A7L	Sub-Lt(A) J A Harris	N/Air S R D Stevenson
L2984/A7P	Lt D C E F Gibson	Sub-Lt M P Gordon-Smith
L2955/A7Q	Sub-Lt(A) R E Bartlett	N/Air L G Richards
L2956/A7R	PO(A) J A Gardner	N/Air H Pickering
800 Squadron		
L2995/A6A	Capt R T Partridge RM	Lt R S Bostock
L2908/A6K	Lt K V V Spurway	PO(A) R F Hart
L2900/A6C	PO(A) H A Monk	PO(A) R S Rolph
L3000/A6F	Lt G E D Finch-Noyes	PO(A) H G Cunningham
L3047/A6H	Mid(A) D T R Martin	L/Air W J Tremeer
L3028/A6G	Mid(A) L H Gallagher	PO(A) W Crawford

There was not a great feeling of confidence among the crews. They knew the odds were stacked against them on this occasion. 'I didn't rate my chances of survival as particularly high,' remembered N/Air Lloyd Richards, gunner onboard Sub-Lt Dick Bartlett's A7Q. Mid(A) Derek Martin added:

> 'The whole fjord would be full of guns. During the short briefing before the raid we were told that they expected that some of us would not return. That didn't sound good. But we had to obey orders – we could do nothing about it. I didn't write a letter to my father, because when he was told about my death, he would think that it happened so suddenly that I didn't expect it either.'

Two minutes after midnight *Ark Royal* began launching the Skuas, all weighed down with the unusually heavy load represented by a 500lb semi-armour piercing bomb beneath their bellies. Lt-Cdr John Casson was to lead the strike with 803 Squadron. At this stage RAF support was still anticipated, the Blenheim fighters having made radio contact with the carrier as early as 22:57, but in the event they were too late to escort the dive-bombers in to the target zone. Capt Dicky Partridge set the scene:

'It was 23:50 that the first of my aircraft sprang into life with a roar, quickly followed by the others. I was airborne at 00:01, the last of my squadron to take-off, so that those already in the air could form up on me as I climbed away from the carrier. We circled in formation waiting for John Casson, the last off, to be joined by his squadron, then both squadrons swung round on a course for the Norwegian coast and Trondheim. We climbed steadily in open formation until we reached a height of 12,000 feet. The weather was good, too good, with a completely clear sky, and maximum visibility. We now settled down to our most economic cruising speed of 140/150 knots which would only be varied later by John Casson's observer's navigation requiring a higher or lower speed to arrive over the target at exactly 02:00. At that moment I liked to think that there were also a dozen or so Beauforts well on their way from Scotland and also navigating to arrive precisely at that time.

'We had been airborne now for well over an hour and ahead of us I could see the first land which Robin [Bostock] told me was the northern end of the island of Froya. All aircraft were nicely in position and so far we had seen nothing, neither ship nor plane. As we passed over the island, in this very clear visibility, I could see a lighthouse and thought it highly probable that the Germans would have an observation post there to give good warning of any attack by sea or air. Now we were crossing over the mainland coast proper and there, confound it, was another lighthouse or coastguard station. I couldn't help but believe that the wires back to Trondheim were humming with the news that an enemy bombing force was approaching, and I could imagine the alarm being sounded at the aerodrome with Me109s and 110s being scrambled one after another.

'John Casson now started to go into a shallow dive, our speed building up to about 200 knots, and I asked Robin how far there was to go. He said he reckoned we were about 25 miles from Trondheim and that we should arrive there in about 10 minutes almost exactly at 02:00. So far, so good. I was looking anxiously ahead for AA bursts in the air, which would mean that the Beauforts were there and I hoped creating havoc with the Messerschmitts at Vaernes airfield. But as yet the air was as clear and still as ever. Speed was now building up to 240 knots, height 9,000 feet, as John Casson manoeuvred to arrive over target on time and at the prearranged height.

'I looked at my watch - it was three minutes to our deadline. There ahead of us I could see quite clearly the town of Trondheim and laying in the fjord the German fleet. I call it a fleet because it appeared to me that there were dozens of ships, including two larger ones that I assumed to be *Scharnhorst* and *Gneisenau*, which were obviously to be our targets if we could reach them. There was still no sign of the Beauforts and I think it was at that moment that John Casson and I knew we would have to go it alone, as we had always suspected.

'Then the German AA fire opened up. I think only those who have experienced it can appreciate the volume of fire that a concentration of warships, supported by a considerable number of shore batteries, can put up, and can understand when I describe this barrage as intense with tracer bullets floating upwards and past us in thick showers. John Casson swung away to port putting his aircraft in open line astern and I did the same to starboard. As I did so I saw a twin-engined Me110 flash past us heading for the other squadron and shortly afterwards a Skua spiralling downwards in flames.'[150]

It seems likely that the Bf110 was that flown by Oblt Gordon Gollob of 3/ZG76, who recorded the first kill at 02:00 and his victim was possibly Mid(A) Len Gallagher's aircraft A6G, in which he and his observer PO(A) Wallace Crawford lost their lives in the resulting crash at Hermstadheia Rissa.[151] One of the 4/JG77 pilots, Obfw Hans-Jacob Arnoldy claimed a second Skua two minutes later, probably Mid(A) Derek Martin's A6H:

'I did not see the two which dealt with me until they were turned in on my tail; neither did my air gunner, though he did say, down the Gosport tubing, 'Just a minute, sir'. Perhaps he had seen them and this was his cool way of saying so, but I do not know. I turned into one fighter and his incendiaries, which I do remember seeing very clearly, missed. However the second fighter of which I was unaware was more successful. His bullets came through the back of the aircraft – and, I now believe, my air gunner, alas – under my seat and between my legs. They shot away all my control columns and the aircraft started to go into a dive which I had no means of stopping. I yelled "jump" several times.'

As Martin had feared, Bill Tremeer had been killed, but he himself descended by parachute into a fjord at Stadsbygd, where a He115 landed close by and taxied towards him:

'I was very conscious of the machine-gun in the nose of the aircraft as it approached and waited – no doubt nervously; but nothing happened until a German airman climbed down on to the port float, called out in clear English, "Wait a minute," and threw me a rope. I climbed into the aircraft, under the pilot. I cannot remember what my feelings were, but they may have been influenced by my surprise at finding two seamen already on board. They in a simply dreadful state. One of them said they were from *Ardent*.'

A section of Bf110s struck next, Skuas being claimed by Ltn Heinrich Köhler, Ltn Rudolf Krzywon, and Obfw Schöb at 02:05, Köhler probably accounting for Lt Ned Finch-Noyes' A6F, the Skua crashing into the rear yard of Schøningdal farm at Møllebakken, the propeller and undercarriage slamming into the farmhouse fotunately without causing injuries to the occupants. Finch-Noyes was killed but his observer, PO(A) Cuts Cunningham had managed to bale out. He was soon captured, however, and became a POW. One of his colleagues (Dickie Rolph) later related:

'Cuts was shot down by two Me110s carrying out a scissors attack. He had the experience of using a smouldering parachute when he had to bale out. He was rescued from the fjord and taken before the German Naval captain for interrogation. On being pressed to admit that he came from the *Ark Royal* he had the pleasure of telling the captain that was impossible since the Germans had already sunk it twice. I understand that the captain was far from amused!'

Obfw Schöb (and his gunner Ogfr Pape) were credited with shooting down Sub-Lt John Harris' aircraft (A7L), No.3 in Lt Filmer's sub-section. Harris was killed when his Skua crashed into a hillside above a farm at Kjora Geitastrand, and his TAG N/Air Stuart Stevenson severely injured.[152] Filmer's A7F followed soon after:

'As we neared Trondheim I was stunned to see the battlecruiser was surrounded by a heavy cruiser and four destroyers. It was painfully evident that the firepower from the six naval ships plus the land batteries was going to be immense. The tracer bullets commenced rising well before we were within striking distance. I carried out my dive-bombing attack and was immediately jumped by two Me110 fighters.'

Both Filmer and his observer Mid(A) Tom McKee, who had been wounded in the attack, survived a wheels-up landing on the fjord at Frostsiejaevet near Trondheim, their aircraft relatively undamaged. They were rescued by Norwegians in a small boat and taken to hospital. Here they were taken prisoner and flown to Germany.[153] Their victor was probably Ltn Krzywon of 3/ZG76 in M8+BL, who recorded his kill at 02:05. Probably one of the last Skuas to be shot down was A7Q crewed by Sub-Lt Dick Bartlett and N/A Lloyd Richards, flying in No.2 position in Lt Gibson's sub-section, the kill being claimed jointly by Obfw Ludwig Fröba and Fw Harbach of 4/JG77, although they were credited with one apiece.[154] Richards watched the drama unfold – and then became part of it:

'On the way in I saw first one aircraft on our right hand side being shot down, immediately followed by another one. Then we were attacked, and both petrol tanks between the pilot and me were hit. Fuel flowed freely into the cockpit, and new hits, shrapnel and bullets, made a terrific noise. My pilot told me he had been hit and asked me to jump. But I couldn't reach the parachute – and immediately afterwards we were in an 80-degree dive towards the target. My legs were above my head. All I could see was the sky, not the fjord, and I had no idea whether my pilot was dead or alive. I could see the altimeter spinning backwards and wondered how we would die – would there be a big bang or not. All I knew was that it would be quick. Suddenly I saw rooftops shooting past below us, and I realised that Bartlett had managed to pull the aircraft out of the dive just in time.'

Severely injured, his stomach torn open and with an aircraft looking like a sieve, Bartlett managed to crash-land on farmland at Soknedal, south of Trondheim:

'During the 60-mile run along the fjord, we felt a deep sense of foreboding, but I also remember the beauty of the rising sun and the electric blue of cloudless sky, as we followed the fjord in a north-easterly heading. Then ahead, we could see the German ships anchored in the harbour just north of the city of Trondheim. Next, the intense and accurate anti-aircraft fire from the ships and shore batteries enveloped the two leading flights as they prepared to dive onto their targets. Simultaneously, the Me109 and Me110 fighters commenced their attacks, relentlessly zeroing in on the vulnerable Skuas in swift attacks from behind and on the beam, swarming around the slowly approaching aircraft. Already the lead aircraft were under fire and I could see Skuas going down in smoke and flames.

'Before even beginning their dive, my flight was attacked by two Me109s from the rear. One hit, striking my Skua in the port wing. The only evasive action I could take was to skid with the rudder when given the alert by Richards, who was gamely firing back with his ancient Lewis machine-gun. On their second pass the 109s hit my starboard wing. Heading to the south, low over the water, toward what I thought would be the relative safety of the city of Trondheim, the aircraft was peppered with machine-gunfire from roof top positions as we clattered, barely under control, over the built up area. A few miles past Trondheim and barely clearing the terrain, my failing engine, now scarcely functioning, suddenly shook loose from the airframe. The aircraft momentarily reared up and flopped out of the sky and, with a great shuddering thump, crashed tail first into a small clearing.'[155]

Bartlett, barely conscious, but with Richards' help was able to stagger clear of the aircraft. Surprisingly, it did not catch fire. Bartlett was bleeding badly from his wounds and unable to move. Richards obtained a mattress from a nearby farmhouse, on which he laid his pilot, who in turn, gave himself a full shot of morphine. Being fully immobilised, he then advised Richards to independently head over the hills for Sweden, which they estimated was only about 30 miles away, but his dash for freedom was brief and he was quickly captured by German troops who arrived on the scene, and taken back to rejoin Bartlett.

Up to this point, it seems that both squadron commanders had survived – but not for long. Capt Dicky Partridge continued:

'We were going to be sitting ducks for these Messerschmitts and I wondered how many of us were ever going to be able to get into a proper dive-bombing position to drop an accurate bomb. Robin suddenly said "Me109 port quarter", and I took violent evasive action so that he shot past and under us. As I pulled round in a very tight turn I could see that all the Skuas of both squadrons were scattered and acting independently and that there were 109s and 110s all over the place. I saw one Skua carrying out what appeared to be a beautifully controlled dive-bombing attack on the further large ship but also had a fleeting glance of his dive getting lower and lower until he hit the water at full power with a horrible crash.

'I asked Robin if there was anything on our tail and he replied 'No'. I decided that it was now or never and that if I was going to get into position to attack I must sacrifice some height in order to build up my speed on the run in. I put the nose down into medium dive and headed at 260 knots towards the nearest pocket battleship. At just under 6,000 feet I was in a position to attack, pulled up to lose speed and came off a stall turn with flaps down into a dive. This dive was started lower than I would have liked and the AA fire coming from the ship was indescribable. At 1,700 feet I released my bomb and, veering violently to port, flaps now raised, continued on down to sea level and headed away across the fjord. Poor old Robin, who must have been having kittens in the rear cockpit whilst all this was going on, now reported that we had had a near miss ahead of the enemy ship and also that at the moment there was nobody on our tail though he had seen two more Skuas crash into the water. After five minutes of flying at zero feet we were well clear of the target area but by no means out of danger. Robin and I had often discussed what to do in this sort of situation. Flying at water or ground level offered the best chance of concealment but little chance of survival if we were attacked by superior forces and the aircraft was hit.

'Flying at any height from 1,000 feet upwards offered less chance of concealment but an obvious chance of baling out. We had both agreed to opt for the chance of baling out and so I was now beginning to climb to gain height. We had reached 3,000 feet when Robin said, "Aircraft slightly above – port bow", and a quick glance showed a single-engined seaplane of all things about to cross in front of and slightly above us. I eased back gently on the stick to raise my nose and as he passed in front of me and slightly above I got in a quick burst with my front guns. This may have been a big mistake on my part; either he hadn't seen me or he had mistaken me for a Me109. At any rate his reaction to my burst of fire was a violent diving turn back towards Trondheim and that was a direction in which I was not going to chase him although even a Skua could have overtaken such an aircraft without too much trouble. But not only did he turn towards Trondheim, he also fired a four-star white Very light similar to the one fired by the submarine we had caught on the surface at Narvik. This could either have been the German recognition signal of the day or it could equally well have been a signal indicating the presence of hostile aircraft.

'After this little incident we were at 4,000 feet, about 20 minutes flying away from Trondheim and not all that far from the coast. I was just beginning to think that we had got away with it when over the intercom Robin said quietly, "Two 109s coming up fast astern." This was the dreaded situation we had often anticipated and had been frightened even to imagine, it scared us so much. We both knew that, barring some sort of miracle, we had really had it this time. Inexplicably, as far as I was concerned, I felt no fear or panic, merely my usual fatalistic calm and a determination to give them a run for their money. Had it been only one Messerschmitt we were dealing with it is just possible we might have got away with it, but two gave us no chance at all. The Me109 was at least 80 mph faster than we were, was more manoeuvrable and was armed with cannon. In spite of this I had a trick or two up my sleeve and felt that if we could survive long enough and at the same time work our way out to sea we could possibly get rid of them; for I knew that shore-based fighter pilots never relished too much flying over water out of sight of land. If we could somehow remain in one piece till we were 50 miles off shore I felt there was a chance that they might give up the chase.

'I felt terribly exposed sitting high up in the Skua's cockpit, with a large expanse of windscreen in front of me which was not bullet-proof. Neither was there any armour under my seat or at my back and the large petrol tanks were not even self-sealing if hit. Robin of course was equally unprotected and had the unnerving view of every attack as it came with only a single Vickers K machine gun to defend us from stern attacks. The odds surely were stacked against us! As soon as Robin shouted they were about to attack in line astern, I went into a 45-degree dive and when they opened fire as my speed built up to 250 knots I suddenly put my flaps down. The result was instant, dramatic and very uncomfortable! We decelerated violently and at the same time shot straight up 500 feet or so and the attacking 109s passed underneath us. It speaks a lot for the ruggedness and strength of the Skua that it could stand this sort of treatment, while I continued to work my way towards the coast. Three times the 109s repeated this type of attack unsuccessfully and I was wondering how long it was going to be before they realized they would have to change their tactics. Unfortunately, not very long. Robin suddenly said 'One attacking from astern and one on starboard beam'. This was decidedly awkward and meant that my 'flap' tactic could make me an easy target if the aircraft on the beam waited until I had avoided the stern attack. So this time I did a really tight turn to starboard and managed to get a quick head-on burst at my beam attacker. Of course this left me more vulnerable to the stern attack and I could see his tracers going past me. I was still working my way towards the coast but our enemies' performance was so superior that they could attack, climb away, circle round and attack again. It couldn't last.

'Robin had just said again, "Attack astern and abeam" when I felt a thud that shook the aircraft and a large piece about the size of a soup plate came away from my starboard wing. It was probably a cannon shell but as it was outboard of the ailerons I still had control of my aircraft. They were circling and climbing ready for another attack - but this time there was no warning of firing from Robin. Suddenly the petrol tank behind my instrument panel, only a foot or two from my lap, went up in a roar of flames. From then on my actions were essentially reflex and must have been carried out at lightning speed.

'I can remember slamming back my cockpit hood and the resulting slipstream drawing a great sheet of flame up between my legs, across my face and out of the cockpit; I can remember hitting the quick-release of my fighting harness, and then the next thing I was aware of was a violent and painful yank at my crotch. Inconsequentially I thought: "That will teach you not to have your parachute harness properly and tightly adjusted!" and there I was at 3,500 feet floating down with a Me109 heading straight for me. As I was bracing myself for him to open fire he swerved to one side and was away.'

Their victor was probably Fw Arnoldy, confirming his second kill of the action, at 02:08.

'I looked around for another parachute there was none. What had happened to Robin? Had he been killed in that last attack on us? Had he been unable to get out? Or was he still in the Skua now spiralling downwards and thinking it was brilliant evasive action I was taking? The Skua hit the fjord below and disappeared in a cloud of spray and wreckage. Robin, my observer, friend and good companion in many good and bad times was dead, but exactly how and when he died we shall never know.

'I was now at 2,000 feet and floating down gently in complete silence. I looked down and saw that I was heading for the centre of a fjord. It wasn't the main Trondheim fjord but an offshoot: even so it appeared to be a mile or two wide. I know the theory of being able to guide a parachute by pulling on the shroud lines, but I tried this with no effect at all other than nearly to collapse the canopy. Gently I drifted down: at 500 feet I was still heading slap for the middle of the fjord. I removed my flying boots and let them drop into the water then, in order to avoid getting tangled up in the parachute, at about 15-20 feet I turned and hit the quickrelease buckle and dropped into the water. As I went under I felt a great searing pain as the salt water came into contact with my burnt face. With my Mae West flotation waistcoat on I soon popped spluttering to the surface and surveyed my situation. From eye level a few inches above the water's surface either shore of the fjord appeared to be miles away and I knew I'd never make it swimming. I also knew that with my floatation waistcoat on I wasn't going to drown. God knows why or how, I was still alive but apparently destined to die of exposure in the icy waters of this remote and isolated Norwegian fjord.

'I had been swimming for about 20 minutes, getting very weak and the shore I was aiming for appeared as far away as ever. Self-preservation is a great spur and I guess I was going to go on swimming until I could swim no more. Suddenly I heard noises that sounded very like those made by oars in rowlocks and looking over my shoulder saw the bows of a small rowing boat bearing down on me. I was too far gone to feel any of the things I ought to have felt, like joy and relief at being rescued at last. I was mentally and physically drained and exhausted and I suspect in a state of deep shock as well. The boat was quickly alongside me and I was seized by the arms and seat of my trousers by two men, hauled on board, thrust into the bottom of the boat and covered quickly and completely with a tarpaulin. As I lay there, gasping and shivering in the dark, I was conscious of the boat being rowed rapidly back to the shore. The boat grounded, I was uncovered, helped out and half carried, half dragged to a farmhouse nestling close to the fjord shore. I had been rescued by two Norwegian fishermen from the farm who had rowed out to me, well knowing that anything moving on land or water was inviting machine-gun attack from the air. To these two gallant men I undoubtedly owe my life.

'My memories of the next 48 hours are vague and hazy. I can remember being stripped and rubbed down in the farm kitchen and being dressed in borrowed clothing, which included a fine knitted traditional Norwegian cardigan. I can remember being examined in a Norwegian doctor's surgery for broken bones or other injuries but can't remember how I got there. It was he who dressed and bandaged my burnt face and gave me a warm drink from a cup with a spout as my lips were too painful for normal drinking, and I think it must have been this doctor who decided that my presence must be reported to the Germans so that I could get proper medical treatment. Fortunately, when my cockpit went up in flames I had had my goggles down and this protected my eyes and saved me from certain blinding. So, save for a burnt face I was still in remarkably good physical condition and had a long and restful night in the farmhouse.

'The next day a car pulled up at the farm with three German NCOs and I was handed over to them and driven away. This was the start of five years, all but one month, as a prisoner of war.' [156]

Lt-Cdr John Casson, the strike leader in A7A, managed to release his bomb but was soon engaged by a Bf109:

'The flak was accurate and concentrated as I dropped my 500lb bomb, missing the quarterdeck of the *Scharnhorst* by a whisker. The Skua was thumped by the flak bursts and I felt it shudder, but there was no sound from Peter Fanshawe in the turret, only the rattle of his Lewis-gun. On full boost I climbed to 2,000 feet and roared up the fjord, the sound echoing and buffeting back from the near vertical cliff walls, but there was an almost unsettling calm after the fierce action. Then I saw a Messerschmitt 109 manoeuvering to attack.

'Hoping that the enemy pilot might be a greenhorn, I half-rolled, dived and levelled out ten feet above the water, leading the Messerschmitt a chase in and out of the fjord, trying to fly the German into a cliff. Discovering that I could just turn my plane inside the Messerschmitt, I roared towards the cliff face, slammed down the Skua's flaps and then turned hard to starboard. The Messerschmitt pilot just turned away. Hard flying had brought us both to the end of the mountains.'

Casson had held off the Messerschmitt for 15 minutes but was now flying down a village street, below roof-top level, taking the tip off a fir tree with his propeller:

'An accidental flick roll caused the Skua to do a high stall, bringing me down again to 50 feet above the water. We were in the open now, making it difficult to outwit the Messerschmitt pilot. I tried to guess the moment when the enemy pilot would fire and then swerve to starboard. Three times the Messerschmitt's tracers passed under my port wing. The fourth time the German took a good, long shot and I heard the rattle and crash as shells and bullets rammed home. A reek of petrol surrounded the plane as Fanshawe spoke for the first time over the intercom: "There's a hole as big as your fist in the bottom of the tank and I've got a bullet in my shoulder."

'I calculated that we had four minutes flying left and no hope of reaching Sweden. Rather than be a sitting duck, I slammed the Skua down on to the water at 100 knots, skidding along the surface. I knew that we had not stalled enough but wanted to get the aircraft down before another attack. Thumping myself in the eye during the ditching, I looked back through a watery haze to see the Messerschmitt bearing down on us. "Jesus! Now he is going to shoot us into the water." But the German throttled back, did a slow circle, waved and flew off.'

They were soon hauled out of the water by Norwegians in a small rowing boat and taken ashore and tended for in a nearby house. But Casson and Fanshawe were soon on their way to the local hospital at Hohemark, where they were later taken prisoner and transferred to Dulug Luft. It would appear that their victor was Fw Erwin Sawallisch of 4/JG77, who claimed the last kill at 02:12.

Only seven Skuas – less than half the force despatched – returned to the carrier. The survivors all related the same tale of woe. Lt Ken Spurway (A6K) recalled that he had followed Capt Partridge as the Skuas dived in line astern. Both aircraft released their bombs at a height of between 3,000 and 2,000 feet. Spurway commented that:

'6K's bomb was released at 3,000 feet and on pulling away, the observer reported that he had seen a flash, possibly caused by 6K's bomb on the port side abaft the funnel. The photograph taken directly after 6K's bomb had fallen shows considerable smoke over the battlecruiser. 6K pulled up to 5,000 feet until clear of the gun area and then dived low over the land to the northward as a Me110 was observed on the starboard beam. An Me109 was observed some distance away. The fighters apparently failed to observe 6K against the dark ground. 6K subsequently returned in company with 6Q, which joined up on leaving the coast.

'Other aircraft were observed to attack the *Hipper*-class cruiser ... but no hits were observed. The weather was hazy with a clear sky, and the movements of aircraft were hard to follow against the ground or water. Two large fires were observed ashore. One in the vicinity of Vaernes aerodrome and the other further west. No Blenheims or Beauforts were sighted. A large number of He115s were observed on the water off the town, and two were seen in the air in the vicinity. A large ball of flame was seen in the sky over the ships by Petty Officer Hart. It is possible that this was an aircraft shot down in flames.'

Another crew to get back was that of PO(A)s Eric Monk and Dickie Rolph in A6C, the latter recalling, with some bitterness:

'The sky was clear of cloud and we could have been seen for miles as we came in from the sea. At the beginning of our glide I could see the hangars on an airfield some miles from Trondheim well alight and on looking up I saw six twin-engined aircraft some 3,000 feet above us and reported to my pilot that we did have the six long-range Blenheims above us. Shortly afterwards these six all put their noses down and their twin tails came into view. I changed my report to Me110s and by this time there were more than six. At this time also, all the AA guns in the world seemed to open up on us, heavy stuff from the ships, batteries along the jetties and main streets of the town, and short-range stuff so thick that there wasn't a gap to get through at all. It looked as if a circle of people were standing around throwing up handfuls of lighted stones.

'The Me110s were almost shoving each other out of the way to have a go. As I started firing at the first one I was sure I was about to accomplish the air gunner's dream by shooting down an attacking fighter because there were flames coming out of the front of the 110. I soon realised that the flames were from his cannon and machine-guns fitted in the central nacelle and his shells and bullets were going above, below and either side of our aircraft! I thought his harmonisation was pretty poor and then realised he was inside his normal harmonisation range. He had to violently alter course as my pilot really did his stuff in literally bringing the Skua to almost a stop.

'The 110 pulled up very sharply followed by others. Each time Monk carried out the same stunt – back throttle, up nose, turn towards. There was one occasion when there was a group of 110s tearing round in a circle just below us, about eight of them, all their rear gunners having a go at just us! I thought it was a bit unfair. I hoped that I was faring better than they were. Finally they gave us the benefit of their departure for which we were thankful. By this time we were miles away from the target area without bombs, having got rid of them during the first attack. Heading north up the fjord away from Trondheim we had a discussion and decided to make for the island given us as a departure point. From there we would set course for the carrier.

'On nearing the coast, with our departure island a long way ahead we met a group of German twin-engined aircraft which we took for Ju88s returning from bombing the Fleet. It was a case of closing one's eyes and hoping you would not be seen. We believe that the Jerries must have done the same for no violence was forthcoming and we simply passed slightly below them and well to one side [these were probably the Blenhims]. On leaving our departure point (the Island of Hitra lighthouse) we climbed so that I could quickly get a good signal from the beam of the homing beacon from which we calculated our course to steer back to the *Ark*. This was successfully obtained and Monk showed great faith in accepting my new course to steer – a difference of some 60-degrees. After what seemed a long time we sighted the *Ark* dead ahead.

'It appeared that much had been going on since our departure some three hours or so before. Fog was responsible for a collision, I believe. There were also some attacks by the Luftwaffe. We were not kept waiting long before being allowed to land on. We were the first back and were hustled up to the 'office' to report to the Vice-Admiral. It went something like this. "Well, Monk, what happened?" "Well, Sir, the bloody fool who laid this trip on ought to have his head tested". "Now, now, tell me all about it". Monk did do that. I was hardly spoken to. I offered a drawing I had made of the ships' positions in Trondheim and the torpedo nets, but no one seemed to want that kind of thing. No one seemed interested in the air fighting part of the trip. We were ushered down to the Wardroom and I was offered a pot of very flat beer – and all I wanted to do was to tell someone how successful our tactics had been in getting the better of a huge gaggle of German fighters. Not a soul seemed interested.'

His pilot, PO(A) Eric Monk, added:

'With our strictly limited number of aircraft now in the *Ark*, inferior in quality to the 109s and 110 we met, our only advantage was that we had dive-brakes and we came to the conclusion that our only real hope was to wait until the enemy opened fire and was closing rapidly, dive down with dive-brakes out and full rudder to left or right to offset the line of sight. The enemy fire should pass to one side and he should rapidly overshoot – immediately pull in dive-brakes and try to get a shot in as the enemy pulled up for a further attack. Not much comfort, but the best we could think of.'[157]

Another to evade and escape was Mid(A) Stephen Griffith in A7G, the only survivor of Lt Filmer's sub-section. Roaring away just above the water, having dropped his bomb, he almost collided with a He115: 'I was so close that all I could do was wave my hand!' he later excitedly recalled. Lt Don Gibson in A7P was the last to return to the carrier. His subsequent report revealed:

'After having flown inshore for about 10 minutes, we turned to the south and approached the target at 10,000 feet, still proceeding at slow speed. Shortly after reaching Trondheim, 803 Squadron formed line astern and 800 Squadron broke away to carry out a separate attack.

'We carried out a shallow dive to 8,000 feet and made our approach. While still north of the target, which was one battle cruiser and one heavy cruiser, heavy anti-aircraft fire developed. By the time I was in a position to attack from north to south along the deck of the battle cruiser, the anti-aircraft fire was exceedingly fierce. Lieutenant-Commander Casson was leading the squadron round to attack from south to north (from bow to stern). As I was the last section to attack, I considered it not worthwhile to expose my aircraft to an extra five minutes of anti-aircraft fire. We attacked from stern to bow of the enemy, being in a perfect position to do so. There appears to be only two survivors of the south to north (bow to stern) attack.

'Although we have no record of having hit the target, our bombs seem to have fallen close around it, one being estimated at 15 feet from its stern. With one exception, all the survivors escaped by low flying in the ground mist. The exception was Sub-Lieutenant Brokensha who circled the area twice to see if he could help anyone.

'Many Me109s were seen to attack Skuas and four Me110s were present, though they held off. I myself, was subjected to a poor-spirited attack by the Me109s when in my dive. One Me110 was driven off by the Skua it attacked. From what we saw, those who were attacked by fighters were those aircraft who [*sic*] climbed after attacking, and did not take advantage of the ground mist. As we had no height and negligible performance, it would have been suicidal to have gone to their assistance.

Lt Gibson added, later:

'Pat Gordon-Smith, my observer, in his matter-of-fact voice, told me that four Messerschmitt 109s were astern of our section and I could see four Messerschmitt 110s on my starboard beam. I could also see Skuas going down in flames; being in a perfect position I therefore led my lot down, attacking from stern to bow. This bombing attack could be compared to the charge of the Light Brigade, had they been attacked by cavalry on their flanks during their approach to the guns, because as well as diving straight at the guns we were being picked off by fighters on the way down. At that sort of moment in life, one is really too busy to be scared.

'My section followed me in the dive and I believe we got one near miss and there may have been one hit. There was a considerable ground mist and on releasing our bomb I went straight on down into the streets. I always say that I left Trondheim by road at about two hundred and fifty miles an hour. I do remember that on the outskirts I saw a horse above us – it was grazing on a bank – but by then we were alone and found the small island from which we were briefed to take departure and this we did. Some ten minutes later, chatting with Pat, I was alarmed to see a formation of twin-engined aircraft ahead, however this turned out to be our Blenheim fighter escort, somewhat late, and Pat called them up on his Aldis lamp and advised them to go home; had they continued they would have been shot down. We were the last of the survivors to land on. After refreshment in the wardroom we turned in.'[158]

His final comment contained a hint of sarcastic humour, for which he was renowned:

'I had learned some important lessons about air warfare and perhaps the most important one is that ideally all future admirals should be shot at in an aeroplane while they are still young. Despite these events I maintained a great admiration for Admiral Wells who was full of fighting spirit and a staunch friend to us young aviators.'[159]

While Mid(A) Derek Martin added:

> 'Many of the higher officers who made decisions at an early stage during the Second World War had no experience of air warfare. The order to attack Trondheim was given without fully realising what it was all about. Both the squadron leaders understood that this was a wrong use of our Naval aircraft, but they could not object.'

Vice-Admiral Wells felt the loss of so many of his young aircrew deeply, and yet, of course, it was he that had planned the mission and despatched them to their fate. In his report he noted that:

> 'Owing to the conditions of light and sky which was clear except for some very light cloud, and to the 50 miles which lay between the coast and the anchorage, surprise was not achieved, and the Skuas met with fighter opposition and intense AA fire.'

He also reserved judgement on other causes:

> 'It is difficult to judge whether the Beauforts' attack on Vaernes aerodrome carried out just before the Skuas arrived served to distract the attention of the defence from the approach of the Skuas, or whether it had an adverse effect against surprise. Many enemy fighters were certainly over the anchorage at the time the Skuas dived to attack, but this may have resulted from the Skuas being reported during their passage from the coast.'

Captain Clement Moody, Director of Naval Aviation at the Admiralty, considered that surprise might have been compromised by two events in particular:

> 'The Squadron Commander of 803 Squadron who appears to have delayed his attack in order to work round the target. His last section of aircraft, who did not wait for him, suffered no loss.
>
> 'It is possible that the Beauforts' attack on Vaernes aerodrome merely stirred up the hornets' nest. It would probably have been better for them to have attacked about 2 hours before. The Skuas attack might then have synchronised with the enemy fighters' refuelling, and the return to bed of the AA guns' crews. As it was, all AA defences must have been fully manned.
>
> 'When the objective is very important, and conditions for surprise not certain beforehand to prevail, it therefore becomes very necessary for the main attack to be delivered in the greatest strength that can be provided with the forces available. This not only results in a lower percentage of aircraft casualties, but is necessary to ensure decisive results. The Skua attack on this occasion had a right to expect (without surprise) only one hit and a 25 per cent chance of a second, and 30 per cent casualties from gunfire plus up to 30 per cent more from fighters.'

The C-in-C, Admiral of the Fleet Sir Charles Forbes, was more forthcoming. He thought that achieving surprise was very difficult against Trondheim:

> '... and I think it is reasonable to assume that the Skuas were reported by coast watchers at least 20 minutes before they arrived over the target. In that time there could have been several fighters at 10,000 feet over the enemy ships.'

With the drama over, work continued on *Scharnhorst*'s propulsion turbine for the centreline shaft, and repairs were completed in ten days. The damage to the starboard shaft was believed to be serious and could only be surveyed in a dry dock. Since it was feared that the shaft had been severed by the explosion, the propeller was lashed to the hull. By 18 June, *Scharnhorst* was running engine trials on the fjord and next day the ship was declared ready to set sail at a maximum 24 knots. She departed for Kiel on 20th June with an escort of three minesweepers.

Next day RAF Coastal Command aircraft spotted the *Scharnhorst* group off the Isle of Utsire, and around 15:00, six torpedo-carrying Swordfish attacked, but were easily repulsed by anti-aircraft fire. At 16:30, nine Beauforts attacked with armour-piercing bombs, but were also driven off by anti-aircraft fire and German fighters. When German interception of British radio messages revealed that much of the British Home Fleet was at sea, the *Scharnhorst* was ordered into Stavanger. Some British warships had closed to within 35 miles of her position when the decision was made. Six Swordfish, three each from 821 and 823 Squadrons flying out of Hatston, carried out an unsuccessful torpedo attack on the *Scharhorst* on **21st June**, as Lt John Stenning (with Lt Victor Smith RAN) in P4144 of 821 Squadron, later wrote:

'The aircraft had a long-range tank in the observer's seat so each aircraft had an observer or a TAG. We took off and flew to the Norwegian coast climbing in fairly open formation. It was a slow business as the aircraft with torpedo and long-range tank plus crew were a bit heavy for the power of the old Pegasus engine. It took nearly two hours to climb to 8,000 feet and reach the Norwegian coast, find our navigation objective and turn north, proceeding up the coast a few miles out to sea. After quite a short time we spotted *Scharnhorst* with a close escort of seven destroyers steaming south at high speed.

'I gave the hand signal for attack formation, pointing my thumbs backwards for line astern. Our sub-flight stayed to the east of the enemy while the other moved to the west. When the flak started it wasn't too accurate and once I started my dive I didn't notice it until after I had dropped my fish – too many things to think about! The destroyers must have been about 1,000-2,000 yards from the battleship. It was quite tricky having to manoeuvre between two destroyers to get inside the screen and have a clear run for the torpedo. It then left very little time to adjust everything and drop the 'fish' within the necessary criteria for a good run, namely, height 50-120 feet above the water – wings level nose not down and not much up – aim off for ship's speed at the right dropping range which had to be 800-1,000 yards - airspeed 80-100 knots.

'The torpedo sight on those Stringbags was two horizontal rows of light bulbs either side of the fuselage ahead of the pilot's cockpit. You had to estimate the target speed and set it so that the correct bulb lit up. I estimated 30 knots but I had never carried out practice attacks on big ships at that speed: most of ours didn't do more than 20-24 knots. Anyway, after dropping I did a violent starboard turn and went like hell at zero feet. I found this was a mistake as all the shots being fired at me ricocheted off the sea all round the aircraft. I was just able to see my torpedo pass through the kick of the wake as *Scharnhorst* altered course – a miss just astern. I got away to the east and circled at about 1,000 feet until two other aircraft joined me. Couldn't wait too long because the fuel situation was getting critical. Smith gave me a course to steer and after four hours we landed at Sumburgh in South Shetlands to refuel. We took off again at 18:25 and landed at Hatston just over an hour later. Four out of six got back and we never heard anything about the other two Swordfish, both from No.823 Squadron.'

Both missing crews – Sub-Lt(A) Maurice White and his TAG N/Air Charlie Hull, and Sub-Lt(A) Len Cater with PO(A) Fred Davis – were lost. That evening, the German group put into Skudenesfjord near Stavanger, where *Scharnhorst* moved round to a relatively safe anchorage in Dusavik Bay, before setting out next morning bound for Kiel.

Despite the severe losses inflicted upon the units and men of the Norwegian Expeditionary Force including those of RN warships and RAF aircraft, the tiny FAA contingent had acquitted itself well in the circumstances. The Admiralty assessed that Home Fleet Skuas and Sea Gladiators (since the beginning of the war) had been engaged in 61 separate combats – mainly with He111s – during which 17 German aircraft had been credited as destroyed and 17 damaged, for the loss of three Skuas in combat, plus two and one Gladiator damaged.

Skuas (48 engagements, 14 enemy aircraft destroyed, 13 damaged; three Skuas lost, two damaged)

Do17/Do215 four engagements, no claims (one Skua lost)
Ju88 five engagements, five destroyed
He111 26 engagements, six destroyed, ten damaged (one Skua lost, one damaged)
Do18 three engagements, two destroyed, one damaged
Do26 two engagements, one destroyed, one damaged (one Skua lost)
He115 five engagements, one damaged
Bf109 two engagements, no claims (one Skua damaged)
Bf110 one engagement, no claims

Sea Gladiators (13 engagements, three enemy aircraft destroyed, four damaged; one Gladiator damaged)

Do17 two engagements, one damaged
Ju87 five engagements, one destroyed, one damaged (one Gladiator damaged)
He111 four engagements, one destroyed, one damaged
He115 two engagements, one destroyed, one damaged

However, these figures do not tally with the 'official' credits awarded to *Ark Royal* and *Glorious* during this period, which were:

Ark Royal:
Destroyed (13): 9 He111, 3 Ju88, 1 He115; Damaged (17): 8 He111, 6 He115, 2 Ju88, 1 'bomber/transport'

Glorious:
Destroyed (7): 4 He111, 1 Ju88, 1 He115, 1 Ju87; Damaged:(3): 3 He115 (plus 1 He111 by ship's gunfire)

The Skua and Sea Gladiator losses listed above are obviously those sustained in air-to-air combat only, and do not show the complete picture. FAA aircraft losses during the Norwegian Campaign, 10 April-21 June were:

Skuas (31)	800 Squadron, 10 lost	801 Squadron, 2 lost
	803 Squadron, 19 lost	
Sea Gladiators (7)	802 Squadron, 6 lost aboard Glorious when sunk	
	804 Squadron, 1 lost	
Swordfish (30)	810 Squadron, 8 lost	816 Squadron, 3 lost
	818 Squadron, 7 lost	820 Squadron, 3 lost
	823 Squadron, 9 lost including 6 aboard Glorious when sunk	
Walruses (3)	700 Squadron, 2 lost	701 Squadron, 1 lost

It had been a tough war so far for the handful of FAA aircrew involved in the Norwegian Campaign, as epitomised by the experiences of Lt Alex Fraser-Harris of 803 Squadron:

> 'At the beginning of the war I was with a Skua squadron in the Orkneys. The first operation we were required to carry out was the bombing of the cruiser *Königsberg* in Bergen Harbour. We took off before daybreak, eighteen aircraft, on a round trip of 600 miles-which was twenty minutes inside our endurance. Seventeen aircraft came back; the *Königsberg* went down in ten minutes, and the BBC announced the same night that the 'RAF have done it again.' That was one trip, and the *Königsberg* was the first ship to be sunk by dive-bombing during the war. Those trips from the Orkneys to Norway went on. It was not only one trip, it was a shuttle service for the next three months, backwards and forwards, with a twenty minute margin of endurance. Some of the aircraft would get back in due course, some forced-landed on the return journey, some forced-landed in Norway. But on the whole they were successful, and I think there were only two of those trips on which some ship belonging to the other side was not sunk. Eventually the Army went into Norway and we embarked in the *Glorious*. From there we carried out the same tactics, dive-bombing, and to the best of our ability giving fighter support to the Army. The Skua, about which we heard a lot at the time, was three things: a dive-bomber, a spotter reconnaissance and a fighter; in point of fact it was none of the three, except a dive-bomber at which it was excellent, although having dropped the bombs it was not fast enough, and you did not always get away. Out of the squadron that went into action from the *Glorious* only three officers are now alive, and one is a prisoner of war in Germany. I was lucky; I was shot down over Norway and just escaped the fate of the *Glorious*. I came back over land.

A greater challenge and threat was yet to come – with the Fleet Air Arm and its aircrew again to the fore. But many of its experienced aircrews had been lost in recent actions.

FOOTNOTES

1 The Walrus was also used by RAF ASR units. The CO of one ASR unit, when asked by a newly posted pilot if he could fly the Walrus, replied:
"You must be off your bloody rocker. It's like flying a brick shithouse. It takes off, flies, and lands, all at the same speed. It wallows all over the place ignoring you flying it, and with the engine at the back it doesn't fly like an aeroplane, in fact it really isn't an aeroplane is it? It's a bloody monstrosity, but God, what would we do without them on this job?" As an after thought he added, "You'll get bloody wet when you go down, and probably have to taxi back on the surface for several hours to Dover Harbour, and then find the bar's closed when you get home, but, be it on your own head." (see *Flying Made My Arms Ache* by Wally Wallens)

2 Extracted from *War in a Stringbag* by Charles Lamb.

3 The crew were held in the Tower of London for some time; two were shot while attempting to escape in 1940.

4 See *War in a Stringbag.*

5 *Ibid.*

6 *Ibid.*

7 Cdr Woodhouse finally succumbed to his ordeal when he died of lung complications on 27 July 1940.

8 See *War in a Stringbag.*

9 Extracted from *It's Really Quite Safe*! by G A Hank Rotherham.

10 See *Anchors Aweigh*! by Kenneth Poolman.

11 *Ibid.*

12 Extracted from *Fleet Air Arm at War* by Ray Sturtivant.

13 Extracted from *Anchors Aweigh*!

14 Pre-war, Lt Charles Evans had been an Osprey floatplane pilot aboard the cruiser HMS *Sussex.*

15 Having learned that there was a shortage of sea-going officers, Lt Bill Robertson requested a return to sea service and in March 1940 was appointed First Officer of the destroyer HMS *Ambuscade.* He survived the war and retired as a Lt-Cdr.

16 See *Anchors Aweigh!*

17 *Ibid.*

18 Extracted from *British Naval Aviation* by Ray Sturtivant.

19 See *Operation Skua* by Major Richard Partridge RM.

20 These included N2265 and N2275 ('hooked' Gladiator IIs), and Sea Gladiators N5504, N5509, N5510, N5538 and N5545.

21 See *War in a Stringbag.*

22 See *It's Really Quite Safe.*

23 Lt-Cdr Phillimore sustained serious leg injuries when the Wellington of 99 Squadron in which he was flying forced-landed on return from a reconnaissance sortie on the night of 20-21 February 1940.

24 See *It's Really Quite Safe.*

25 See *Supermaine Walrus* by Lt-Cdr G W R Nicholl.

26 Article 23 of Convention (II) with Respect to the Laws and Customs of War, The Hague 1899: According to this principle are especially 'forbidden': (f) Making improper use of a flag of truce, of the national flag or of the military insignia and uniform of the enemy, as well as the distinctive badges of the Geneva Convention.

27 See *Ark Royal* by Kenneth Poolman.

28 Captain Patrick Dove, Master of the *Africa Star*, later wrote of his experiences aboard *Graf Spee* in a booklet entitled *I was Graf Spee's Prisoner.*

29 *Ibid.*

30 See *Hunt the Altmark* by Richard Wiggan.

31 See *I was Graf Spee's Prisoner.*

32 *Ibid.*

33 See *Graf Spee* by Michael Powell.

34 *Ibid.*

35 Lt Lewin was awarded the DSC for his performance, while Lt Kearney received a Mentioned in Despatches, the first honours gained by the FAA during WWII.

36 See *Ark Royal* by William Jameson.

37 *Ibid.*

38 See *Anchors Aweigh!*

39 See *Ark Royal.*

40 See *Turns of Fate* by Ken Dimbleby.

41 See *Anchors Aweigh!*

42 See *Haul, Taut and Belay* by Donald Gibson

43 These were: Skuas L2935, L2965, L3004, L3013, L3014, L3106, L3018, L3023; and Rocs L3101, L3102, L3103, L3105, L3153 and L3156.

44 27-year-old James Isbister, a married man with a baby son, was killed outright when a bomb exploded as he stepped outside his cottage at the Bridge of Waithe, four miles east of Stromness in the Orkneys. Six other people were wounded.

45 See *Haul, Taut and Belay.*

[46] 29-year-old Lt William Paulet Lucy, known as Billy to family and friends, was the son of a former Malayan rubber planter who had settled at Sutton Valence in Kent, where Billy was born, the second of five children. Younger brother Bernard had died prewar in Malaya as a result of tropical fever.
[47] See *Operation Skua.*
[48] *Devonshire's* Walrus L2257 suffered damage to all mainplanes and had to be put ashore for repair.
[49] See *Haul, Taut and Belay.*
[50] Comment by Prime Minister Winston Churchill.
[51] See *Operation Skua.*
[52] *Ibid.*
[53] See *Anchors Aweigh!*
[54] See *Blackburn Skua & Roc* by Matthew Willis.
[55] See *Operation Skua.*
[56] *Ibid.*
[57] See *Skua.*
[58] See *Anchors Aweigh!*
[59] See *Operation Skua.*
[60] *Ibid.*
[61] *Ibid.*
[62] *Ibid.*
[63] See *Anchors Aweigh!*
[64] See *Operation Skua.*
[65] See *Skua.*
[66] See *British Naval Aviation.*
[67] See *Anchors Aweigh!*
[68] *Ibid.*
[69] *Ibid.*
[70] Extracted from *TAG in a Stringbag* by Les Sayer and Vernon Ball.
[71] *Ibid.*
[72] See *The Swordfish Story* by Ray Sturtivant.
[73] Lt Marcus Donati was lost when the SS *Almeda Star* was torpedoed by *U-96* some 350 miles west of the Isle of Lewis on 17 January 1941. In total, 140 members of the FAA were lost when the ship was sunk.
[74] Midshpmn Dammers' injured leg was amputated and he was later fitted with an artificial limb. He became an instructor but was killed in 1942 in a flying accident.
[75] See *Anchors Aweigh!*
[76] See *Fleet Air Arm at War.*
[77] Thirteen Ju52/3m transports of KGrzbv.102 took off from Berlin-Tempelhof on 12 April to carry alpine troops of 2/AR112 *Gebirgsbatterie* and supplies to Narvik. Two of the aircraft (SE+JZ and CN+BS of 1/102) got lost in bad weather and force landed. The remaining 11 landed on the frozen Lake Hartvigvann; these were CA+JY (6657); CO+EI (6791); DB+BP (6694); DB+RB (6697); DB+RC (6631); DB+RD (6693); DB+QU (6654); NR+A- (6054) VB+UP (6821); SE+KC (6664); 1Z+BY (6134). In the 1980s several of these were recovered from the lake.
[78] *Ibid.*
[79] Extracted from *Norwegian Patrol* by Gron Edwards.
[80] He111 claimed shot down per N/Air Lionel Miles' logbook.
[81] The other members of the crew of K6+FH were Ltn z.See Max Keil, Fk.Obgfr Werner Merg and Uffz Jacob Ims.
[82] Extracted from *The Supermarine Walrus.*
[83] Admiral Lord Cork and Orrery – William Henry Dudley Boyle, 12th Earl of Cork and 12th Earl of Orrery.
[84] The Arado crashed in the Clyde on 26 April while being flown by Wg Cdr J F X McKenna , who survived the incident.
[85] See *British Naval Aviation.*
[86] *Ibid.*
[87] See *Haul, Taut and Belay.*
[88] See *Lost Voices of the Royal Navy* by Max Arthur.
[89] See *Carrier Glorious* by John Winton.
[90] *Ibid.*
[91] *Ibid.*
[92] One would imagine that Ken Brown's father had great aspirations for his son, whose second name was Admiral.
[93] Extracted from *TAG in a Stringbag.*
[94] Extracted from *After the Battle No.28.*
[95] They were later transferred to England, spending the rest of the war as prisoners in Canada. The Heinkel remained on the mountainside for many years in a remarkably undamaged condition, although stripped of removable items by souvenir hunters, and of paint by the weather. Finally it was recovered by enthusiasts and was restored in 1979. In August of that year the three Germans and the two surviving Fleet Air Arm Skua crewmembers – John Collett and Reg Davies – met at Gardermoen for the roll-out of the aircraft.
[96] See *Blackburn Skua and Roc* by Matthew Willis.
[97] See *Anchors Aweigh!*
[98] See *Carrier Glorious.*
[99] 35-year-old T/Lt(A) William Erwin Gibson Taylor, who had formerly served with both the USN and USMC, volunteered to join the FAA in early 1939 and was snapped up due to his

experience. In October he was persuaded to resign his commission and join the RAF to help form the first US Eagle Squadron.

[100] See *Operation Skua.*

[101] Extracted from *Find, Fix and Strike* by Terence Horsley.

[102] See *Operation Skua.*

[103] See *Find, Fix and Strike.*

[104] *Ibid.*

[105] See *Operation Skua.*

[106] See *Find, Fix and Strike.* Dicky Partridge's *Operation Skua* has a fuller and slightly different version of this adventure.

[107] See *The First Pathfinders* by Kenneth Wakefield.

[108] *Ibid.*

[109] See *Carrier Glorious* by John Winton.

[110] 34-year-old PO(A) Stanley Andrews was killed in a flying accident on 17 January 1941.

[111] Donald Willis later joined the RAF's 121 Eagle Squadron before transferring to the USAF; he became a Major and was shot down over Holland in April 1944 while flying a P-38. He evaded capture and eventually reached Gibraltar, from where he was flown back to the UK.

[112] The He115s were F.58 and F.64, which arrived at Sollum Voe on 7 June, followed next day by F.56; they were later sold to the British Government and became BV184-187.

[113] Sub-Lt (A) Woodrow Adams eventually died of his injuries on 5 October 1940.

[114] Extracted from *TAG in a Stringbag.*

[115] See *Operation Skua.*

[116] Fw Karl Grube, Uffz Helmut Bennighoff, and Uffz Werner Wamser.

[117] There is confusion as to whether this aircraft was lost on this date, although it apparently appears on the QMR later in the year.

[118] Escorted by two destroyers, *Resolution* departed for Scapa Flow, where she arrived without further incident five days later. The battleship's Swordfish floatplane had been damaged in the bombing and the aircraft was later shipped back to the UK aboard the steamer *Blackheath.*

[119] Adapted from *Find, Fix and Strike.*

[120] Both Flt Lt Hull and Lt Lydekker were evacuated to the UK. After recovering from his injuries Lyddecker returned to his duty as the Armament Officer on the Air Staff of HMS *Furious.* He was lost during the sinking of HMS *Avenger* in November 1942. Flt Lt Hull was killed during the Battle of Britain.

[121] Extracted verbatim from *Carrier Glorious.*

[122] *Ibid.*

[123] *Ibid.*

[124] *Ibid.*

[125] *Ibid.*

[126] Extracted from *The Sea Eagles Volume I* by Chris Goss.

[127] Extracted from *Carrier Glorious.*

[128] *Ibid.*

[129] *Ibid.*

[130] John Casson was the son of Sir Lewis Casson and Dame Sybil Thorndike, the celebrated actress.

[131] See *Aces, Warriors and Wingmen* by Wayne Ralph.

[132] See *Carrier Glorious.*

[133] See *Straight and Level* by Air Chief Marshal Sir Kenneth Cross.

[134] *Ibid.*

[135] See *British Naval Aviation.*

[136] There is a signal from C-in-C Home Fleet dated 6 June 1940 to *"Proceed to Scapa to enable a court-martial to be held"*. At the time official reasons for *Glorious* to sail back have been stated:

1) The *Glorious* had carried out the mission for which she had been despatched (the retrieval of RAF Hurricane and Gladiator fighters that were now on board, having landed for the first time on an aircraft carrier)
2) She could contribute less to the safety of the evacuation convoys, which were the Fleet's next main concern, than she herself would need in the way of protection.
3) It is considered to be doubtful whether, after five days at sea off Norway, she had sufficient fuel to return to base with the desired 33 per cent reserve remaining.
4) Although the Admiralty required that the ship's company was to be sent on leave from Devonport on completion of the operation, the C-in-C Home Fleet had stated that she was first to proceed to Scapa Flow to hold an outstanding court-martial.

[137] See *Carrier Glorious.*

[138] Although Commander Heath requested a court-martial to enable him to defend his actions, this could not be permitted due to the death of Captain D'Oyly-Hughes. However, he was able to make his case to the subsequent Board of Inquiry and eventually received a letter from the Admiralty, stating: "Their Lordships have had under review the circumstances which led to your leaving HMS *Glorious* in May 1940, and I am now able to

inform you that in the official view of the Admiralty no charges involving your honour or professional reputation stand against you. The notation of the reason for your removal from the Glorious has been erased from your record." But, by then, the damage had been done.

139 *Ibid.*

140 *Ibid.*

141 *Ibid.*

142 *Ibid.*

143 See *Straight and Level.*

144 Post war Bob Kearsley met the German pilot and they became firm friends.

145 Oblt Böcking and his crew were lost; the others were Fw Wilhelm Nordhorn, Fw Heinz Neidhardt, and Fw Erich Rau. SdFhr Vogel of *Lw Kriegsberichter Kompanie 1*, a war reporter, was also aboard this aircraft and died with the others.

146 See *Aces, Warriors and Wingmen.*

147 The official record states that no Swordfish were in the air prior to the attack, although one source (*Flying Marines* by Major Allan Marsh RM) suggests that two aircraft from 823 Squadron were in fact airborne, one flown by Lt Aubrey Parnell RM, and a second that included Mid(A) Arthur Keep as observer. Parnell's aircraft ditched en route to Hatston and the crew were rescued, while Keep's aircraft landed safely at Hatston. In-depth research now suggests that neither aircraft/crew was aboard *Glorious* when she was sunk, but were operating from Hatston on that date.

148 The Carley float was essentially an oval-shaped roll of canvas, painted to make it watertight and stuffed with kapok or granulated cork. Inside the oval, a wooden lattice deck was laced with ropes, and another rope ran around the outside rim for men to cling to. The Carley float had no 'right' or 'wrong way up'. The wooden deck would settle in the water whichever way the float fell. But as the floats were all free-flooding the survivors' feet and legs were in sea-water. Most of the floats held twenty-five men, but some of the larger floats were designed for fifty. None of *Glorious'* Carley floats had any food or drinking water in them, and few of them even had a paddle. Some survivors retrieved oars from the sea. (*Carrier Glorious*)

149 See *Haul, Taut and Belay.*

150 See *Operation Skua.*

151 One source credits Oblt Gollob with shooting down Lt Filmer's aircraft, but his victim apparently went down in flames, it was more likely to have been Mid(A) Gallagher's aircraft.

152 N/Air Stuart Stevenson was taken prisoner and eventually succumbed to his injuries almost a year later (31 May 1941).

153 While a POW, Lt Filmer made repeated attempts to escape. Once he and five others jumped at night from a train travelling at about 25mph, but were recaptured next day. Another time he hid in the false bottom of a box filled with empty food tins and was carried out to a rubbish dump. While the guard was distracted, he slithered out and hid in a hut until darkness fell and walked away from the camp. After ten days he reached the Danish border, where he was caught again. Later he helped with the tunnel at Stalag Luft III for the Great Escape in April 1944. Finally, with several thousand other POWs, he marched hundreds of miles in freezing conditions from south-east of Berlin to the port of Lubeck to avoid the advancing Russians.

154 One source credits Sub-Lt Bartlett's Skua to Ltn Köhler of 3/ZG76 but from Bartlett's account it would seem that it fell to a Bf109.

155 See *One Man's War.*

156 See *Operation Skua.*

157 See *Anchors Aweigh!*

158 See *Haul, Taut and Belay.*

159 *Ibid.*

An undated photograph of an unidentified Sea Gladiator on which the two-bladed Watts propeller is clearly evident. *FAA Museum*

An unidentified Sea Gladiator seen at Hatston. *FAA Museum*

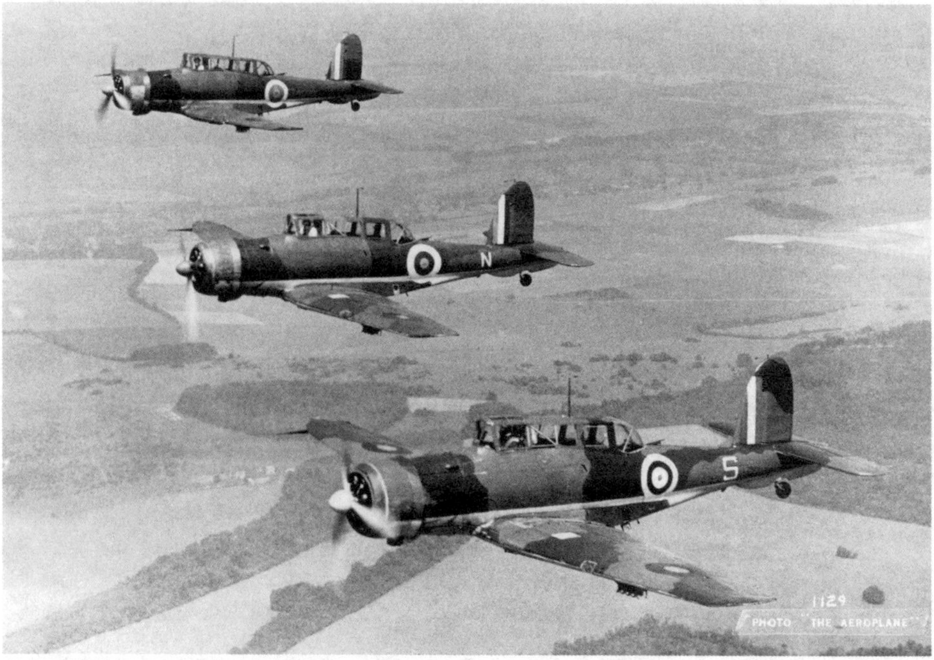

Skuas in camouflage. Although the other aircrafts' serials are not apparent that of 'S' is either L2928 or L2929. Both aircraft appear to have been coded 'S' at some stage of their service lives with 759 and possibly 769 Squadrons respectively. *via NAM*

Roc L3059. Hopeless as a fighter even with a wheeled undercarriage, this familiar image suffices to illustrate how impossible the Roc appeared as a float equipped fighter which could scarcely achieve a top speed of 190 mph; 170 mph at sea level! It was though quite usual for the Admiralty to adapt selected aircraft types to accommodate floats, there was many a precedence for this; however, by 1940 the primacy of the high-performance landplane was very evident. Even so, 805 Squadron was formed on 4th May 1940 as a Roc seaplane fighter unit, it having been proposed that it would operate from Norwegian fjords with perhaps 18 such aircraft. *via NAM*

Walrus L2191 '42' seen at Farnborough in 1938. When photographed '42' was allocated to 712 Squadron (nee 712 Flight) and served aboard the light cruisers HMS' *Newcastle* and *Southampton* of the 2nd Cruiser Squadron from May 1938 to May 1939. Thereafter L2191 served with 765 and 796 Squadrons until at least September 1943. *via NAM*

Fairey Seafox K857?. Perhaps the least known type of operational biplane with which the Fleet Air Arm was equipped at the beginning of World War II was the Seafox, an aircraft designed to be operated by and catapulted from light cruisers as a reconnaissance seaplane. Quite large and rather underpowered, the Seafox could be identified by having an open cockpit for the pilot whilst the observer enjoyed an enclosed canopy and their only means of defence; a single .303 mg, (when carried). Excluding two prototypes, Seafox production ran to 64 machines and the type remained in service until approximately mid-1943 at which point any surviving Seafoxes were withdrawn. *FAA Museum*

Seafox K8582 of 718 Squadron being launched from it's parent vessel, the light cruiser HMS *Ajax*; it being one of two Seafoxes aboard the ship during the action against *Graf Spee* at the River Plate in 1939. At the time that this photograph was taken, K8582's vertical fin was painted black with the ship's badge superimposed upon it. The items below the lower mainplane appear bomb-like albeit minus fins; the Seafox was designed to carry two 100lb bombs or eight 20lb bombs. *FAA Museum*

Sub-Lt(A) Dick Bartlett, 803 Squadron, POW June 1940.

Lt(A) John Collett, Observer, 801 Squadron.

Sub-Lt(A) Guy Brokensha, 803 Squadron, DSC.

PO(A) Reg Davies, 801 Squadron TAG.

Lt-Cdr Peter Bramwell, CO, 801 Squadron.

Lt(A) Moose Martin, 801 Squadron.

Captain Les 'Skeet' Harris DSC, RM, 803 Squadron.

Major Richard 'Birdy' Partridge DSO, RM,
800 Squadron, POW June 1940

APPENDIX I

FAA Aircrew Operational Fatalities September 1939-June 1940 (Home Fleet) Roll of Honour

10/9/39 Swordfish P4090 822 Sqn KoAS
Lt W A H Playfair
Sub-Lt(A) H A Wheatman (O)
N/Air F Frizzell (TAG)

14/9/39 Skua L2873 803 Sqn KiA
PO(A) G V McKay (O)
Skua L2957
PO(A) J Simpson (O)

17/9/39 811 Sqn KiA (HMS *Courageous*)
Lt H J C Walton-Wilson (O)
Lt A F Ingram (O)
Lt(A) T D M MacDonald
PO(A) B J Owen
N/Air R J W Byrne (TAG)
N/Air A Marsh (TAG)
Sub-Lt(A) D F Williams
Sub-Lt(A) G J B Pollard (O)

23/10/39 Roc L3063 803 Sqn KoAS
PO(A) L R Tregillis
N/Air R E Eason (TAG)

31/10/39 Walrus L2261 HMS *Sussex* KoAS
Lt(A) S M Bird
Lt C H E Osmaston (O)
L/Air W H Brown (TAG)

25/11/39 Swordfish L2774 810 Sqn KoAS
L/Air E H Shayler (TAG)

8/12/39 Skua L2880 800 Sqn KoAS
Sub-Lt(A) P T Bethell

11/1/40 Skua L2946 803 Sqn KoAS
Mid(A) J D W Barr
L/Air G E Uren (TAG)

9/4/40 Skua L2948 803 Sqn KoAS
PO(A) W E Chinn
N/Air T G L Burgess (TAG)

10/4/40 Skua L2923 803 Sqn KiA (Flak)
Lt B J Smeeton
Mid(A) F Watkinson (O)

13/4/40 Swordfish U3C 818 Sqn KiA (Flak)
Sub-Lt(A) G R Hampden
N/Air R Dale (TAG)

13-14/4/40 Wellington L4339; attached to
38 Sqn RAF KiA (Bf109)
Sub-Lt(A) L C Franklin (O)

14/4/40 Skua L2881 803 Sqn KiA (Flak)
Capt E D McIver RM
L/Air A A Barnard (TAG)

18/4/40 T P4214 816 Sqn KiA
Lt(A) F Whittingham
(hit HT wire)

19/4/40 Swordfish P4163 818 Sqn KiA (Flak)
Lt C R D Messenger (O)
L/Air T Cutler (TAG)

20/4/40 Skua L2999 800 Sqn KiA (FTR)
Mid(A) J R Crossley
PO(A) M Hall (TAG)

24/4/40 Walrus L2316 700 Sqn KiA
(believed Do18)
PO(A) C L Smeathers
Mid(A) P L Furber (O)
N/Air C E Adams (TAG)

25/4/40 Swordfish L2790 810 Sqn KiA (Flak)
Lt A A Pardoe
PO(A) L M Lloyd (TAG)

26/4/40 Skua L2991 803 Sqn KiA
(He111 return fire)
PO(A) K G Baldwin (TAG)

27/4/40 Skua L2931 801 Sqn KiA
(He111 return fire)
Lt W C A Church
Sub-Lt(A) D G Willis (O)

9/5/40 Blenheim IV L9482; attached to
254 Sqn KiA (Flak)
Lt(A) R Nuthall (O)

14/5/40 Skua L2925 803 Sqn KiA
(He111 return fire)
Lt W P Lucy
Lt M C E Hanson (O)

17/5/40 Swordfish 823 Sqn KoAS
(engine failure)
Sub-Lt H A Mourilyan
N/Air R Parkinson (TAG)

18/5/40 Walrus P5647 HMS *Devonshire*
KiA (He111 return fire)
Lt R W Benson-Dare
L/Air B M Hill (TAG)

9/6/40 802 Sqn KiA HMS *Glorious*
Lt J F Marmont
Lt D N H Ogilvy
Lt N E Ward
Lt G D D'E Lyver
Capt R J W Nott RM
Capt J R Owens RM

Lt(A) G H J Feeny
Lt(A) R J B Miles

823 Sqn KiA HMS *Glorious*
Lt-Cdr C J T Stephens (O)
Lt J L Hallewell
Lt S F W Hebblethwaite (O)
Lt G Starkey
Lt B J C Wise (O)
Sub-Lt(A) J H Radclift
Sub-Lt(A) G P Ritchie
Sub-Lt (A) J M Franklin (O)
Sub-Lt(A) J F Shillitoe (O)
PO(A) E H Puntis (O)
L/Air B Brett (TAG)
L/Air A W Crichton (TAG)
L/Air J Heath (TAG)
L/Air W H Hill (TAG)
L/Air J Houldsworth (TAG)
L/Air P McN McLennan (TAG)
N/Air W H Burns (TAG)
N/Air D C Morton (TAG)

13/6/40 Skua L3028 800 Sqn KiA (Bf110)
Mid(A) L H Gallagher
PO(A) W Crawford (TAG)

Skua L2992 803 Sqn KiA (Bf110)
Sub-Lt(A) J A Harris
N/Air S R D Stevenson (TAG)
POW – died from injuries 31/5/41

Skua L3000 800 Sqn KiA (Bf110)
Lt G E D Finch-Noyes

Skua L4007 800 Sqn KiA (Bf109)
L/Air W J Tremeer (TAG)

Skua L2995 800 Sqn KiA (Bf109)
Lt R S Bostock (O)

21/6/40 Swordfish 823 Sqn KiA (Flak)
Sub-Lt(A) M P White
N/Air C Hull (TAG)

Swordfish 823 Sqn KiA (Flak)
Sub-Lt(A) L B Cater
PO(A) F Davis (TAG)

APPENDIX II

FAA Combat Claims, Home Fleet, September 1939 – June 1940

26/9/39	Lt B S McEwen PO(A) B S Seymour (O)	Skua L2873 803 Sqn	Do18 M7+YK 2/KüFlGr 506 destroyed
	PO(A) H A Monk L/Air L C S Eccleshall (TAG)	Skua 800 Sqn	He59 M2+JK 3/KüFlGr 106 damaged
20/3/40	Lt E W T Taylour Lt R S Bostock (O)	Skua L3028 800 Sqn	He111 6/KG26 destroyed shared with RAF
	Lt W P Lucy Lt M C E Hanson (O)	Skua L2925 803 Sqn	He111 2 /KG26 c/landed (w/o)
10/4/40	Sub-Lt(A) M F Fell PO(A) G W Peacock PO(A) A W Sabey	Sea Gladiator N5510 804 Sqn Sea Gladiator N5538 804 Sqn Sea Gladiator N5509 804 Sqn	He111 2 /KG26
	Lt R M Smeeton	Sea Gladiator N2275 804 Sqn	He111 2 /KG26 destroyed
14/4/40:	Lt W P Lucy Lt M C E Hanson (O)	Skua L2925 803 Sqn	
	Lt A B Fraser-Harris L/Air G S Russell (TAG)	Skua L2910 803 Sqn	He115 1 /KüFlGr 106 (on water)
	Capt E D McIver RM L/Air A A Barnard (TAG)	Skua L2881 803 Sqn	
17/4/40	Lt H E R Torin Mid(A) T A McKee (O)	Skua L203 803 Sqn	Do18 probable (possibly M2+KK 2 /KüFlGr 106)
	Sub-Lt I H Easton L/Air F Costan (TAG)	Skua L3010 803 Sqn	
	Lt L A Harris RM PO(A) S E Andrews (O)	Skua L2991 803Sqn	
	Sub-Lt(A) G W Brokensha N/Air A J Hayman (TAG)	Skua L2905 803 Sqn	He111 possible 1 /KG26 (damaged)
	Sub-Lt(A) P N Charlton L/Air A Ashby (TAG)	Skua L2916 803 Sqn	
	Lt A B Fraser-Harris L/Air G S Russell (TAG)	Skua L2910 803 Sqn	
	Lt-Cdr H P Bramwell Lt J W Collett (O)	Skua L3005 801 Sqn	

	Lt(A) W H Martyn L/Air R W C Davies (TAG)	Skua L2917 801 Sqn	Do18 K6+FH 1 /KüFlGr 406 destroyed
	Sub-Lt(A) B F Wigginton N/Air E J Adlam (TAG)	Skua L2912 801 Sqn	
24/4/40	Lt L A Harris RM PO(A) K G Baldwin (TAG	Skua L2881 803 Sqn	
	Lt C H Filmer N/Air H Pickering (TAG)	Skua L2991 803 Sqn	He111 5J+JT 9 /KG54 crash-landed (w/o)
	Sub-Lt I H Easton N/Air A J Hayman (TAG)	Skua L3010 803 Sqn	
	Lt W P Lucy Lt M C E Hanson (O)	Skua L2925 803 Sqn	
	Lt A B Fraser-Harris L/Air G S Russell (TAG	Skua L2910 803 Sqn	He111 5J+AT 9 /KG54 crash-landed (w/o)
	Lt J M Christian N/Air S G A Wright (TAG)	Skua L2924 803 Sqn	
25/4/40	Lt W P Lucy Lt M C E Hanson (O)	Skua L2925 803 Sqn	
	Lt A B Fraser-Harris L/Air G S Russell (TAG)	Skua L2910 803 Sqn	
	Lt J M Christian N/Air S G A Wright (TAG)	Skua L2924 803 Sqn	4 He115 destroyed + 3 damaged I/KüFlGr 506 (in harbour)
	Lt L A Harris RM PO(A) K G Badwin (TAG)	Skua L2881 803 Sqn	
	Lt C H Filmer N/Air H Pickering (TAG)	Skua L2991 803 Sqn	
	Lt G R Callingham N/Air D A Prime (TAG)	Skua L3028 800 Sqn	He115 (2 /KüFlGr 506) destroyed
26/4/40	Lt(A) W H Martyn N/Air R W C Davies (TAG)	Skua L2915 801 Sqn	He111 5J+CN 5 /KG54 destroyed
	Lt-Cdr H P Bramwell Lt J W Collett (O)	Skua L2881 801 Sqn	
	Sub-Lt(A) B Wigginton N/Air E J Adlam (TAG)	Skua L2997 801 Sqn	+ He111 probable
	Lt W P Lucy Lt M C E Hanson (O)	Skua L2925 803 Sqn	

	Lt C H Filmer PO(A) K G Baldwin (TAG)	Skua L2991 803 Sqn	2 He111s damaged
	Lt J M Christian N/Air S G Wright (TAG)	Skua L2924 803 Sqn	
	Lt W P Lucy Lt M C E Hanson (O)	Skua L2925 803 Sqn	He111 L1+KT 9 /LG1 destroyed
	Lt J M Christian N/Air S G A Wright (TAG)	Skua L2924 803 Sqn	
	Lt G E D Finch-Noyes PO(A) H G Cunningahm (O)	Skua L3000 800 Sqn	
	Lt K V V Spurway PO(A) W Crawford (O)	Skua L2908 800 Sqn	He115 1 /KüFlGr 506 damaged
	Lt J A Rooper L/Air V H M Cordwell (O)	Skua L3001 800 Sqn	
27/4/40	Lt R M Smeeton	Gladiator N2275 804 Sqn	
	Lt (A) W E G Taylor (US)	Gladiator N2272 804 Sqn	He111 1 (F)/122
	Sub-Lt(A) R R Lamb	Gladiator N2274 804 Sqn	force-landed, w/o
	Capt R J Partridge RM/ Lt R S Bostock (O)	Skua L2995 800 Sqn	
	Lt E W T Taylour/ PO(A) R F Hart (O)	Skua L3028 800 Sqn	He111 1H+CT 9 /KG26 force-landed, w/o
	Sub-Lt(A) B St A H Hurle-Hobbs N/Air R E Northfield (TAG)	Skua L3047 800 Sqn	
	Lt L A Harris RM/ N/Air F Culliford (TAG)	Skua L2910 803 Sqn	He111 1H+JP 7 /KG26 crash-landed, w/o
	Sub-Lt(A) G W Brokensha PO(A) S E Andrews (O)	Skua L2905 803 Sqn	
	Lt G E D Finch-Noyes PO(A) H G Cunningham (O)	Skua L3000 800 Sqn	
	PO(A) H A Monk L/Air L C S Eccleshall (TAG)	Skua L3028 800 Sqn	He111 2 /KGr 100 force-landed, w/o
	Mid(A) L H Gallagher N/Air G W Halifax (TAG)	Skua L2938 800 Sqn	

	Lt(A) W C A Church Sub-Lt(A) D G Willis (O)	Skua L2931 801 Sqn	
	Lt R C Hay RM N/Air S A Bass (TAG)	Skua A7H 801 Sqn	He111 2 /KGr 100 destroyed
	PO(A) H C Kimber N/Air L W Miles (TAG)	Skua L2912 801 Sqn	
	Lt R L Strange PO(A) N Reid (O)	Skua L2963 801 Sqn	
	Sub-Lt(A) J B Marsh N/Air G R Nicholson (TAG)	Skua L2912 801 Sqn	He111 4 /LG1 destroyed
	Mid(A) G C Baldwin L/Air S R Smailes (TAG)	Skua A7H 801 Sqn	
28/4/40	Lt K V V Spurway PO(A) W Crawford (O)	Skua L2908 800 Sqn	
	Lt J A Rooper L/Air V H M Cordwell (O)	Skua L3024 800 Sqn	
	Mid(A) L H Gallagher L/Air W J Tremeer (TAG)	Skua L2938 800 Sqn	5 He115s destroyed in harbour I/KüFlGr 506
	Lt R L Strange PO(A) N Reid (O)	Skua L2963 801 Sqn	
	Sub-Lt(A) J B Marsh N/Air G R Nicholson (TAG)	Skua A7H 801 Sqn	
	PO(A) H C Kimber N/Air L W Miles (TAG)	Skua L2961 801 Sqn	
	Lt W P Lucy Lt M C E Hanson (O)	Skua L2925 803 Sqn	Ju88 4D+EH I/KG30 destroyed
	PO(A) A G Johnson L/Air F Costan (TAG)	Skua L2992 803 Sqn	
	Lt W P Lucy Lt M C E Hanson (O)	Skua L2925 803 Sqn	2 He111 destroyed 4 /KG26
	Sub-Lt(A) G W Brokensha PO(A) S E Andrews (O)	Skua L2905 803 Sqn	
	Sub-Lt(A) G W Brokensha PO(A) S E Andrews (O)	Skua L2905 803 Sqn	He111 probable
	PO(A) A G Johnson L/Air F Costan (TAG)	Skua L2992 803 Sqn	He111 probable

	Lt G E D Finch-Noyes PO(A) H G Cunningham (O)	Skua L3000 800 Sqn	
	Lt E W T Taylour PO(A) R F Hart (O)	Skua L3028 800 Sqn	He111 8/KG26 destroyed
	PO(A) H A Monk L/Air L C S Eccleshall (TAG)	Skua L2938 800 Sqn	
	Lt G E D Finch-Noyes PO(A) H G Cunningham (O)	Skua L3000 800 Sqn	2 He111 damaged
	Lt E W T Taylour PO(A) R F Hart (O)	Skua L3028 800 Sqn	He111 damaged
	PO(A) H A Monk L/Air L C S Eccleshall (TAG)	Skua L2938 800 Sqn	He111 damaged
1/5/40	Unidentified pilot Unidentified pilot	Sea Gladiator 804 Sqn Sea Gladiator 804 Sqn	Do17 damaged 1(F)/120
	Lt-Cdr J C Cockburn	Sea Gladiator N2265 804 Sqn	Ju87 damaged I/StG1
	Lt J F Marmont Lt(A) R J B Miles (possibly)	Sea Gladiator 6A 802 Sqn Sea Gladiator 6B 802 Sqn	Ju87 destroyed I/StG1
7/5/40	Lt(A) T E Gray N/Air H Pickering (TAG)	Skua L3030 803 Sqn	He111 8 /KG26 badly damaged
	Lt W P Lucy Lt M C E Hanson (O)	Skua L2925 803 Sqn	
8/5/40	Lt L A Harris RM Lt J H R Medlicot-Vereker (O)	Skua L2910 803 Sqn	
	Sub-Lt P N Charlton, Sub-Lt(A) N/Air F Culliford (TAG)	Skua L2916 803 Sqn	Do26 P5+BH KrzbV 108 destroyed
	PO(A) A G Johnson L/Air F Costan (TAG)	Skua L2992 803 Sqn	
	Mid(A) A S Griffith N/Air F P Dooley (TAG)	Skua L3961 803 Sqn He111 damaged	Ju88 damaged,
10/5/40	PO(A) H A Glover N/Air H T Chatterley (TAG)	Skua L3046 803 Sqn	He111 unknown result (possibly Ju88 4D+FH Z/KG30 f/landed, w/o)

12/5/40	Lt J A Rooper PO(A) W Crawford (O)	Skua L3001 800 Sqn	
	Mid(A) R W Kearsley L/Air L C S Eccleshall (TAG)	Skua L3024 800 Sqn	Engaged He111 & Do17 – no result observed
	PO(A) L E Burston	Skua L2938 800 Sqn	Possibly He111 F6+DH 1(F)/122 crashed into mountain
14/5/40	Lt W P Lucy Lt M C E Hanson (O)	Skua L2925 803 Sqn	He111 + He111 damaged
	Lt(A) T E Gray L/Air A G Clayton (TAG)	Skua L2918 803 Sqn	He111 Stab II/KG26 c/landed, badly damaged
15/5/40	Lt L A Harris RM Lt J H R Medlicot-Vereker (O)	Skua L2910 803 Sqn	Ju88 possibly 4D+RH 2 /K30
	PO(A) A G Johnson L/Air F Costan (TAG)	Skua L2992 803 Sqn	
16/5/40	Lt L A Harris RM Lt J H R Medlicot-Vereker (O)	Skua L2910 803 Sqn	Ju88
	PO(A) H A Glover N/Air S G A Wright (TAG)	Skua L3046 803 Sqn	
	Sub-Lt I H Easton L/Air A J Hayman (TAG)	Skua L3019 803 Sqn	Ju88
	Mid(A) A S Griffith N/Air F P Dooley (TAG)	Skua L2961 803 Sqn	Ju88 Ju88 6 /KG30 FTR
	Sub-Lt(A) B H St A H Hurle-Hobbs N/Air R E Northfield (TAG)	Skua L3049 800 Sqn	Ju88 4D+AP 6 /KG30
	Mid(A) R W Kearsley L/Air L C S Eccleshall (TAG	Skua L3024 800 Sqn	
18/5/40	Lt G E D Finch-Noyes PO(A) H G Cunningham (O)	Skua L3000 800 Sqn	
	Mid(A) R W Kearsley L/Air L C S Eccleshall (TAG)	Sklua L3028 800 Sqn	He111 damaged – possibly 3 /KG26
	Mid(A) L H Gallagher L/Air W J Tremeer (TAG)	Skua L3047 800 Sqn	
	Lt K V V Spurway PO(A) W Crawford (O)	Skua L2908 800 Sqn	

	Lt J A Rooper L/Air V H M Cordwell (O)	Skua L3024 800 Sqn	2 Bv138 strafed and sunk KGzbV 108
	Unidentified crew	Skua 800 Sqn	
	Unidentified crew	Skua 800 Sqn	
27/5/40	Lt A J G Lydekker	Gladiator N5705 attached 263 Sqn RAF	Ju87 I/StG1
28/5/40	Lt D N H Ogilvy Lt G D D'E Lyver Lt(A) G H J Feeny	Sea Gladiator N5527 802 Sqn Sea Gladiator N5530 802 Sqn Sea Gladiator N5526 802 Sqn	 He115 2 /KüFlGr 506
9/6/40	Lt D C E F Gibson Sub-Lt M P Gordon-Smith (O)	Skua L2984 803 Sqn	
	Sub-Lt(A) R E Bartlett N/Air L G Richard (TAG)	Skua L2995 803 Sqn	He111 5 /KG26
	PO(A) A W Theobald N/Air F J L de Frias (TAG)	Skua L2956 803 Sqn	
10/6/40	Lt-Cdr J Casson Lt P E Fanshawe (O)	Skua L2992 803 Sqn	
	Sub-Lt(A) G W Brokensha PO(A) S E Andrews (O)	Skua L2997 803 Sqn	He115 2 /KüFlGr 106
	PO(A) T F Riddler L/Air H T Chatterley (TAG)	Skua L2915 803 Sqn	

APPENDIX III

Other Notable Successes Gained by the FAA During the Norway Campaign

10/4/40 Walrus claimed U-boat [U-50] sunk in conjunction with HMS *Hero* - not confirmed

Skuas of 800 and 803 Squadrons bombed and sank cruiser *Königsberg*

Swordfish floatplane HMS *Devonshire* bombed and sank U-64

15/4/40 Swordfish of 816/818 Squadrons destroyed two Ju52/3m of 3/KGzbV.102 on the ground and damaged several others.

17/4/40 HMS *Suffolk*'s gunfire destroyed four He115 of I/KüFlGr.106, five He59s, and a BV138 of KGzbV.108 at Sola. Walruses attempted to spot fall of fire.

25/4/40 Swordfish of 810/818 Squadrons destroyed seven Ju87s of 1/StG1 and one Ju52 of KGzbV.107 on the ground.

Three Skuas of 803 Squadron set fire to two oilers.

9/5/40 Minesweeper M.134 sunk by Skuas of 806 Squadron

13/6/40 *Scharnhorst* damaged by Skuas of 800 and 803 Squadrons.

APPENDIX IV

Principal Types of German Aircraft in Service 1939 – 1940

Arado Ar 196
Two-seat, single-engined, ship-board reconnaissance and coastal patrol float seaplane. Max speed 194mph at 3,280ft. Armament – 2x 20mm cannon and 2x 7.9mm mgs.

Dornier 17
Twin-engined medium bomber. Max speed (loaded) 255mph at 13,100ft. Armament – multiple 7.9mm mgs.

Dornier 18
Four-seat, twin-engined maritime patrol and reconnaissance flying boat. Max speed 166mph at 6,560ft. Armament – 1x 20mm cannon plus 7.9mm mgs.

Dornier 24
Three-engined, air-sea rescue and transport flying boat. Max speed 206mph at 8,500ft. Armament – 1x 20mm cannon plus 7.9mm mgs.

Dornier 26
Four-engined long-range maritime reconnaissance and transport flying boat. Max speed 201mph at 8,500ft. Armament – 1x 20mm cannon plus 7.9mm mgs.

Heinkel 59
Four-seat, twin-engined torpedo-bomber and reconnaissance float biplane. Max speed 137mph at sea level. Armament – two or more 7.9mm mgs.

Heinkel 111
Five-seat, twin-engined medium bomber. Max speed 247mph at 16,000ft. Armament – combination of fixed and flexible 7.9mm mgs.

Heinkel 115
Three-seat, twin-engined torpedo-bomber float seaplane. Max speed 186mph at 3,200ft. Armament – several 7.9 mgs.

Junkers 52
Multi-seat, three-engined transport. Max speed 172mph at 3,000ft. Armament 7.9mm mgs.

Junkers 87 (Stuka)
Two-seat, single-engined dive-bomber. Max speed 238mph at 13,400ft. Armament – 3x 7.9mm mgs.

Junkers 88
Four-seat, twin-engined level and dive-bomber. Max speed 280mph at 18,000ft. Armament – combination of fixed and flexible 7.9mm mgs.

Messerschmitt Bf109E
Single-seat, single-engined fighter, Max speed 348mph at 14,500ft. Armament – 2x 20mm cannon plus 2x 7.9mm mgs.

Messerschmitt Bf110C
Two or three-seat, twin-engined long-range fighter. Max speed 336mph at 19,600ft. Armament – 2x 20mm cannon 5x 7.9mm mgs.

BIBLIOGRAPHY

Aces, Warriors & Wingmen: Wayne Ralph
Aircraft Carriers of the World, 1914 to the present: Roger Chesneau
Anchors Aweigh!: Kenneth Poolman
Ark Royal: William Jameson
Ark Royal: Kenneth Poolman
Battleships of World War 1: Anthony Preston
Blackburn Skua & Roc: Matthew Willis
Bombs Gone – The development of British air-dropped weapons from 1912: J A MacBean & A Hogben
British And Empire Warships of the Second World War: H T Lenton
British Battleships 1884-1904: R A Burt
British Carrier Aviation: Norman Friedman
British Naval Aviation: Ray Sturtivant
Carrier Glorious: John Winton
Fairey Swordfish & Albacore: W A Harrison
Fledgling Eagles: Christopher Shores *et al*
Fleet Air Arm Aircraft 1939-1945: Ray Sturtivant & Mick Burrow
Fleet Air Arm at War: Ray Sturtivant
Find, Fix & Strike: Terence Horsley
Flying Marines: Major Allan Marsh RM
Graf Spee: Michael Powell
Haul, Taut & Belay: Sir Donald Gibson
Hitler's Northern War; The Luftwaffe's ill-fated campaign 1940-1945: Adam R A Claasen
Hitler's U-Boat War, (Vol 1) The Hunters 1939-1942: Clay Blair
It's Really Quite Safe! Hank Rotherham
I was Gree Spee's Prisoner: Captain Patrick Dove
Kaigun ...the Imperial Japanese Navy, 1887-1941: David C Evans & Mark R Peattie
Lost Voices of the Royal Navy: Max Arthur
Naval Weapons of WWII: John Campbell
Nelson to Vanguard: D K Brown
Norwegian Patrol: Gron Edwards
One Man's War: Stuart E Soward
Operation Skua: Major Richard Partridge RM
Seven Seas Nine Lives: Richard Pike
Skua: Peter C Smith
Squadrons of the Fleet Air Arm: Ray Sturtivant & Theo Ballance
Straight & Level: Air Chief Marshal Sir Kenneth Cross
Supermarine Walrus: G W R Nicholl
TAG on a Stringbag: Les Sayer & Vernon Ball
The Fleet Air Arm History: Lt-Cdr J Waterman
The First Pathfinders: Kenneth Wakefield
The Grand Fleet: D K Brown
The Imperial Japanese Navy: A J Watts & B G Gordon
The Right Of The Line The RAF in the European War 1939-1945: John Terraine
The Sea Eagles Volume I: Chris Goss
The Swordfish Story: Ray Sturtivant
Turns of Fate: Ken Dimbleby
U-Boat Fact File, Detailed Service Histories of the Submarines Operated by the Kriegsmarine 1935-1945: Peter Sharpe
War in a Stringbag: Charles Lamb

SELECT GLOSSARY

AA	Anti-Aircraft
C-in-C	Commander-in-Chief
D/F	Direction Finding
DLT Sqn	Deck Landing Training Squadron
FAA	Fleet Air Arm
Flak	AA fire (from the German Fliegerabwehrkanone)
GP	General Purpose (bomb)
MV	Motor Vessel
MTB	Motor Torpedo Boat
POW	Prisoner of War
RAF	Royal Air Force
RAFVR	Royal Air Force Volunteer Reserve
RAN	Royal Australian Navy
recce	Reconnaissance
RN	Royal Navy
RNNAS	Royal Norwegian Naval Air Service
RNZN	Royal New Zealand Navy
RNAS	Royal Navy Air Service / Royal Navy Air Station
RFC	Royal Flying Corps
R/T	Radio telegraphy
TAG	Telegraphist Air Gunner
W/T	Wireless telegraphy

FAA ranks

Lt(A)	Lieutenant(Air)
Sub-Lt(A)	Sub-Lieutenant(Air)
Mid(A)	Midshipman(Air)
PO(A)	Petty Officer(Airman)
L/Air	Leading Airman
N/Air	Naval Airman

Luftwaffe / RAF / RN rank comparisons

Obstlt	Oberstleutant	Wing Commander (W/C)	Commander (Cdr)
Maj	Major	Squadron Leader (S/Ldr)	Lt-Commander (Lt-Cdr)
Hptm	Hauptmann	Flight Lieutenant (F/Lt)	Lieutenant (Lt)
Oblt	Oberleutnant	Flying Officer (Flg Off)	Sub-Lieutenant (Sub-Lt)
Ltn	Leutnant	Pilot Officer (P/O)	Midshipman (Mid)
Obfw	Oberfeldwebel	Flight Sergeant (F/Sgt)	Petty Officer (PO)
Fw	Feldwebel	Sergeant (Sgt)	
Uffz	Unteroffizier	Corporal (Cpl)	
Obgfr	Obergefreiter	Leading Aircraftman (LAC)	
Gfr	Gefreiter	Aircraftman 1st Class (AC1)	

Luftwaffe unit designations

JG	Jagdgeschwader	Fighter Wing
KG	Kampfgeschwader	Bomber Wing
KGr.	Kampfgruppe	Bomber Group
KüFlGr.	Küstenfliegergruppe	Coastal Flying Group
ObdL	Oberbefehlshaber der Luftwaffe	Luftwaffe High Command Reconnaissance Group
ZG	Zerstorergeschwader	Fighter Wing (Bf110 equipped long-range fighter unit)

RN/RM PERSONNEL

RAF PERSONNEL

RNNAS PERSONNEL

LUFTWAFFE PERSONNEL

KRIEGSMARINE PERSONNEL

OTHERS